Yahweh's Coming of Age

Yahweh's Coming of Age

Jason Bembry

Winona Lake, Indiana
EISENBRAUNS
2011

© 2011 by Eisenbrauns Inc.
All rights reserved
Printed in the United States of America

www.eisenbrauns.com

Library of Congress Cataloging-in-Publication Data

Bembry, Jason.
  Yahweh's coming of age / Jason Bembry.
       p.   cm.
  Includes bibliographical references and indexes.
  ISBN 978-1-57506-172-6 (hardback : alk. paper)
    1. God (Judaism)—Age. 2. Bible. O.T.—Criticism, interpretation, etc.
  I. Title.
  BM610.B37   2011
  296.3′112—dc22
                                                              2011008537

The paper used in this publication meets the minimum requirements of the American National Standard for Information Sciences—Permanence of Paper for Printed Library Materials, ANSI Z39.48-1984.♾™

Contents

Preface vii

Introduction 1

Part 1

OLD AGE IN BIBLICAL AND UGARITIC LITERATURE

Chapter 1. The Biblical Evidence 5
   Previous Works on Old Age 5
   The Lexicon of Old Age 8
   Old Age Terminology in the Pentateuch 16
   The Deuteronomistic History 29
   Old Age in the Prophets 38
   Wisdom Literature 42
   Interpretive Models for Qoheleth 12:1–7 47
   Analysis of Qoheleth 11:7–12:7 49
   Ruth 56
   Lamentations 58
   Daniel 58
   Ezra-Nehemiah 58
   1–2 Chronicles 59
   Conclusion 60

Chapter 2. The Ugaritic Evidence 61
   Epigraphic Sources 62
   Iconographic Sources 78
   Conclusion 86

Part 2

AGING YAHWEH

Chapter 3. Why Yahweh Is Not Old 91
   Yahweh: Eternal, Not Elderly 91
   Yahweh as a Selective Conflation of El and Baal 94
   Yahweh versus the "Other Gods" 104

Chapter 4. Yahweh Comes of Age 107
   Daniel 7: Preliminary Matters 107
   Canaanite Antecedents of the Ancient of Days 113
   Hellenistic Antecedents for the Ancient of Days? 146
   Conclusion 148

Indexes 151
   Index of Authors 151
   Index of Scripture 155
   Index of Other Ancient Literature 161

Preface

This book began in conversations that I had in 2000 with my doctoral adviser, Jo Ann Hackett. Her timely feedback and direction assisted me greatly as the original dissertation progressed. Jon Levenson also provided good assistance and direction as I developed the two-trajectories idea. John Huehnergard gave me important input regarding the lexicon of old age in Hebrew, Ugaritic, and other cognate languages as well as regarding grammatical issues. My use of the archaeological data regarding the iconography of the deities from Ugarit and figurines from Palestine benefited greatly from the insight of Lawrence Stager. My fellow students from Harvard proved helpful in this project as well. In particular, I want to mention Gene McGarry, whose friendship and scholarship have been and continue to be one of the great gifts from my time in Boston. After completing the dissertation in 2004, I asked Gene to help me shape the manuscript for publication, and his editorial insight proved valuable once again. So I want to express my thanks to my good friend Gene and to these four professors, to whom I will always be grateful—for the excellent education I received from them and the valuable assistance they provided on this project. I was assisted with proofreading by Mr. Nathaniel Greene and Ms. Elizabeth Scott.

I would be remiss if I did not also mention my parents, Wallace and Anne Bembry, who provided generous support throughout my doctoral program. My debt to them is incalculable. My sons, Logan, Jack, and Miles, are due special thanks for putting up with me during the long hours I had to be away from them. The highest appreciation is reserved for my wife, Fay, who has supported me throughout this process with much love, patience, and understanding. It is to her that this book is affectionately dedicated.

Note to the Reader

Abbreviations in this volume follow the list provided in the *Society of Biblical Literature Handbook of Style for Ancient Near Eastern, Biblical, and Early Christian Studies* (ed. P. H. Alexander et al.; Peabody, MA: Hendrickson, 1999) §8.4.2.

Introduction

In the Judeo-Christian tradition, the deity Yahweh is often portrayed as an old man. One of the epithets used of Yahweh in the Hebrew Bible, the Ancient of Days, is a source for this depiction of God as elderly. Yet when we look closely at the early traditions of biblical Israel, we see a different picture. We see a relatively youthful God, a warrior who defends his people. So we might ask how the transformation of Yahweh from youthful God to elderly God took place in Israel's traditions. This book is an examination of the question: How did God become old? Asking this kind of question of an ancient culture through the use of textual and archaeological data culled from the past is not an easy undertaking. The biblical texts are not always pristine snapshots of a given moment. Because the biblical texts have been retouched numerous times by later redactors, it is a challenge to know precisely when God is portrayed a certain way at a certain time in Israel's past.

Texts from the ancient Near East outside the Bible present obstacles as well. These texts, especially the texts most relevant to this book, are partially preserved, and the modern interpretation of some of them rests on scholarly reconstruction. Archaeological data are not without obstacles of their own. The dirt, the pottery, and the figurines do not speak, and so each discovered fragment must be painstakingly integrated into reconstructed stratigraphy. Thus, sometimes it seems that scholars of the ancient Near East are working with confetti, tiny scraps of data that must be put together with great care. Despite the challenges of ancient texts and archaeological remains, however, theories can be tested and probable solutions can be proffered. This book constitutes such an endeavor.

In order to answer the question regarding Yahweh's coming of age, I examine the way that old age is portrayed in the Hebrew Bible. Texts that explicitly or even implicitly depict the aged are considered in chap. 1. From this investigation, we are allowed a glimpse into the way ancient Israelites viewed aging and the aged. I then turn in chap. 2 to making a similar foray into the world of ancient Ugarit in order to see the way that this culture viewed senescence. The primary lens through which I make this examination is the corpus of texts written in Ugaritic, one of the greatest textual collections discovered in the 20th century. These texts, in a language quite close to ancient Hebrew, provide a window onto an ancient culture just north of Israel from the Late Bronze

Age. Unlike many archaeological sites in Syria–Palestine, the ancient site of Ugarit provides a relatively pristine snapshot of Late Bronze Age life because it was relatively undisturbed after its destruction ca. 1187 B.C.E. In addition to the Ugaritic texts, I also examine the iconography of some of the deities in the Ugaritic pantheon to see how the relative ages of major gods are depicted artistically.

In chap. 3, I begin to look at the transformation of Yahweh from a young and virile God to the elderly Ancient of Days. I begin with an examination of the imagery used of Yahweh and argue that he is indeed a youthful warrior deity in early Israelite tradition. I look at the way that Israel's God takes on attributes shared with the Ugaritic deities Baal and El. Then, in chap. 4, I address the question raised at the beginning in earnest, explaining how Yahweh becomes an aged God, the Ancient of Days in Daniel 7. The transformation takes place at the intersection of two trajectories of development in the traditions of Israel. One trajectory is the way that apocalyptic traditions seen in the book of Daniel recast old Canaanite mythic imagery, which can be seen in texts from Ugarit as well as early biblical texts. This trajectory allows Yahweh to take on qualities, such as senescence, that were not associated with him during most of Israel's history but were associated with El in the Canaanite traditions. A second trajectory that yields a depiction of Israel's God as elderly is the development of the idea of Yahweh as a father. The more comfortable the biblical tradents became with portraying Yahweh as a father to the people Israel, a metaphor that was not embraced in the early traditions, the easier it became for the people to think of Yahweh as occupying a stage of the human life cycle. If Yahweh is a father, then perhaps he looks like and can age as a human father. These two trajectories came together in the 2nd century B.C.E., the chronological backdrop for Daniel 7, and found expression in a new epithet for Yahweh: Ancient of Days.

Part 1

OLD AGE IN
BIBLICAL AND UGARITIC LITERATURE

Chapter 1

The Biblical Evidence

From a human perspective, the process of aging is inevitable for all beings. Even so, cultures respond differently to this inescapable reality; some societies actively embrace the onset of old age, while others fiercely resist it. As David Hackett Fischer points out in his book *Growing Old in America*, the way the elderly are portrayed in America has drastically changed from colonial days to the present. Compare the respect afforded Ben Franklin with the popular portrayal of Abraham Simpson in Matt Groening's *The Simpsons*. The white powdered wig was a mainstay of colonial fashion, in sharp contrast with the present avoidance of all things perceived to be old.[1] As Margaret Gullette has argued, aging itself has become synonymous with decline, to be avoided at all costs.[2] A cult of youth has taken root and flowered in our time. This transformation may help explain the dearth of studies on old age in the ancient world compared with the number of studies in other fields of inquiry. In light of the relative paucity of studies on aging in the Bible and the ancient Near East, this study is designed to address this virtual void. In the first part of this study, I examine how old age is portrayed in the ancient West Semitic world as attested in the Hebrew Bible and the cuneiform tablets of the Kingdom of Ugarit. To the extent possible, part 1 will provide a glimpse into the way these two cultures within the broader West Semitic world viewed senescence. In part 2, I will address the question why old-age imagery was initially eschewed in the portrayal of Israel's God and only later embraced.

Previous Works on Old Age

Reference to a few studies that prove to be exceptions to the general avoidance of this topic is in order. A book entitled *Biblical Perspectives*

---

1. In colonial days, men's jackets were tailored to give their shoulders a stooped look in order to make men look older than they were. See David Hackett Fischer, *Growing Old in America* (New York: Oxford University Press, 1977) 84.
2. Gullette's book is a cultural critique of the way age is viewed in America. She notes that aging is often associated with decline in every facet of one's humanity, while the maturity, wisdom, and insight that may accompany old age are appreciably downplayed. See Margaret M. Gullette, *Aged by Culture* (Chicago: University of Chicago Press, 2004) 11–13.

on Aging by J. Gordon Harris, from 1987, is one of only two scholarly monographs of note on the subject in the last 25 years. While providing a satisfactory overview of the biblical picture, Harris's book does not sufficiently address critical issues. His work also betrays a priori pejorative assumptions about the nature of extrabiblical sources and the cultures from which they derive. This is best seen in his assessment of Ugarit as a city in decline that lost its traditional values because of its monarchy and the concomitant bureaucracy. He assumes that the elderly are degraded in Ugarit because it is a city-state sloughing off rural sensibilities.[3] Another part of Harris's work that plots a similar trajectory is his assumption that this same development is seen in the tension between the gods Baal and El. For him, Baal represents the younger culture that is trying to decenter the older traditions epitomized by El.[4] Such urban-rural and old-young dichotomies are too simplistic to account for the data. The second monograph is Rachel Z. Dulin's *Crown of Glory: A Biblical View of Aging*, from 1988. Dulin describes her work as the product of a phenomenological approach designed to "gather themes which comprise the multifaceted view of biblical old age."[5] Dulin's book is helpful in that it examines many facets of old age portrayed in the Hebrew Bible. Yet it is essentially descriptive and avoids addressing deeper issues that I raise in this study. It lacks technical linguistic sophistication and a broader view of the cultures of the ancient Levant—namely, Ugarit.

Two dissertations, one from 1997 and the other from 1998, also address old age but do not adequately account for the material at Ugarit and the Bible. Joel Ajayi's 1997 dissertation from Baylor University entitled *Wisdom and Old Age in Israel* is a biblical-theological examination of the connection between the aged and wisdom. Ajayi's work is limited to the dyad of wisdom and old age, and so he addresses a select portion of the Hebrew Bible without examining all old-age motifs in the canon.[6] Ajayi's work fails, however, to address contrary evidence, namely stories that depict the aged as unwise. He assures his reader that Isaac is actually wise when he is fooled by Jacob, because the aged patriarch knows the divine plan for Jacob's ascendancy.[7] Ajayi is also quite certain that David is not at all senile in old age, despite the suggestion of his impo-

---

3. J. Gordon Harris, *Biblical Perspectives on Aging* (Philadelphia: Fortress, 1987) 26.
4. Ibid.
5. Rachel Z. Dulin, *A Crown of Glory: A Biblical View of Aging* (New York: Paulist Press, 1988) 5.
6. Joel Ajayi, *Wisdom and Old Age in Ancient Israel* (Ph.D. diss., Baylor University, 1997) 34.
7. Ibid., 174.

tence and confusion in 1 Kings 1-2.[8] Ajayi's work also lacks controls that might allow him to establish who is actually to be reckoned "old." He assumes, for example, that Saul is old and David is young, even though Saul is nowhere described as old.[9]

Milton Eng's 1998 Drew University dissertation, *The Days of Our Years*, is a lexical-semantic study of the life cycle in biblical Israel.[10] The bulk of Eng's work is lexical, providing interesting information on the meaning of individual terms but adding little to the broader understanding of the way old age is conceived in the community of Israel.

This book seeks to fill in these gaps in previous scholarship by presenting a critical study of the available biblical and Ugaritic sources on old age and then using these data to solve a critical problem about the portrayal of Israel's God. The work within these pages seeks to mirror in some ways the rapidly growing work in gerontology in other scholarly areas that reflects a larger trend of concern about old age in American culture. Since the abstract notion of old age is rarely a subject of explicit discussion among the biblical and Ugaritic writers, this study must tease out references to old age in the entire corpus, ranging from narratives, legal material, and wisdom writing in the Bible to mostly narrative texts from Ugarit. I will begin with a systematic examination of all terminology related to old age, ranging from single words (*zāqēn, yāšîš, śêbâ*) and phrases (*zāqēn mě'ōd, mělē' yāmîm*) to lengthy expressions (*ḥādal lihyōt lěśārâ 'ōraḥ kannāšîm*) noting aspects of old age in Hebrew and Ugaritic, with some assistance from cognate languages. These words, along with synonyms that appear in parallel cola in Hebrew and Ugaritic verse as well as antonyms (*na'ar, yeled bāḥûr*) with which they are contrasted will be included. Because *old* or *elderly* is a relative category, not specifically defined in the Bible or in the Ugaritic corpus, analysis of this sort must proceed with caution.

Sociology has provided many helpful insights for the study of the ancient Near East in general and biblical studies in particular. Sociological examinations of old age among people from various cultures, especially individuals from preindustrial societies, can provide interesting models for comparison with the biblical world. The classic work in this arena is Leo Simmons's 1945 work, *The Role of the Aged in Primitive Society*. As a sociologist, Simmons conducted studies in Africa, Asia, and North and

---

8. Ibid., 232.
9. Ibid., 223. Certainly we may assume that David is younger than Saul, but this does not mean that the two men epitomize old age and youth in the way that Ajayi desires. A similar example of this desire is Ajayi's assumption that Hushai is old and Ahithophel is young (ibid., 229).
10. Milton Eng, *The Days of Our Years* (Ph.D. Diss., Drew University, 1998).

South America to determine patterns and unique phenomena among the world's preindustrial population in their approach to the elderly. As is often true of a pioneering work in any field, Simmons has been criticized for some of his methodology.[11] Even so, Simmons should be credited with introducing the cross-cultural study of aging and laying the groundwork for further investigation.[12] The book most formative for the present study has been David Gutmann's *Reclaimed Powers*, a work that provides numerous insights from examinations of cultures in modern Israel and South America, and of Navajo Native American communities.[13] Citations of these works and a few others from the field of anthropological and gerontological studies will appear occasionally in this study.

The Lexicon of Old Age

The most frequent of all old-age terminology in the Hebrew Bible is the word *zāqēn*, an adjective associated with the noun *zāqān* 'beard', which is attested in many Semitic languages. The etymology suggests that this adjective referred to men with beards as opposed to men who could not yet grow them, originally referring perhaps to adult males in general.[14] Yet in the Hebrew Bible, *zāqēn* is used of old men (and *mutatis mutandis* women) and of "elders" who serve as officials. The verb *zqn* 'to be old' or 'to grow old' appears in both Biblical Hebrew and Old Aramaic.[15] Hebrew is unique among Semitic languages, however, in that it

---

11. Nancy Foner, *Ages in Conflict: A Cross-Cultural Perspective on Inequality between Old and Young* (New York: Columbia University Press, 1984) 27. Foner points out that many of the writers Simmons relied on for his conclusions neither spoke the languages nor lived with the people whom they were assessing for a sufficient period of time. Solon Kimball also questioned Simmons's results, remarking that "there is the ever present danger that the use of isolated cultural facts, called 'traits', outside their context may produce distortion of meaning." See Solon Kimball, "Review of Leo Simmons, *The Role of the Aged in Primitive Society*," *American Review of Sociology* 52 (1946) 287, quoted in Ellen Rhoads Holmes and Lowell D. Holmes, *Other Cultures, Elder Years* (Thousand Oaks, CA: Sage, 1995) 96.

12. Ibid., 96.

13. David Gutmann, *Reclaimed Powers: Toward a New Psychology of Men and Women in Later Life* (New York: Basic Books, 1987).

14. J. Conrad, "*zāqēn*," *Theological Dictionary of the Old Testament* (hereafter *TDOT*; ed. G. Johannes Botterweck and Helmer Ringgren; trans. J. T. Willis, G. W. Bromiley, and D. E. Green; Grand Rapids, MI: Eerdmans, 1974–) 4:124.

15. See Sefire ii B 8 (KAI 223) where the verb appears in the imperfect (*yzqn*) with the meaning 'to be old'. Jacob Hoftijzer and K. Jongeling, *Dictionary of North-West Semitic Inscriptions* (hereafter *DNWSI*; Leiden: Brill, 1995) 1:339. The verb in this line is paired with the form *wybʿ* which is from the root *nbʿ* 'to bubble forth'. Fitzmyer translates the paired verbs as '*babbling* and growing old', which a son would say about

employs the noun *zāqēn* to refer to elders.[16] The stative verb *zāqēn* is attested 18 times in the Hebrew Bible, the adjective (or noun) 187 times.[17] In the LXX, *zāqēn* is rendered 127 times with *presbyteros*, and 23 times with *presbytēs*, 26 times by *gerousia*, and 3 times each with *gerōn* and *anēr*. In Deut 31:28, *ziqnê šibṭêkem* is rendered with *phylarchous*.[18] The verbal forms are typically rendered with the verb *gēraskein* or *gēran* (14 times).

A synonym of *zāqēn* that appears with far less frequency (only 19 times) is *śêbâ*, a noun that derives from the Semitic root *śyb* 'to be gray'. In Akkadian, the noun *šībum* 'old man, elder'[19] is attested in the Old Babylonian period, but it is unclear whether the original meaning was 'old' and then later took on the meaning 'gray' or vice versa.[20] The word *šībum* denotes the person while the Hebrew term *śêbâ* describes the condition of being old. The corresponding Akkadian verb is *šiābum* 'to age, to become old'.[21] In the Amarna archive, Letter 137 is from an old man who says, *šībāti* 'I am old' (line 29).[22] Four times in the Bible, *śêbâ* is modified with *ṭōbâ* 'good' to describe the good quality of the old age a person had achieved at death; the combination is used of Abraham (Gen 15:15, 25:8), Gideon (Judg 8:32), and David (1 Chr 29:28). The use of *śêbâ* in the Bible is a metonomy to denote senescence. Twice within the Joseph story, the phrase "my *śêbâ*" is used as a self-designation by Jacob, who is worried about descending to Sheol in "grief" (Gen 42:38) or "calamity" (Gen 44:29). Judah uses the same word to refer to his elderly father in Gen 44:31. David uses the term in a similar manner in his instructions to Solomon just before he dies. The aged king orders Solomon to

---

his ruling father whom he was seeking to overthrow. See Joseph A. Fitzmyer, *The Aramaic Inscriptions of Sefire* (BEO 19/A; Rome: Pontifical Biblical Institute, 1995) 129.

16. Biblical Aramaic, most other forms of Aramaic, and Akkadian use variations of the word *šību* or *śāb* (occurring 5 times in Ezra 5) from a verb meaning 'to be old' and expressed in Hebrew as *śyb*.

17. Because the 3ms form of the stative verb is identical to the singular noun and the masculine singular adjectival form, these statistics could be altered slightly depending upon the way these ambiguous forms are parsed. Forms of this sort will be noted in our fuller discussion of individual occurrences.

18. Conrad, "*zāqēn*," 124.

19. Wolfram von Soden and Bruno Meissner, *Akkadisches Handwörterbuch; unter Benutzung des lexikalischen Nachlasses von Bruno Meissner (1868–1947)* (hereafter *AHw*; 3 vols.; Wiesbaden: Harrassowitz, 1965–81) 1228b.

20. Heinz-Josef Fabry, "*śêbâ*," in *Theologisches Wörterbuch zum Alten Testament* (hereafter *TWAT*; ed. G. Johannes Botterweck and Helmer Ringgren; Stuttgart: Kohlhammer, 1970–) 7:752.

21. Erica Reiner et al., eds., *The Assyrian Dictionary* (hereafter *CAD*; Chicago: Oriental Institute, 1956–) Š/1 19a.

22. William Moran, *The Amarna Letters* (Baltimore, MD: Johns Hopkins University Press, 1992) 218.

prevent Joab's *śêbâ* from descending to Sheol in peace (1 Kgs 2:6) and to bring Shimei's *śêbâ* down to Sheol in blood (1 Kgs 2:9).

The word is used in parallel with *ziqnâ* 'old age' in Isa 46:4 and Ps 71:18. A similar meaning is found in Ps 92:15, where the righteous are said to bear fruit like a tree in *śêbâ*. In Proverbs, *śêbâ* is called "the beauty of old men" (20:29) and a "crown of glory" attained through a righteous life (16:31). Both usages in Proverbs retain the more literal sense of "gray hair" by calling *śêbâ* a "crown" or by comparing *śêbâ* with the "strength" of youth (20:29) as outward manifestations of age. On one occasion *śêbâ* is used to refer to the elderly in general (that is, 'old people' or more likely 'old men'). Lev 19:32 says, "You shall stand before *śêbâ*," without the definite article or any other modifiers. Deut 32:25 uses the phrase "man of *śêbâ*" as a contrast with "suckling child" to speak of the ranges of human life. In Hos 7:9, Ephraim is said to be "sprinkled with *śêbâ*, yet he knows it not." The reference here is the more literal sense of *śêbâ*, whether it is "gray hair" or "gray mold."[23] An even more enigmatic use of *śêbâ* is found in Job 41:24[32], where it is said that Yahweh leaves a path (wake) behind himself, and he considers the deep *lĕśêbâ* 'to be hoary' (?).

Ugaritic attests the adjective *šb* 'gray' and the noun *šbt* 'gray hair', often placed in construct with *dqn* 'beard' to yield *šb(t) dqn* 'grayness of beard' (KTU 1.3 V 24–25 and 1.4 V 4).[24] The verb *šyb* 'to become gray, old' is not attested in Ugaritic.[25] The reflex of this root, *śyb*, is broadly attested in Imperial Aramaic, used four times in the Aḥiqar text as an adjective 'old' (lines 6 and 17) and as a substantive 'old man' (lines 26 and 35).[26] Palestinian Aramaic uses this word to mean 'elder'.[27] It is attested five times in Biblical Aramaic (Ezra 5:5, 9; 6:7, 8, 14) where, however, it appears in construct or otherwise determined through a

---

23. See Shalom Paul, "The Image of the Oven and the Cake in Hosea VII 4–10," *VT* 18 (1968) 119–20.

24. The word *dqn* in Ugaritic is also used as a PN. The person(s) with this name often appear in lists of craftsmen (KTU 4.98 17; 4.141 II 9; 4.183 II 26; 4.609 23) or royal guards (4.33 37; 4.54 3). Yet there is only one use of *dqn* in the formula *bn dqn* (4.787 10).

25. The dictionary of G. del Olmo Lete and J. Sanmartín (*Dictionary of the Ugaritic Language in the Alphabetic Tradition* [trans. W. G. E. Watson; 2nd rev. ed.; Leiden: Brill, 2003]) does not include this root. Gordon does include the word in his glossary, but it is noted as a hypothetical verbal root from which the noun/adjective is derived. See Cyrus Gordon, *Ugaritic Textbook* (hereafter *UT*; rev. ed., AnOr 38; Rome: Pontifical Biblical Institute, 1998) 489, §2407.

26. Albert E. Cowley, *Aramaic Papyri of the Fifth Century* (Oxford: Clarendon, 1923) 212–13.

27. Joseph A. Fitzmyer and Daniel J. Harrington, *A Manual of Palestinian Aramaic* (Rome: Pontifical Biblical Institute, 1978) #89. See pp. 172–73, 229.

genitive, with the meaning 'old age'. The lexeme is also attested in other Semitic language groups. Arabic has *šāba* (*šby*) 'to become old' and *šayb* 'old, gray-haired', and Ethiopic yields *šeba* and *šibat* 'gray-haired', and corresponding forms exist in Amharic and Tigre.[28] In the Hebrew Bible, the verbal form is used only twice (1 Sam 12:2 and Job 15:10). In 1 Sam 12:2, Samuel says *zāqantî wā-śabtî* 'I am old and I am gray-headed'. The participle form appears in Job 15:10 parallel with *yāšîš* 'aged', when Eliphaz the Temanite says, "The gray-headed one and the aged are on our side," presumably to lend credence to his point. The substantive infinitive *śêb* appears only once (1 Kgs 14:4) when the eyes of Ahijah from Shiloh are described as being "fixed" from 'old age'.

The term *yāšîš* is used in Job to denote old age (Job 12:12, 15:10, 29:8, 32:6). It seems to have an original meaning of 'weak', but it is never used in this sense alone.[29] A variant of this word, *yāšēš*, appears in 2 Chr 36:17, where it is paired with *zāqēn* to indicate the ruthless nature of the Chaldeans, who slaughtered young and old when they captured Judah.

Several idioms are employed in Hebrew to denote old age. One of the more common expressions is *'ōrek yāmîm* 'length of days', which is often used to denote long life (Deut 30:20; Job 12:12; Ps 21:5; 91:16; Prov 3:2, 16).[30] A similar expression appears in the Aramaic inscription from Tell Fekheriyeh: *lm'rk ywmwh w lkbr šnwh* 'to lengthen his days and increase his years'.[31] The Ugaritic text KTU 2.23 20 employs the same expression to pronounce a blessing: *urk ym bʿly* '(may) my lord (have) a length of days'. Another frequently used idiom is *yāmîm rabbîm* 'many days', which has the general sense of "a long time" in most cases but occasionally is used to refer to one's old age (1 Kgs 3:11, Job 38:21, 2 Chr 1:11). Two variations on this phrase, *rōb yāmîm* (Zech 8:4) and *rōb šānîm* (Job 32:7) should be included here, along with the verbal use of *rbb* 'to be many' to describe days (Job 29:18) or years (Prov 4:10). A similar expression, *šānîm rabbōt* 'many years', is used to describe the span of a

---

28. Fabry, "*śêbâ*," 753.
29. Conrad, "*zāqēn*," 123.
30. Sometimes this phrase simply refers to a long time without reference to one's age (Ps 23:6, 93:5; Lam 5:20).
31. Lines 7–8. See Ali Abou-Assaf, P. Bordreuil, and A. Millard, *La statue de Tell Fekherye et son inscription bilingue assyro-araméenne* (Paris: Éditions Recherche sur les civilisations, 1982) 23. See also Abraham Malamat, "Longevity: Biblical Concepts and Some Ancient Near Eastern Parallels," in *Vorträge gehalten auf der 28. Rencontre assyriologique internationale in Wien, 6.–10. Juli 1981* (AfO Beiheft 19; Horn, Austria: Berger, 1982) 215. Malamat also suggests that one of the inscriptions found at Kuntillet Ajrud attests a similar usage. K. Ajrud 7 begins with the line *brk . ymm*, and Malamat suggests emending the initial *b* to *'* (n. 2).

long life in Qoh 6:3. The phrase *mĕlēʾ yāmîm* 'full of days' occurs once in Jer 6:11, parallel with *zāqēn*.

As I noted above, most old-age teminology by far includes forms of the root *zqn*, most frequently the noun *zāqēn*. Because this term is central to understanding the biblical view of what it means to be old, it is necessary to attempt a basic definition at the outset of this study. Because the precise meaning of *zāqēn* is not fully articulated in the Hebrew Bible, we must infer its semantic range from its usage, bearing in mind the possible nuances given to the term by the numerous authors of the texts as well as the actual chronological span associated with the term. Every occurrence of an old-age term is considered in detail in this chapter. Thus, the terms outlined above will be noted and discussed within their own contexts.

At this point, therefore, I merely want to list some terms with which *zāqēn* is associated, sometimes synonymously and sometimes antithetically, in order to demonstrate the complicated nature of a term that is used to denote old age as well as a type of leader—even used as an honorary title. The word *zāqēn* is paralleled with *ʾāb* 'father', Deut 32:7; *ḥōrîm* 'nobles', 1 Kgs 21:8, 11; "all the people at the gate," Ruth 4:11; *śar* 'prince', Ps 105:22, Lam 5:12, 2 Kgs 10:1 ("*śārîm* of Jezreel, the elders," with no *waw* between them), Ezra 10:8, Isa 3:14, 1 Chr 15:25; *ʾōmānîm* 'entrusted ones', 2 Kgs 10:1, 5; *roʾš* 'head', Josh 23:2 (others listed too),[32] 24:1 (others listed too); Deut 5:23, 29:9 (others listed too); *rāʾšê hāʾābōt* 'heads of the fathers', Ezra 3:12; *šōṭēr* 'official', Num 11:16, Deut 29:9 (others listed too); Deut 31:28; Josh 23:2 (others listed too), 24:1 (others listed too); *šōpēṭ* 'judge', Deut 21:2, Ezra 10:4; Josh 23:2 (others listed too), 24:1 (others listed too); *ḥākām* 'wise one', Ezek 27:9; *melek* 'king' (in this case, the pretender Absalom), 2 Sam 17:15; *naʿar* 'youth', Gen 19:4, Exod 10:9, Deut 28:50, Jer 51:22, Esth 3:13, Ps 37:25, Isa 3:5, 20:4; Lam 2:21; *ʿōlālîm* 'children', Ezek 9:6, Joel 2:16; *bāḥûr* 'young man', Jer 31:13, Joel 3:1, Prov 20:29, Lam 5:14; *yĕlādîm* 'youths', Zech 8:4–5; *neʾĕmānîm* 'trusted ones', Job 12:20; *kōhānîm* 'priests', Deut 31:9, Lam 1:19, 4:16; Ezek 7:26, Jer 29:1 (others listed too); *kol hāʿām* 'all the people', Ruth 4:9, and 4:4 (with "my people").

Because the noun *zāqēn* accounts for most of the uses of the root *zqn* in the Hebrew Bible, it is worthy of special attention. While it can certainly refer to one who is old, *zāqēn* is also used to denote a specific office of leadership in Israel, usually rendered 'elder'. Lawrence Stager

---

32. By "others listed too," I mean that the terms are not a strict pair, because other groups of people are mentioned as well. I am labeling it this way to indicate that, while *zāqēn* is parallel with this term, it may also be related to the others in the list.

has argued that *zāqēn* denotes a head of a household, the mature counterpart to *naʿar*, often rendered 'youth'.[33] In this usage, age is probably not relevant, because one could conceivably become head of a household at a relatively young age if the *paterfamilias* had died when he was relatively young.[34] John MacDonald has even argued that *zāqēn* marks one with a social status analogous to medieval nobles.[35] In monographs focused on the term *naʿar*, Hans-Peter Stähli and Carolyn Leeb establish a more basic idea of status indicated by *naʿar* and *zāqēn*.[36] Leeb's is the more helpful of the two studies for our purposes, because she suggests that *zāqēn* is used to designate a head of household, a position that was probably not open to individuals who are called *naʿar*.[37] While the class status of *naʿar* and *zāqēn* can be debated, the substantive point for my purposes is that *zāqēn* can denote one who is not necessarily considered "old."[38]

This, of course, presents a challenge to any study seeking to understand how old age was viewed in biblical Israel. A certain circularity would obtain if one were to assume that anyone indentified with a form of *zāqēn* was "old" and then use the description of that person to understand what it means to be (a) *zāqēn*. To avoid this problem, I will attempt to isolate the occasions when *zāqēn* is being used to refer only to a status position, be it head of a household and/or city leader, and to eliminate those descriptions from this investigation of old age. In addition, I will not consider it sufficient evidence that a person is "old" if he or she is merely referred to as *zāqēn*. That is, to be considered old in this study, a biblical figure must be identified as old by more than the term *zāqēn*, either contextually or lexically. The role of "elders" as a political body, therefore, is not treated in this study.[39] In what follows, the polyvalence

---

33. Lawrence Stager, "The Archaeology of the Family," *BASOR* 260 (1985) 26.
34. Ibid.
35. John MacDonald, "The Status and Role of the Naʿar in Israelite Society," *JNES* 35 (1976) 167.
36. Hans-Peter Stähli, *Knabe-Jüngling-Knecht: Untersuchung zum Begriff* נער *im Alten Testament* (BBET 7; Frankfurt am Main: Peter Lang, 1978). Stähli argues that a *naʿar* is simply one who is unmarried and in a dependent relationship (p. 275). Carolyn S. Leeb, *Away from the Father's House: The Social Location of* naʿar *and* naʿarah *in Ancient Israel* (JSOTSup 301; Sheffield: Sheffield Academic Press, 2000) 19.
37. Ibid., 18.
38. Leeb (ibid., 19) argues that the assumed "high-born" status of a *naʿar* may not apply in every case because someone's dependent status may have precluded him from the kind of land ownership requisite to lead a household and thus hold such a status.
39. Several studies are available on elders as a body of leaders in the Hebrew Bible. See Hanoch Reviv, *The Elders in Ancient Israel: A Study of a Biblical Institution* (trans. Lucy Plitmann; Jerusalem: Magnes, 1989); Timothy Willis, *The Elders of the*

of *zāqēn* will necessitate careful consideration of contextual clues in each story.

One additional matter remains before we look at the Hebrew Bible. A precise definition of the word *old* in reference to a person cannot be found in our sources. One could argue that a clear definition does not exist even in our own time. I would suggest that individuals were considered old in biblical Israel when they began to present outward features associated with old age: wrinkled skin and gray hair.[40] For men, gray beards also marked them as old, while for women the mark of old age, though not outward, would probably be the onset of menopause.[41] The data for calculating life expectancy in ancient Israel are slight, and calculating it with real precision is impossible. Yet the evidence that is available suggests that most people did not live beyond their 40s. If data from Neo-Assyrian and Neo-Babylonian cuneiform sources are applicable in determining age patterns for ancient Israel, men would have married for the first time, on average, between the ages of 26 and 32, while women would have been only 14 to 20 at the time of their first marriage.[42] This pattern of age difference of more than a decade is also currently reflected in marriage customs in the Middle East, where a bride is in her early teens and a groom is at least in his middle 20s when they marry for the first time.[43] Given the approximate life expectancy of 40 to 50 years, therefore, a male would not often live to see his male offspring marry.[44]

City; A Study of the Elder-Laws in Deuteronomy (SBLMS 55; Atlanta: Society of Biblical Literature, 2001); and John L. McKenzie, "The Elders in the Old Testament," *Bib* 40 (1959) 522–40. I also found O. Seesemann's work helpful though it is quite old. See Otto Seesemann, *Die Ältesten im Alten Testament* (Ph.D. dissertation, University of Leipzig, 1895).

40. Rivkah Harris notes that gray hair was the distinguishing characteristic of old age in Mesopotamia. See Rivkah Harris, *Gender and Aging in Mesopotamia: The Gilgamesh Epic and Other Ancient Literature* (Norman, OK: Oklahoma University Press, 2000) 51.

41. While menopause does not present obvious outward manifestations, cross-cultural evidence suggests that roles for postmenopausal Israelite women may have changed, as they do for many in the world's populations. The LoDagga women of Ghana are given broader power when they enter menopause because they are viewed as asexual at that point. Some Amerindian women were allowed to become shamans after menopause. See Gutmann, *Reclaimed Powers*, 159.

42. Martha T. Roth, "Age at Marriage and the Household: A Study of Neo-Babylonian and Assyrian Forms," *Comparitive Studies in Society and History* 29 (1987) 737.

43. John Gulick, *The Middle East: An Anthropological Perspective* (Pacific Palisades, CA: Goodyear, 1976) 183. Cited in Roth, "Age at Marriage," 737.

44. Roth suggests that the age at which a man would marry effectively coincided with his realizing his patrimony at the death of his father. The passing of one's father and subsequent acquisition of his inheritance may have been the point at which a

As we will see later in this chapter, the ages attributed to the antedeluvian fathers and the early leaders of Israel cannot be used to estimate the average age of the Israelite population. The tendency to attribute a long life to the heroes of old to elevate their reputation was all too common among the early sources. Age overstatement has been shown to be common even into the present among the world's cultures.[45] Yet even so, when we turn, for example, to the kings of Judah and Israel in the DH, the ages given to them are basically what we expect in light of our own experience. The ages given for these kings range from 21 to 66, and the average is 44; of course, one must allow for the possible margin of error when computing the reigns of kings in the ancient world.[46] It is difficult to know whether this sort of information is even helpful in approximating life expectancy in ancient Israel. Wolff notes that these rulers probably had the best access to a varied diet, as well as freedom from the hard labor that the masses surely knew all too well.[47] In keeping with the extremely high ages attributed to the early ancestors, the claim that Jehoida the priest died at the age of 130 (2 Chr 24:15) is likely inflated, despite being close to the modern record for longevity.[48] Nabonidus's mother was said to have died at the age of 104.[49] Yet such a long lifespan was surely quite rare, and the vast majority died at what we would call an "early age," long before reaching the 120-year maximum decreed by Yahweh (Gen 6:3). Even the seven or eight decades mentioned in Ps 90:10 were an allotment that relatively few enjoyed.

When we move beyond the textual evidence, we see that it is corroborated by archaeology. Assessing the approximate age of death from skeletal remains sheds further light on lifespans in the ancient world. Unfortunately the best osteological evidence comes from the Second Temple period, which is later than most of the texts examined in this

---

man was able to marry and thus may help explain why men married at an older age than women. See Roth, "Age at Marriage," 737.

45. Holmes and Holmes, *Other Cultures, Elder Years*, 44.

46. Hans W. Wolff, *Anthropology of the Old Testament* (trans. Margaret Khol; Philadelphia: Fortress, 1974) 119.

47. Ibid.

48. The current world record for longevity is held by Jeanne Louise Calment, who lived to be 122; she was born on February 21, 1875, and died on August 4, 1997.

49. Other ages of a few Babylonians have been approximated by M. A. Dandamayev. The Babylonian scribe Aplā, son of Bēl-iddina, descendant of Egibi, was around 90 when he died. Dandamayev lists several other scribes who had careers that lasted 40 years, which would probably have meant that they lived to be at least 60. See M. A. Dandamayev, "About Life Expectancy in Babylonia in the First Millennium B.C.," in *Death in Mesopotamia* (ed. Bendt Alster; Copenhagen: Akademisk Forlag, 1980) 184.

study.⁵⁰ Rachel Hachlili and Patricia Smith uncovered 31 individual skeletons from the Herodian period in Jericho. Of these, 10 were infants 0–5 years; one juvenile aged 11–12; 2 adolescents aged 16–18; 2 young females and 3 males aged 20–39; 3 females and 2 males aged 40–50; and 2 females and 4 males over 50 at death.⁵¹ Extrapolating from the evidence of the tombs at Jericho shows that 38% died before age 20, substantially less than the figure from the Greek world at the same time (48%).⁵² The mortality rate among infants, assessed at approximately 33%, is also attested in other areas in Palestine.⁵³ This figure is also lower than infant mortality rates from the greater Mediterranean world in the same period.⁵⁴ The evidence from these tombs is quite limited, however, and they probably reflect an upper socioeconomic stratum in Jerusalem and Jericho.⁵⁵ That being the case, the extant evidence only provides a picture of individuals who could afford good burial, and it may thus be conjectured that the life expectancy of those who could not would be appreciably less.

At this point, I want to examine the Hebrew Bible to offer a survey of old-age depiction. I have elected to proceed from book to book in canonical order in this survey rather than, say, thematically, in order to give the reader an easier approach to this material.

Old Age Terminology in the Pentateuch

I now turn to an examination of the Pentateuch and the portrayal of old age therein. My object of inquiry will, first of all, be the figures who are labeled "old," bearing in mind the special attention that the term *zāqēn* is to receive. Old age as a motif will also feature in the study of these books. This motif is especially relevant to the narratives of the patriarchs, which frequently employ old age as a backdrop for the work of God in their lives. An examination of these two facets of the Hebrew Bible is designed to determine how old age was viewed in Israel. Understanding this will serve as the groundwork for my quest to understand

---

50. Patricia Smith and Joseph Zias, "Skeletal Remains from the Late Hellenistic French Hill Tomb," *IEJ* 30 (1980) 109.

51. Rachel Hachlili and Patricia Smith, "The Genealogy of the Goliath Family," *BASOR* 235 (1979) 67. The percentage of individuals living beyond 50 is slightly greater at Jericho than Jerusalem, suggesting that the conditions there were perhaps more favorable to its inhabitants. See Rachel Hachlili et al., "The Jewish Necropolis at Jericho," *Current Anthropology* 22 (1981) 701.

52. Hachlili and Smith, "Genealogy of the Goliath Family," 67.

53. Smith and Zias, "Skeletal Remains," 111.

54. Ibid., 114.

55. Ibid., 115.

why Yahweh is not explicitly portrayed with old-age imagery in most of Israel's history.

Before I begin with an examination of the relevant texts, a few words are in order regarding the Hebrew Bible as an object of critical study. It is well established that the received text represents a composition that has been worked and reworked over centuries. A consensus exists in biblical scholarship that P is responsible for providing ages for the various characters in the stories.[56] Yet J and E are the main sources for examples of old age as a narrative motif and of the portrayal of the aged in general. Thus, the vast majority of relevant data available from the Pentateuch are heavily mediated through the work of J, E, and subsequently P. Although the age that P ascribes to many figures in the Pentateuch may indicate that someone reached old age, we will consider an individual to be old only if he or she is so described in other ways. Numerical age alone will not serve to mark someone as "old."

A ground rule of this sort proves its immediate import in Genesis, where within the primeval history of Genesis 1–11 many biblical figures are said to live unbelievably long lives. In chaps. 5 and 11, extreme ages ranging from 777 to 969 are reported for ten *Urväter* from Adam to Noah, and only Enoch, snatched from the earth at a relatively youthful 365, can be singled out as an exception. Such high numbers are seen in the Sumerian King List, in which the lifespans of some kings are measured in millennia.[57] The practice of attributing extraordinarily long lifespans to primeval ancestors was widespread in the ancient world.[58] Although proportionally less, the high ages attributed to the patriarchs and leaders of Israel down to the period of the settlement are probably meant to mark the connection that these men had with the heroes of old.[59] It is likely that assumptions regarding longevity and piety may have contributed to the extreme ages credited to these men by the biblical writers.

---

56. Julius Wellhausen, *Prolegomena to the History of Israel* (Scholars Press Reprints and Translations; Atlanta: Scholars Press, 1994) 337; repr. of *Prolegomena to the History of Israel* (trans. J. Sutherland Black and Allan Enzies, with preface by W. Robertson Smith; Edinburgh: Black, 1885); trans. of *Prolegomena zur Geschichte Israels* (2nd ed.; Berlin: Reimer, 1883). See also John Skinner, *Genesis* (Edinburgh: T. & T. Clark, 1910) 127; and E. A. Speiser, *Genesis* (AB 1; Garden City, NY: Doubleday, 1964) 41.

57. See Thorkild Jacobsen, *The Sumerian King List* (Chicago: University of Chicago Press, 1939) 71–77; lines 1–45 of the text list kings who reigned for up to 108,000 years.

58. Claus Westermann, *Genesis 1–11* (trans. John J. Scullion; London: SPCK, 1984) 351.

59. Josef Scharbert, "Das Alter und die Alten in der Bibel," *Saeculum* 30 (1979) 341.

The first mention of a person's age outside of the mythological material of Genesis 1–11 illustrates the need to distinguish between who is old and who has simply lived for many years. At the beginning of the Abraham stories, we discover, courtesy of P, that Abraham[60] is 75, though no other indication of old age is provided. That he is childless at this age is, for the most part, a departure from his forebears as indicated by the Shemite lineage in 11:10–26. Shem was 100 when he had his first son, Arpachshad, who was 35 when he had his first son, Shelah, who became a father at 30, when Eber was born. Eber was 34 when his son Peleg was born; Peleg had his first son, Reu, at 30. Reu was 32 when he fathered Serug, who sired Nahor at the age of 30. Nahor fathered Terah at 29. Thus far in the lineage, each man had fathered his first son by the age of 35, with the exception of Shem.

The pattern shifts with Terah who, at 70, was over twice the average age of his most immediate ancestors when Abraham is born. Abraham's childless state at 75 is, therefore, somewhat alarming to the audience, and it establishes the context for the primary problem our protagonist faces—childlessness. Because old age is not specifically mentioned here and Abraham is not called "old," we may simply say that Abraham's period of childlessness is, in comparison with many of his ancestors, at an extreme variance. In fact, it even exceeds that of his father, who was approximately twice the average age of his ancestors when he entered fatherhood. So, while we cannot say with certainty that Abraham was viewed as "old," we may say that he was likely considered old to be childless.

The portrayal of Abraham and Sarah with explicit old-age terminology and imagery begins in Gen 18:11, where Abraham and Sarah are, for the first time, referred to as *zĕqēnîm* 'old', a term immediately qualified with the phrase *bā'îm bayyāmîm* 'ones advanced in years'. The Aramaic reflex of this latter phrase will be used to refer to Yahweh in Daniel 7. This qualification allows us to understand the plural of *zāqēn* as meaning 'old' rather than denoting an honorific title. This verse also demonstrates that Sarah is postmenopausal, with the phrase *ḥādal lihyōt lĕśārâ 'ōraḥ kannāšîm* 'the way of women had ceased to be for Sarah'. Here again is further qualification of the notion of being described as *zĕqēnîm*. The emphasis on infertility in old age is clearly indicated. The description of the couple in Gen 18:11 allows the reader to assume a connection between the couple's infertility in Gen 17:17 and their senescence. Gen 17:17 portrays the patriarch laughing at the prospect of an elderly couple, a man of 100 years and his wife of 90 years, hav-

---

60. Although the patriarch is initially called Abram, I have elected, for the purposes of consistency and clarity, to refer to him always as Abraham.

ing a child. Here, indeed, is the only place in Genesis where someone's numeric age occurs in direct discourse rather than in narration. In the texts of Genesis 17 and 18, the motif of old age that will be the backdrop for the Abraham-Sarah stories is established. The tenor of the two stories provides a common understanding of old age as a time when fertility ceases in women.

The following verse continues this theme with the laughter of Sarah in response to the news of her imminent pregnancy. Here she refers to her state as *'aḥarê bĕlōtî* 'after I have become worn out', she calls her husband *zāqēn*, and she wonders whether she will have *ʿednâ*. The verb *blh* is used of clothing in Deut 8:4, 29:4, and (along with sandals) in Josh 9:13; of bones that have dried up in Ps 32:3; and of an afflicted man in Job 13:28.[61] The verb's proximity to the description of Abraham as "old" suggests its synonymous relationship with old-age imagery and expresses the pejorative description of old age here in this story. The word *ʿednâ* has had an interesting translational history.[62] While it is often rendered in English translations as 'pleasure' (RSV, KJV) the more likely meaning is 'fertility', which is contextually appropriate.[63]

Her childless state plus the age provided by P heighten the narrative anxiety over Sarah's barren womb in old age. While lack of an heir was certainly a problem for men, women were forced to bear a disproportionate burden of suffering in the wake of childlessness, because they were likely to outlive their husbands, and there would be no male to provide for them in their widowhood. The sense of hopelessness that seems to accompany Sarah's words here actually follows a pattern that has been documented by Lowenthal, Thurner, and Chiriboga. Their data suggest that the female entry into a more independent existence after middle age is often preceded by a period of malaise and

---

61. The verb *blh* is also used of clothing in Isa 50:9, Ps 102:27, and Isa 51:6. In each of these examples, the garment's becoming worn is used as a simile for the wearing away of the heavens and the earth (Ps 102:27) one's enemies (Isa 50:9) and the earth (Isa 51:6).

62. The translations include *heôs tou nun* 'until now' in the Vaticanus LXX; a similar rendering of *akmē* 'as yet' in Symmachus's translation, which assumes the word to be *ʿadenâ* 'hitherto, still', as in Qoh 4:2 and 4:3. See Francis Brown, S. R. Driver, and Charles A. Briggs, *The New Brown, Driver, Briggs, Gesenius Hebrew and English Lexicon* (hereafter BDB; Peabody, MA: Hendrickson, 1979) 725b; *truphêria* 'voluptuousness' in Aquila's Greek translation; and 'conception' in *Tg. Pseudo-Jonathan*. BDB has 'sexual delight' (p. 726b).

63. The Old Aramaic verb *ʿdn* means 'to be fruitful', and so the noun here could mean 'fertility'. See B. Kedar-Kopfstein, "*ʿēden*" *TDOT* 10:486. Kedar-Kopfstein mentions this possibility but opts for the more traditional translation 'enjoyment'. For more on the Old Aramaic Tell Fekheriyeh inscription attesting *ʿdn* 'to enrich, make abundant', see A. R. Millard, "The Etymology of Eden," *VT* 34 (1984) 105.

hopelessness.⁶⁴ Gutmann uses their work to argue that women tend to acquire a more assertive role in their later years.⁶⁵ This is true for Sarah, who appears somewhat despondent here but shows great assertiveness toward her husband in Gen 21:10. This literary representation of Abraham's seeming passivity and Sarah's assertive disposition suggests that the biblical writers were conscious of a drop in assertiveness in men and a parallel rise in this quality among women as they age. These changes were perhaps correlated with the decrease in testosterone levels in men and their increase in women as they approach old age.⁶⁶

The phenomenon is documented for men and women in cultures the world over. Gutmann argues that this male-female exchange in assertiveness in old age is an intercultural phenomenon. He even finds parallel evidence in the primate world.⁶⁷

In the story of Lot in the city of Sodom, the narrator describes the gathering of men around his house as ranging *minnaʿar wĕʿad zāqēn* 'from a youth to an elder person' (Gen 19:4). The polyvalence of *zāqēn* is a critical factor here, especially in proximity to *naʿar*, because both terms may refer to either the age or the status of individuals in the city.⁶⁸ The narrator could be indicating the range of the status of the men who had come to the house that evening.⁶⁹ The LXX does little to resolve the problem, because it renders *zāqēn* with the genitive of *presbyteros*, which carries the same semantic variation as the Hebrew. Since there are no other indicators of age in this story regarding these men, this story cannot provide evidence for our understanding of old age.

Senescence plays a clearer role in the episode later in the same chapter when Lot is staying in a cave with his two daughters (Gen 19:30–38). The daughters say, *ʾābînû zāqēn* 'our father is old' (19:31) and they plan to impregnate themselves using him. Contextually, *zāqēn* in this instance has little to do with status and everything to do with senescence.⁷⁰ The daughters' primary concern is probably for Lot's waning life, if he is esteemed as old in their minds. So it is his age and not his possible honorific status that is at issue. Waiting to ascertain whether a possible

---

64. Marjorie Fiske Lowenthal, Majda Thurner, and David Chiriboga, *Four Stages of Life* (San Francisco: Jossey-Bass, 1975) 152.
65. Gutmann, *Reclaimed Powers*, 157.
66. Ibid., 182.
67. Idem, *The Human Elder in Nature, Culture, and Society* (Boulder, CO: Westview, 1997) 178.
68. Stager, "Archaeology of the Family," 26.
69. MacDonald, "Status and Role of the Nʿr," 167. MacDonald argues that the two groups comprise the fighting men of the city.
70. The LXX again uses *presbyteros* here, as it does earlier in the chapter regarding the men of Sodom.

mate survived the overthrow that they had experienced does not seem to be an option. The fact that a man who was *zāqēn* was assumed to possess the ability to impregnate also tells us something about the way the aged were imagined. The ancients were obviously well aware that even old men could father a child, as Abraham's ability to impregnate Hagar indicates. Even so, the portrayal of Lot as an old man duped by his daughters is by no means a flattering portrayal of old age. Lot's drunkenness and apparent ignorance of the encounters may be a part of a larger attempt to portray Lot as a comic foil to Abraham.[71] In any case, old age coincides with vulnerability. Whether the reader is supposed to connect this vulnerability with Lot's old age or with Lot's role as a schlemiel who just happens to be old is impossible to know. The fact that the episode has a connection to the senescent vulnerability of Isaac is suggestive of the former.

Just as the daughters of Lot bring forth sons of a union with an old man (Gen 19:37–38) so too Sarah bears a son in Abraham's old age (*zĕqēnāyw*, Gen 21:7). This episode again plays on the narrative motif of old age, insofar as what an audience might reasonably conclude based on the couple's old age is overturned by the power of the patriarch's God. Who would have assumed that Abraham could sire a child and that Sarah would nurse a baby at their age? The assumed sterility of the aged woman is disproved with the arrival of Isaac.

Just before he sends his servant away to acquire a wife for his son Isaac, Abraham is once again said to be *zāqēn bā' bayyāmîm* 'old, advanced in years' (24:1) echoing the same words used of Sarah and him in Gen 18:11. As before, the qualification of *bā' bayyāmîm* indicates that *zāqēn* here refers to age rather than an honorific status. Incidentally, the servant entrusted with the mission to find a wife for Isaac in Gen 24:2 is *'abdô zĕqan bêtô* 'his servant, the oldest in his house', which likely reaffirms the status that age brings. Of course, this does not automatically mean that this man is old, but I assume that *zāqēn* in this context refers to age, because it is unlikely that this servant would be an "elder" of a community while serving Abraham in a dependent position.

The story of Abraham's purchase of the cave at Machpelah to serve as a family burial ground has been attributed to P by virtually all critical commentators.[72] Nowhere in this story is Abraham's aged status cited.

---

71. Joel Kaminsky has noted possible humor in the stories of Isaac in Genesis. It seems to me that Kaminsky's insight could be applied to Lot's portrayal as well. See Joel Kaminsky, "Humor and the Theology of Hope: Isaac as a Humorous Figure," *Int* 54 (2000) 370.

72. Claus Westermann, *Genesis 12–36* (trans. John J. Scullion; Minneapolis: Fortress, 1995) 371; Gerhard von Rad, *Genesis* (trans. John H. Marks; Philadelphia: Westminster, 1961) 241; however, see Speiser (*Genesis*, 173), who thinks it is mostly J.

Yet in keeping with P's narrative chronology, where Abraham and Sarah have been described with a number of senescent terms and phrases, I have deemed this episode appropriate to the docket of elderly concerns. When Abraham purchases this plot to bury his wife, Sarah, we witness the concern of an elderly man for the proper burial of loved ones and, implicitly, of himself—a concern, as Herbert Brichto has noted, that may elucidate an Israelite view of the afterlife.[73] This story of acquisition reflects a worldwide recognition of the importance of property for security in old age.[74]

The account of Abraham's death is accompanied by the comment that he was 175 and that he died *bĕśêbâ ṭôbâ zāqēn wĕśābêaʿ* 'in a good old age, old and full [of years]' (Gen 25:8). This is in keeping with the promise given by God in Gen 15:15. Here for the first time we see a report of death that is accompanied by an assessment of the person's life in terms of his age and quality of life. The juxtaposition of *zāqēn* and *śābēaʿ* is yet another indicator of the use of *zāqēn* to denote age rather than a specific title or office. This assessment of Abraham's life establishes a pattern to which many will aspire and that some biblical figures will actually repeat, as we will see in the lives of Isaac and Jacob.

Besides Sarah's infertility, another facet of senescent infirmity is seen in Isaac, who is blind in his old age (Gen 27:1). Genesis 27 begins, *wayhî kî zāqēn yiṣḥāq wattikhênâ ʿēnāyw mērĕʾōt* 'When Isaac was old, his eyes were dimmed so that he could not see'. The association of *zāqēn* and visual infirmity guarantees that *zāqēn* must refer to age. Isaac himself says, *zāqantî* 'I am old' (Gen 27:2) adding that he does not know the day of his death—although he assumes it is imminent, given the request he addresses to his servant. The verbal form of the root *zqn* juxtaposed with what appears to be a statement about the proximity of death indicates that *zāqēn* must refer strictly to Isaac's age without indicating his status as head of household. The narrative motif of old age first employed in the stories of Abraham and Sarah is thus extended to the next generation. The picture of old age here is, again, infirmity. Yet rather than impotence or barrenness, the focus is on eyesight.

The motif of deceiving the elderly, reminiscent of the story of Lot and his daughters, reappears, again implying the vulnerable nature of the aged. At the behest of his mother, Jacob deceives his father and receives the paternal blessing, the bestowal of which, as we discover later in Genesis, is one of the hallmarks of an elderly father. The deception

---

73. Herbert Brichto, "Kin, Cult, Land and Afterlife: A Biblical Complex," *HUCA* 44 (1973) 9–10.

74. Leo Simmons, *The Role of the Aged in Primitive Society* (New Haven, CT: Yale University Press, 1945) 36.

turns on an exploitation of Isaac's concern for food, which is a common transcultural phenomenon among seniors.[75] Like Lot, Isaac is fooled by family members—this time, his wife and son. Unlike Lot, however, Isaac discovers the deception almost immediately, even though it is too late. This recurrent motif of deceiving the elderly indicates a negative portrayal of old age.

Isaac's age at death is given as 180 (Gen 35:28), and he is said to be *zāqēn ûśēbaʿ yāmîm* 'old and full [lit., 'satisfied'] of days' (Gen 35:29).[76] Yet, before he dies, Isaac pronounces a blessing on Jacob as the latter leaves for Paddan Aram to seek a wife (Gen 28:1). Once again, the feature of an elderly father pronouncing a blessing on his son serves an important narrative function.

Jacob is the patriarch for whom we have the most detailed "biography," from his birth to his death at the end of Genesis. His youngest son, Joseph, is referred to as a *ben zĕqūnîm* (Gen 37:3) usually rendered 'a son of [Jacob's] old age'. This form is seen earlier in the Abraham story (Gen 21:2, 7) when Sarah gives birth to Isaac, a son *lizqūnāyw* 'for his old age'. A bit later in the Joseph story (Gen 44:20), Benjamin is referred to as a *yeled zĕqūnîm* 'a boy of old age', a title similar to the title given to Joseph. It is possible that the form *zĕqūnîm*, an abstract of the root *zqn*, may refer to the status of one who heads a household. In this case, the phrase would mean that Joseph was born at a time after Jacob had become the head of his patrimonial household. Yet the traditional understanding of *zĕqūnîm*, supported by the LXX's *huios gērous* 'son of old age', as an abstract noun connoting old age is more likely, in light of the way that forms of *zqn* have been employed in the previous parts of Genesis. Because the form *zĕqūnîm* only occurs in these patriarchal stories in Genesis, stories that often employ the topos of old age as a backdrop, it is quite likely that *zĕqūnîm* carries the nuance of old age rather than indicating a title or status.

If we may assume that the traditional way of understanding is the best interpretation of *ben zĕqūnîm*, having a child at an advanced age is portrayed positively. Yet Jacob's joy over Joseph turns to sorrow when the other sons sell Joseph into slavery and lead their father to believe that he is dead (37:31–32). Jacob also endures the loss of Rachel, his favorite wife, who died while delivering Benjamin (35:17–19) another

---

75. Ibid. See also Gutmann, *The Human Elder*, 114. Simmons (*Role of the Aged*, 26) assumes that this obsession is based on a desire to ward off approaching death, while Gutmann (p. 118) suggests it is more closely related to the comfort that good food brings and the concomitant reminiscence of maternal care.

76. Note that this is the fuller locution of the phrase used in Gen 25:8, *zāqēn wĕśābēaʿ* 'old and satisfied'. This truncated version assumes that the reader understood *śābēaʿ* to refer to 'days'.

son born in his old age. In Gen 44:20, Judah refers to Benjamin as *yeled zĕqūnîm qāṭān* 'a little boy of old age' when he pleads for the boy's release to Joseph, whom the brothers have not yet recognized. As before, the LXX's locution understands *zĕqūnîm* to indicate senescence, rendering *paidion neōteron gērōs* 'little child of old age'. In this verse, Judah refers to Jacob as *ʾāb zāqēn*, which could be rendered either 'an old father' or 'a father, an old man'. Earlier, Joseph had asked the brothers about their father, saying, *hăšālôm ʾăbîkem hazzāqēn* 'How is your elderly father?' (or 'your father, the elderly one?', Gen 43:27). In both instances, however, the LXX translates *zāqēn* as *presbyteros* and retains the ambiguity of the Hebrew in regard to age or honorific title.

Of the patriarchs, Jacob has arguably the worst experience in old age. He says as much about his life in Gen 47:9: *mĕʿaṭ wĕrāʿîm hāyû yĕmê šĕnê ḥayyay* 'few and unpleasant have been the days of the years of my life'. He continues his lament by saying that the sum of his years had not reached those of his forefathers. So in Jacob's own view, his life had been worse than that of his ancestors in terms of quality and quantity. Gen 48:1 signals the decline of Jacob in his final years, when Joseph receives the report that *ʾābîkā ḥōleh* 'your father is ill'. A few verses later, we learn that *ʿênê yiśrāʾēl kābĕdû mizzōqen lōʾ yûkal lirʾōt* 'Israel's eyes were heavy from old age so that he could not see' (48:10). The form *zōqen*, a hapax legomenon, must mean 'old age' without reference to status. The particular infirmity of old age that was seen in Isaac is repeated in his son.

However, unlike Isaac's, Jacob's blindness is not an occasion for his deception at the hands of others. In fact, Jacob's blindness plays an interesting role in the blessing that he pronounces on Joseph's sons. In the blessing that the aged *paterfamilias* bestows on Ephraim and Manasseh (Gen 48:19–20), Jacob continues the tradition handed to him. Jacob's very opportunity to deliver the blessing here is couched as a serendipitous blessing for the aged man himself: he hardly expected to pronounce a blessing on his grandchildren, because he previously thought that he would never see his son, their father, again. However, there is a twist on the usual custom, whereby Jacob actually gives the primary blessing to the younger rather than the older. Joseph tries to correct his blind father, but Jacob assures him that he knows what he is doing. Though the patriarch is blind, his cognitive functions are still keen. The blessing also demonstrates the prerogative given to a senescent *paterfamilias* whereby he may adopt his grandchildren in order to bless them with a son's share of the inheritance.[77] The portrayal of Jacob in old age

---

77. Speiser, *Genesis*, 357. See also von Rad, *Genesis*, 410.

is one of a feeble body said to be sick and blind, yet containing an alert and clever mind.

Genesis 49 continues this portrayal of the aged Jacob in the recording of the blessing he gives to all of his sons shortly before his death. Although the poem may have originally comprised discrete tribal sayings,[78] the collection thereof constitutes the blessing that the dying patriarch pronounces on his sons. As in the old poetry of Judges 5, praise and blame are meted out to the addressees, another indication of the prerogative given to an aged patriarch. Though Gaster notes that these deathbed blessings stem from a popular belief that the dying are prescient, his examples are derived from the Greek world.[79] The more likely explanation, in my opinion, is that, in the narrative world of Genesis, these patriarchs are extraordinary figures, as their extreme old age indicates. As such, even their blessings on their children are couched in what appear to be predictions of the future. Their blessings also confirm the favorable opinion of these groups in the mind of later tradents of these texts.

Old age is not a prominent theme in the book of Exodus. In keeping with its *Tendenz*, P provides the age at death of Levi (137, 6:16) Kohath (133, 6:18) Amram (137, 6:20) and Moses and Aaron (80 and 83, respectively, 7:7) all from the priestly tribe of Levi. The profundity of the exodus events is twice expressed in terms of the current generation's relationship to preceding or following generations. Thus, Moses is told in 10:2 that he will be able to tell his grandchildren how Yahweh made sport of the Egyptians, while in 10:6 the locust plague is said to be worse than what anyone's grandfather had seen. On one occasion, Moses speaks of all Israelites leaving Egypt, saying, "We will go *binʿārênû ûbizqēnênû*" 'with our youths and with our elderly' " (Exod 10:9). In this verse, we see an interesting pairing of *zāqēn* 'elderly' and *naʿar* 'youth' in addition to "sons and daughters" and "flocks and herds." I suspect that *binʿārênû ûbizqēnênû* are general references to ages here, hence my translation. Yet it is possible that with these two groups Moses indicates social groups such as "dependents and leaders."[80]

Leviticus has the fewest references to old age in the Pentateuch. In 19:3 occurs the command, *ʾîš ʿimmô wěʾābîw tîrāʾû* 'Each one of you

---

78. Claus Westermann, *Genesis 37–50* (trans. John J. Scullion; Minneapolis: Augsburg, 1986) 221.

79. Theodor H. Gaster, *Myth, Legend, and Custom in the Old Testament* (New York: Harper & Row, 1969) 214. His examples are Xenophon and Aristotle.

80. This grouping may indicate a distinction between a *naʿar* and merely a son and may also demonstrate that a *naʿar* is a youth of social standing who represents a potential elder, as Stager suggests ("Archaeology of the Family," 25).

must revere his mother and his father'. Although this is not a specific command to take care of parents in old age, this verse sets the stage for the more specific command that comes later in this chapter. Although Leviticus has rather limited references to old age, in 19:32 is found the most forthright biblical command to respect the aged. The verse reads: *mippĕnê śêbâ tāqûm wĕhādartā pĕnê zāqēn* 'you must rise up before the hoary head and honor the face of an old man'.[81] This expression is unmatched in the Hebrew Bible in its commitment to safeguard the honor of the elderly. The command is connected to the further enjoinder to "fear your God" in the second part of the verse.

A similar instruction is seen in the Egyptian "Instruction of Ani" dating back to the Eighteenth Dynasty, when the father tells his son, "You should not sit when another who is older than you is standing."[82] Such behavior was also practiced in Sparta and dictated in Plato's *Republic*.[83] The command to rise may be intended to guarantee a comfortable seat for the elderly. This seems to be the case in Job 29:8, where both young and old rise for Job in the context of preparing a seat in the city square. Yet *qûm* + *mippĕnê* 'to rise before' can be an act of honor in itself, which appears to be the case in Gen 31:35, when Rachel apologizes to her father for not standing up when he enters her tent. The verb *qûm* is also used with the Hishtaphel of *ḥwh* 'to bow' in several places where honor is expressed (Gen 23:7; Exod 33:10; 1 Sam 20:41, 25:41; Isa 49:7). Of course, in these passages the act of bowing probably carries the weight of the intended honor; the act of standing merely places the person in the proper stance for bowing. In any case, the idea of deference to the elderly is commanded here more clearly than in any other text of the Hebrew Bible.

In Lev 27:3–7, there is an assessment regarding the value of people who are vowed to Yahweh according to age. Listed in the chart on p. 27 are the valuations of persons described in this text. Men aged 20–60 have the highest value—50 shekels—which, however, drops considerably after age 60. This reflects their capacity for labor, which surely decreased in men over 60. That 60 is the upper age limit for prime value suggests that there were men who worked up to that point, even though external evidence indicates that individuals of this age were probably rare.

---

81. The pairing of the forms *śêbâ* and *zāqēn*, as was suggested above, indicates that *zāqēn* here is to be translated 'old man'.

82. J. Gordon Harris, *Biblical Perspectives*, 23; John Wilson, trans., "Instruction of Ani," in *Ancient Near Eastern Texts Relating to the Old Testament* (hereafter *ANET*; ed. James B. Pritchard; Princeton: Princeton University Press, 1969) 420.

83. Ephraim David, *Old Age in Sparta* (Amsterdam: Hakkert, 1991) 64, 66.

Gender	Age	Worth
male	20–60 years	50 shekels
female	20–60 years	30 shekels
male	5–20 years	20 shekels
female	5–20 years	10 shekels
male	1 month–5 years	5 shekels
female	1 month–5 years	3 shekels
male	60 + years	15 shekels
female	60 + years	10 shekels

The book of Numbers does not broaden our view of old age in biblical Israel to a significant degree. Yet on a few occasions it does provide a window on retirement and on the optimal age for warriors. Two censuses are commanded by God to number the men, aged 20 and above, who can serve as warriors (1:2-3, 26:2). According to Num 8:24, Levites aged 25 and older are to serve in the tent of meeting.[84] The very next verse establishes a kind of retirement for Levites at age 50, when they are to cease doing manual labor. Like the valuation of different ages in Lev 27:3-7, the upper age limit of 50 suggests that, albeit rarely so, there were some men who did manual labor at this age.[85]

Before we examine Deuteronomy's portrayal of old age, a few words about the composition of Deuteronomy are in order. The *Forschungsgeschichte* of Deuteronomy's composition is long and distinguished. Noth's foundational work, *Überlieferungsgeschichtliche Studien* (1943), serves as the text to which all react.[86] Noth's contribution has been to frame the work of the Deuteronomistic Historian from Deuteronomy to 2 Kings and to posit a single exilic author. Frank Cross has refined Noth's position with his theory of a double redaction, positing a pre-exilic author designated Dtr^1, whose work was then supplemented by an exilic author, Dtr^2.[87] A further refinement was applied to the study of Deuteronomy by Jon Levenson, who suggested that the law corpus, designated Dtn, was known to Dtr^1 but was only inserted by Dtr^2 during

---

84. See Num 4:3, where the lower age limit is 30 years.
85. The only specific age cited for an individual in Numbers is that of Aaron, who dies at the age of 123 (33:38-39).
86. Martin Noth, *Überlieferungsgeschichtliche Studien* (Halle: Max Niemeyer, 1943).
87. Frank Moore Cross, *Canaanite Myth and Hebrew Epic* (Cambridge: Harvard University Press, 1973) 278-89.

the exile.[88] Although there have been some attempts to resurrect Noth's position,[89] I find Cross's position to be the most likely, and Levenson's refinement thereof addresses the incongruity between the law and Dtr[1]'s position regarding the monarchy. In what follows, I have adopted the schema of Dtr[1], Dtr[2], and Dtn to mark the appropriate source.

One of the recurring notions in the book of Deuteronomy is the promise that "your days will be prolonged in the land." While it is possible that this line may refer to the life of Israel as a whole in the land, it may also be understood to reflect a gift of longevity at the individual level. Certainly the threat of exile, directed to the nation as a whole, has parallels in the greater context of Deuteronomy. Yet the way in which this promise could apply to individual life on the land cannot be ignored. This promise and the potential threat to it are seen eight times in the book (Deut 4:40; 5:16; 6:2; 11:9, 21; 25:15; 30:18, 20). All but 11:21 and 30:20 employ the Hiphil form of the verb *'rk* 'to lengthen'.[90] They are roughly split between Levenson's Dtr[2] (4:40, 30:18, 30:20) and Dtn (5:16; 6:2; 11:9, 21; 25:15). Not surprisingly, the verb does not appear in Dtr[1], since conditionality is not a part of Dtr[1]'s framework.[91]

In two places (28:50 and 32:25), old age is contrasted with youth in descriptions of the ruthlessness with which foreign nations will punish Israel for unfaithfulness. These nations will have no regard for the young (*naʿar* in 28:50, *yōnēq* 'nursing child' in 32:25) or the old (*zāqēn* in 28:50, *îš śêbâ* 'man of gray hair' in 32:25) as they destroy the people.[92]

Moses is portrayed as the quintessential old man in Deut 34:7, where he is said to be 120 years old; this is the only age mentioned in the book.[93] Even so, Moses is nowhere called *zāqēn*. The closest the text comes to indicating any old-age infirmity for Moses is found in Deut 31:2, where he himself says, after declaring his age, "I am no longer able to go out and come in." Despite the years he has lived, we are told (again, in Deut 34:7) that his eyes were not dim and that his vigor (or

---

88. Jon D. Levenson, "Who Inserted the Book of Torah?" *HTR* 68 (1977) 203–33.

89. See Hans-Detlef Hoffmann, *Reform und Reformen* (Zurich: Theologischer Verlag, 1980); and Brian Peckham, *The Composition of the Deuteronomistic History* (HSM 35; Atlanta: Scholars Press, 1985).

90. In 11:21, the form is *yirbû* from the verb *rbh*, and 30:20 has the phrase *'ōrek yāmeykā* 'length of your days'.

91. Levenson, "Who Inserted?" 227.

92. Deut 28:50 is another text that tests MacDonald's assumption that all references to *naʿar* indicate a high-born youth. The verb that takes *naʿar* as its object is *yāḥōn* 'to have compassion', while the *zāqēn* occurs with the phrase "lift the faces." The verb *ḥnn* more likely indicates the compassion one would have for a child *qua* child, rather than an acknowledgment of his status. See MacDonald, "Status and Role of the Naʿar," 167.

93. His age is also mentioned in Deut 31:2, where Moses declares it to be 120.

"freshness") was not diminished. Because the combination of Moses' extreme old age and good health are probably attempts to connect him to the mythological figures and patriarchs who also achieved extreme old age, his age can in no way be used to compute actual life expectancy in early Israel.[94] Note the contrast between this description of Moses' vigor and the vulnerability of old age seen in Lot (Gen 19:31) and Isaac (Gen 27:1-2). By presenting Moses as an exceptional figure even at an advanced age, the Deuteronomist establishes old age as the time to dispense the wisdom gleaned from a lifetime of communion with the God of Israel. This is seen most clearly in the way Deuteronomy is framed as the final sermon of Moses. Though on a lesser scale, the same is true of Joshua, who will address the people at the age of 110.

The Deuteronomistic History

When we turn to the work of the Deuteronomistic Historians in the books following Deuteronomy, only Joshua is portrayed as old in the book that bears his name. Twice we are told that Joshua was *zāqēn bā' bayyāmîm* 'old, one who is advanced in days' (13:1a, 23:1).[95] This phrase is also used of Abraham and Sarah in Gen 18:11 and then Abraham alone in Gen 24:1. The identical usages of this formula are possibly an attempt to connect Joshua to Abraham, perhaps to convey the notion that Joshua has taken the land promised to the patriarch. As I noted regarding the locution in Genesis, the qualification provided by the phrase *bā' bayyāmîm* suggests that *zāqēn* in this sense bespeaks age rather than status.

In 13:1b, Yahweh repeats a varied version of the phrase by employing suffix-conjugation forms of the verbs *zqn* and *bw'* in a direct address to Joshua; *'attâ zāqantâ bā'tā bayyāmîm* 'you have become old; you have become advanced in days'. This statement of Yahweh finds its parallel on the lips of Joshua in 23:2 when he says, *'ănî zāqantî bā'tî bayyāmîm* 'I have become old; I have become advanced in days'. The use of the verbal forms further supports the idea that *zāqēn*, when used in the phrase *zāqēn bā' bayyāmîm*, refers to age rather than a leadership status. Joshua employs an idiom denoting old age when he says, *wĕhinnēh 'ānōkî hōlēk hayyôm bĕderek kol hā'āreṣ* 'today, I am about to go the way of all the earth' (Josh 23:14). His age at death is given as 110 (Josh 24:29) which is the age at which Joseph died (Gen 50:22). Like Moses, Joshua is portrayed as exhorting the people to remain faithful as he prepares to die.

---

94. Scharbert, "Das Alter und die Alten," 342.
95. It is equally possible to parse *zāqēn* as a Qal stative 3ms form from *zqn* rather than an adjective. The form *bā'* could also be understood as a 3ms Qal suffix conjugation of *bw'*.

This portrayal of an aged leader delivering a final discourse underlines the idea that the aged have wisdom to impart and as such is a positive depiction of old age.

In Judges, the only age mentioned is that of Joshua who is, in agreement with the parallel passage in the Joshua account, 110 when he dies (2:8). Note that this age approaches the age of Moses but falls short by ten years, reflecting the biblical idea that no one bests the great leader of the exodus among the leaders of Israel in the DH's purview.[96] The only figure portrayed as *zāqēn* is the unnamed man who takes in the Levite and his concubine and their servant (19:16, 17, 20, and 22). In 19:16, he is called *'îš zāqēn* 'an old man', while in 19:17 and 20, he is called *hā'îš hazzāqēn* 'the old man'. Finally, in 19:22 he is called *hā'îš ba'al habbayit hazzāqēn* 'the man, the owner of the house, the old man'. This *zāqēn* is a sojourner in Gibeah from the hill country of Ephraim. All that we know of him is that he is a sojourner, working in the field when the guests arrive, and that he is the owner of a house. As a *gēr* 'sojourner', or better 'client', in the Ephraimite hill country, this man is probably a dependent of someone in Gibeah. However, as an "owner of a house," he has a certain independent status as well.

In light of these facts, it does not appear that *zāqēn* in this context should denote status, because his position as a client in a land outside his tribal patrimony seems to preclude having status. So *zāqēn* here more likely refers to his age. Though he is a sojourner in Gibeah, this man is the only local to provide hospitality to the guests. In this respect he is portrayed in a positive light. However, he is the one who offers the gang of rapists his own daughter and the Levite's concubine. In the narrative world of Judges 19, no obvious indicators are given whereby the actions of this old man are to be assessed. Thus the portrayal of old age in this character is somewhat mixed. The unnamed old man is laboring in a field as a client, and he is a hospitable homeowner and a father; yet our Western sensibilities suggest that we should question his actions, even condemn him for his lack of concern for the women in his care. The lack of any explicit condemnation of him in the story, however, may suggest that the tradents of this text saw his willingness to sacrifice his own daughter and his guest's concubine in a positive light, reserving their ire for the Benjaminites. Because the man's old age does not seem to be related to a positive or negative portrayal in this story, the episode's contribution to our inquiry is limited.

There are four people in 1–2 Samuel who are called *zāqēn* 'old': Eli (1 Sam 2:22, 4:18), Samuel (1 Sam 8:1, 12:2), Jesse (1 Sam 17:12), and

---

96. The Chronicler notes that Jehoiada the priest reached 130 years (2 Chr 24:15).

Barzillai (2 Sam 19:33). Eli and Barzillai are called *zāqēn mĕ'ōd* 'very old' (1 Sam 2:22 and 2 Sam 19:33, respectively). Their ages are provided in the text: Eli was 98 (1 Sam 4:15) and Barzillai was 80 (2 Sam 19:33, 36) and both men experienced some adversity in old age. Eli's eyes are set so that he cannot see (1 Sam 4:15) though he is said to be *derek mĕṣappeh* 'watching the road' for the return of the army, among whom are his two wayward sons (1 Sam 4:13). Earlier in the story, Eli's eyes are beginning to become 'dim' (*kēhōt*, 1 Sam 3:2) which is the same verbal root used of Isaac's condition in Gen 27:1. Upon hearing the news of the loss of the ark, Eli falls off his seat backward and breaks his neck (1 Sam 4:18). He dies because *zāqēn hā'îš wĕkābēd* 'the man was old and fat'. The presence of *kābēd* suggests that *zāqēn* be parsed as an adjective as well. That *kābēd* should be understood as 'fat' is supported by the LXX's translation *barus* 'heavy in weight'.[97]

The loss of eyesight provides a contextual clue that *zāqēn* here denotes his age rather than his status. Eli's sons are a grave disappointment to their father because of their wickedness. They ignore their father's admonition (1 Sam 2:23–25) and thereby bring a curse upon Eli's house from an unnamed man of God who declares to the elderly priest that all descendants will be cut off from both his house and the house of his father and that there will be no *zāqēn* in his house (1 Sam 2:31–32).[98] The polyvalence of *zāqēn* makes this curse especially poignant. Its reference to 'an old man' is certainly applicable, because the sons will die before their father, and so they will not attain old age. Yet neither will either of these sons become a head of household, and so Eli's house will have no head after he dies. As a result, Eli's house will have no representation at the village level either. The portrayal of Eli as an old man expands the biblical view of senescence slightly. It continues the pattern of old-age infirmity seen in Isaac and Jacob—especially the debility of impaired vision. Although it must be inferred, Eli's loss of sight may be connected to a critique of failing to see the wicked ways of his sons. Their indulgence may also be connected to his own indulgence, which is perhaps portrayed in his portly stature. The nuance of the curse is, furthermore, an interesting portrayal of old age because the state of *zāqēn* in all its connotations is denied to Eli's house. All in all, the portrayal of Eli in old age is of infirmity, tragedy, and loss.

An interesting contrast to Eli is the elderly Gileadite Barzillai, who supplied David and his entourage during Absalom's revolt (2 Sam 17:27).

---

97. Henry George Liddell, Robert Scott, and Henry Stuart Jones, *A Greek-English Lexicon* (hereafter *LSJ*; 9th ed.; Oxford: Clarendon, 1961) 308a.

98. Despite this curse, Eli is said to have descendants in 1 Sam 14:3 and 1 Kgs 2:27.

In 2 Sam 19:33, we are told that Barzillai is *zāqēn mĕʾōd* 'very old'. Here the adverb *mĕʾōd* indicates that *zāqēn* is an adjective denoting age rather than status. In 19:34, David invites the elderly Barzillai to return with him to Jerusalem. In the MT of v. 34, David says *kilkaltî ʾōtĕkā* 'I will support you'. Yet the LXX traditions (except Alexandrinus) attest *to gēras sou* 'your old age' in place of *ʾōtĕkā* 'you'. McCarter rightly restores the reading attested by the LXX traditions, *śêbātĕkā*, although he offers no explanation for the different readings.[99] There may be a connection with the form *bĕšîbātô* in v. 33, which is usually rendered 'when he stayed'. The presence of the *yod* in this form is odd (the expected form is *bĕšibtô*) and may actually mask the form *bĕśêbātô* 'in his old age', which is indeed attested in two Hebrew manuscripts.[100]

Because Barzillai is 80 at this point, he certainly could be said to have provided for David in his (that is, Barzillai's) old age. Barzillai escorts the king to the Jordan River, no mean feat for an octogenarian, and this despite Barzillai's claim that he cannot taste what he eats or drinks, nor can he hear the voices of men and women singers (2 Sam 19:36). A similar complaint is attested in the Insiger Papyrus from the Hellenistic period. An Egyptian wisdom teacher laments, "Sixty years are past, all is past. When his heart loves wine, he can no longer drink to drunkenness. When he likes food, he can no longer eat as he once did. When his heart desires a woman, that moment no longer comes."[101] Barzillai recounts these infirmities to David as he declines the king's invitation to join him in Jerusalem. As an old man, Barzillai knows his remaining days are few. He does not want to be a burden to the king, and yet Barzillai seizes the opportunity to provide for Chimham, who may be his son.[102] The story of Barzillai provides one of the most informative descriptions of old age available in the Hebrew Bible.

The life of Samuel is recounted from birth to death (and even beyond) in these two books. He is the only one who is called "old" in direct speech (1 Sam 8:5) in 1–2 Samuel, and he is the only figure to

---

99. P. Kyle McCarter, *II Samuel* (AB 9; Garden City, NY: Doubleday, 1984) 414. LXX Alexandrinus attests 'your house'.

100. Wellhausen says, "durch ihren [i.e., the presence of a marginal gloss of שיבת for the MT's את in v. 34] zufälligen Einfluss ist hier שבת in שיבת verändert." Julius Wellhausen, *Der Text der Bücher Samuelis* (Göttingen: Vandenhoeck & Ruprecht, 1871) 205. The two Hebrew manuscripts are mentioned in the BHS critical apparatus.

101. Quoted in Willy Schottroff, "Alter als soziales Problem in der hebräischen Bibel," in *Was ist der Mensch . . . ? Beitrage zur Anthropologie des Alten Testaments, Hans Walter Wolff zum 80. Geburtstag* (ed. Frank Crusemann, Christof Hardmeier, and Rainer Kessler; Munich: Chr. Kaiser, 1992) 64 (my translation).

102. The LXX adds "my son" in 2 Sam 19:38.

admit being old (1 Sam 12:2). In his old age, Samuel appointed his sons as judges (1 Sam 8:1) yet like the sons of Eli, Samuel's sons were not respected among the elders (1 Sam 8:4-5). Samuel makes an encore appearance during the story of Saul's visit to Endor, when he is summoned from beyond the grave to foretell Saul's imminent demise. When the "witch" sees him, she says he is *'îš zāqēn* 'an old man' (1 Sam 28:14).[103] Her description is most likely a reference to Samuel's age because his appearance alone would not have denoted the honorific status that *zāqēn* can denote in certain contexts. Though the news that Samuel brings is quite grim for Saul, the portrayal of Samuel as an old man whose word is sought has a connection to the notion that the aged offer wise counsel, seen in the description of Moses and Joshua as well as in the wisdom texts of Job 8:8 and 12:12. Of course, we cannot rule out the possibility that Samuel speaks wisdom not because he is old but because he is dead. That he is imagined as an "old man" even in death, however, suggests that wisdom and old age are a coordinate pair.

The brief description of David's father, Jesse, as *zāqēn bā' ba'ănāšîm* 'old, entering among men' in 1 Sam 17:12 is, as McCarter observes, "an impossible combination" and should probably be read *bā' baššānîm* 'advanced in *years*', which is attested in the Lucianic tradition of the LXX as well as the Syriac.[104] Although he thinks it is less likely, McCarter also suggests the possibility of reconstructing the phrase *zāqēn bā'ănāšîm* 'old among men'.[105] If this reconstruction is accepted, one could argue that *zāqēn* may be employed here to refer to a status that Jesse had. He is clearly the head of a household, and a large one at that. With three sons old enough to fight in Saul's army, Jesse probably was approaching or perhaps even had surpassed the presumed average life expectancy in Israel. In the end, both renderings are possible; it is, therefore, probably best to avoid the assumption that Jesse's age is an important component of his presentation in the narrative.

The portrayal of David in old age, like the portrayal of Barzillai, provides another fascinating window into biblical perceptions of the aged. The case of David is unique in that it is a story of power transferred from old king to heir and the problems that obtain in such circumstances. In 1 Kings 1, it is immediately apparent that David is not only *zāqēn mě'ōd* 'very old' (1 Kgs 1:15) and *bā' bayyāmîm* 'advanced in days'

---

103. It is tempting to suggest that the "witch" in this story is an old woman in light of cross-cultural evidence that links witchcraft and old women. Our text provides no evidence for this, however. See Gutmann, *Reclaimed Powers*, 174-76.

104. P. Kyle McCarter, *I Samuel* (AB 8; Garden City, N.Y.: Doubleday, 1980) 301.

105. Ibid.

(1 Kgs 1:1), but he is also unable to get warm.[106] The rather candid portrayal of the enfeebled king describes his need for a young virgin to provide warmth for him. Though she is beautiful, the once-great king is unable to be intimate with her. That the reference to a lack of warmth may serve as a double entendre alluding to David's impotence is quite possible. The verb used here, *yḥm* (or perhaps *ḥmm*) is used elsewhere in contexts of sexuality (Gen 30:41 and Ps 51:7). The vulnerability of this quintessential Israelite king, the model for all others to follow according to the Deuteronomistic Historians, is expanded to the political arena when Adonijah has proclaimed himself king in his father's place (1 Kgs 1:5).

Literarily, what is true of David sexually is assumed to be true politically.[107] This sexual-political connection is strengthened by the appearance of the verb *ydʿ*, used sexually when the narrator speaks of David's not "knowing" Abishag in 1:4 and denoting cognition (and possibly connoting senility) when Nathan says that David does not know about his son Adonijah's proclamation as king (1:11). The contrast to the elderly, impotent monarch is this son, who in 1:6 is described as *ṭôb tōʾar mĕʾōd* 'quite attractive'.[108] The tenuous status of David's power structure is indicated by the actions of Joab, the military commander, and Abiathar the priest, who both support Adonijah. While it is true that some members of David's entourage remain loyal to him, it is clear from Nathan's instructions to Bathsheba that the remains of this structure are not sufficient to protect her and Solomon. Nathan's actions suggest that either David has forgotten a promise made to Bathsheba or that no such promise existed and Nathan is taking advantage of the king's impaired condition to effect a response to the pretender Adonijah that Nathan deems appropriate. However, whether David is senile is not clearly in-

---

106. Schottroff suggests that this text may reflect an ancient belief, fully articulated by Aristotle, that aging was the result of a process of cooling of the body, producing both gray hair and the state that David is in here. See Schottroff, "Alter als soziales Problem," 65.

107. This is perhaps another example of the two bodies of the king discussed by Mark Hamilton in his book, *The Body Royal: The Social Poetics of Kingship in Ancient Israel* (Leiden: Brill, 2005). Hamilton has applied the work of E. H. Kantorowicz to the kings in the Hebrew Bible to show that they, like their medieval counterparts, were assumed to possess two bodies, one biosocial and the other sociopolitical. I suggest that some of Hamilton's discussion of Saul's death (pp. 160–70) can be applied to David's impotence. Hamilton even notes (p. 163) that "the end of sexual function is an index of death itself."

108. Again, Hamilton's work is helpful. His discussion of Absalom's body as the locus of the contest between him and his father (ibid., 208–9) can be applied to David and Adonijah here. The frailty of David's two bodies (biosocial and sociopolitical) is contrasted with the strength and beauty of the body of his son.

dicated in the text.[109] For whatever reason, Nathan is compelled to remind or perhaps manipulate David with the aid of Bathsheba, so as to achieve what each of them wants from the elderly king: the enthronement of Solomon.[110]

After the throne is secured for Solomon, David instructs this son to exact vengeance on some unfavored subjects. First the elderly king says, "Do not let [Joab's] gray hair descend to Sheol in peace" (1 Kgs 2:6). Then David enjoins Solomon to "bring Shimei's gray hair down to Sheol in blood" (2:9). Both men had offended David during his reign: Joab by ruthlessly killing both Abner (2 Sam 3:27) and Amasa (2 Sam 20:10), military men to whom David had made overtures, and Shimei by publicly insulting the fugitive king during Absalom's rebellion (2 Sam 16:5-8).

The Deuteronomistic depiction of David in old age is multifaceted. While he is cold and calculating when he encourages Solomon to exact revenge on his enemies, he is also helpless and feeble in his personal life and political power. The old king must be assisted by the young Abishag at home and by Bathsheba and Nathan at court in order to deal successfully with his own physical and political decline.

Old age features prominently in the Deuteronomistic portrayal of David's heir. In Solomon's tenure as king, he was asked by God to request whatever he wished (1 Kgs 3:5). Because Solomon did not request riches and honor or long life, God promised him the riches and honor. Yet long life was not given to him in this manner. In characteristic Dtr^2 fashion, long life was predicated on obedience to the commands. Thus God said, "If you walk in my ways, keeping my statutes and commands like David your father, I will lengthen your days" (1 Kgs 3:14).

Solomon is also portrayed in old age, although not with the amount of detail accorded to David. The Deuteronomistic Historian remarks that Solomon's heart was led astray by his foreign wives to serve other gods lĕ‘ēt ziqnat šĕlōmōh 'at the time of Solomon's old age' (1 Kgs 11:4). Here, like his father, David, Solomon is portrayed as weak in advanced age. However, David's weakness is physical and political, while Solomon's is seen in his religious heterodoxy and submission to his wives. According to the Deuteronomistic Historian, his wives had led him to be unfaithful to Yahweh, and this literary account of Solomon's apostasy

---

109. The king's symptoms of lack of heat retention, likely erectile dysfunction, and partial memory loss may indicate a type of vascular dementia. See Eugene Braunwald et al., eds., *Harrison's Priciples of Internal Medicine* (15th ed.; New York: McGraw-Hill, 2001) 2395.

110. An interesting contrast to this portrayal of David in 1 Kings is seen in the parallel account in Chronicles, which betrays no knowledge of an aged and impotent David (1 Chronicles 28-29).

may owe something to the general phenomenon, discussed by Gutmann, of increased passivity among men as they age; the DH notes that this heterodoxy took place late in Solomon's life.[111] God's promise of "many days" was predicated on faithful adherence to the laws, as we witnessed in 1 Kgs 3:14. Portraying this rebellion in Solomon's old age enabled the Deuteronomistic Historian to avoid the problem of reconciling Solomon's old age with his disobedience.

A more subtle version of senescent weakness is seen in the accession of Rehoboam, when the young king is faced with choosing between the advice of the zĕqēnîm 'elders' who had stood before his father (1 Kgs 12:6) and the advice of his peers, referred to as yĕlādîm 'youths' (1 Kgs 12:8). Although we are not told exactly who these zĕqēnîm are, we may surmise that they are elder courtiers.[112] Although they are called simply zĕqēnîm, I hesitate to designate them strictly as 'elders', because they are contrasted with the yĕlādîm, who were probably close in age to Rehoboam. The word zĕqēnîm in this context is best understood as 'statesmen'.[113] Although I have not included politically active "elders" in this study, Rehoboam's "elders" deserve attention precisely because they are contrasted with their younger counterparts in this story.

The story is framed as a classic generational conflict. The attitude of these elder advisers may have appeared to the young king to be the attitude of an older generation, but the outcome demonstrates that they were in fact more in tune with the present reality.[114] Rehoboam's rejection of the advice of the zĕqēnîm in deference to the advice of the yĕlādîm serves as a cautionary tale in the Deuteronomistic History, because the outcome sets in motion the division of the kingdom. Thus we have here an interesting example of the Deuteronomistic Historian's

---

111. Gutmann, *Reclaimed Powers*, 157.
112. Reviv, *The Elders in Ancient Israel*, 101.
113. Mordechai Cogan, *1 Kings* (AB 10; New York: Doubleday, 2000) 347. DeVries's notion that these men are "veterans" cannot be sustained. The military connotation of this term fits neither the context nor the preponderance of occurrences of zĕqēnîm. See Simon J. DeVries, *1 Kings* (WBC 12; Waco, TX: Word, 1985) 156. We should also note that Malamat's insistence that "elders" and "youths" here stand for a bicameral legislature simply lacks substantive proof. See A. Malamat, "Kingship and Council in Israel and Sumer: A Parallel" *JNES* 22 (1963) 251. Malamat later suggests that, although the term yĕlādîm is "inappropriate to a political institution of any sort," the "young men" were actually in their late 30s or early 40s, a generation younger than the "old guard' under King David. See A. Malamat, "Organs of Statecraft in the Israelite Monarchy," *BA* 28 (1965) 44. Yet given the life expectancy data, it is quite unlikely that groups of this sort would have existed in sufficient numbers to sustain the two-house political institution posited by Malamat.
114. D. Geoffrey Evans, "Rehoboam's Advisers at Shechem, and Political Institutions in Israel and Sumer," *JNES* 25 (1966) 279.

associating wisdom with a group that is the older counterpart to a group called *yĕlādîm*.[115]

Following hard upon this story, however, the Deuteronomistic Historian demonstrates that wisdom and old age are not necessarily synonymous in his account of the old prophet of Bethel[116] and the man of God from Judah (1 Kings 13). The prophet of Bethel is called *nābî' 'eḥād zāqēn* 'an old prophet' in 13:11 and *hannābî' hazzāqēn* 'the old prophet' in 13:25. In both instances, *zāqēn* indicates his age rather than serving as a title indicative of leadership. The prophet is clearly the head of a household, because he is the father of at least two sons. Here the advice of the older prophet is a lie that leads to the destruction of the Judahite man of God. The old prophet places the body in his own grave and requests that his son bury him next to the Judahite when he dies, suggesting real sympathy for the dead man of God. Yet how the reader should evaluate the old prophet is not immediately clear. Despite his seemingly compassionate care for the man's body, the text as it stands leads the reader to conclude that the old prophet has deceived the man of God. Even if we accept the suggestion that the reference to his deception in v. 18 is from a later hand,[117] we are still left with the divine repudiation of the old prophet's words to the man of God, and the old prophet remains a morally ambiguous figure. In addition, it is not clear whether the old prophet's age is a contributing factor to his behavior or is merely incidental to his portrayal.

In addition to King David, who suffers the infirmities of old age, a few other characters in 1-2 Kings have health problems in their later years. The prophet Ahijah, for example, is not able to see *kî qāmû 'ēnāyw miśśêbô* 'because his eyes were set from his old age' (1 Kgs 14:4). Even so, his awareness is acute, as his knowledge of the queen's identity demonstrates. The aged Ahijah then delivers a condemnation of the house of Jeroboam to the wayward king's wife (1 Kgs 14:7-16). The aged prophet is physically limited but possesses undiminished mental and prophetic ability attributable to direct divine intervention.

An additional report of senescent physical ailment is the notice regarding the Judahite King Asa: *raq lĕ'ēt ziqnātô ḥālâ 'et raglāyw* 'except, at the time of his old age, he was diseased in his feet' (1 Kgs 15:23). The

---

115. Note, however, that I am not assuming that these *zĕqēnîm* are considered "old." Even so, it is rather clear that the author is portraying this group as *older* than the *yĕlādîm*, thus demonstrating that this *older* group has the sage advice that Rehoboam would do well to heed.

116. This prophet is said to be from Samaria in 2 Kgs 23:18. The problem of the redaction history of these two sections of Kings has not yet been fully solved.

117. DeVries, *1 Kings*, 171.

nature of this debility is unknown, but interpreters have suggested a host of answers ranging from gout to "peripheral obstructive vascular disease with ensuing gangrene."[118] The Hebrew use of *regel* (in the dual form) to refer to the genitals also complicates the matter.[119]

One final comment regarding physical problems in old age is taken from the story of the Shunamite woman and her husband. In his description of the couple's childless state, Elisha's servant Gehazi says *wĕʾîšâ zāqēn* 'and her husband is old' (2 Kgs 4:14). Context suggests that *zāqēn* is to be taken as a reference to age rather than status because Gehazi is hardly likely to adduce the man's status as a cause for his infertility. Both the couple's lamentable state and its subsequent reversal echo motifs from the patriarchal narratives.

Old Age in the Prophets

In this section, I will look at the larger works of Isaiah, Jeremiah, and Ezekiel first and then address the collection of the so-called minor prophets. As I noted above, canonical order is followed for ease of access to episodes referring to some facet of old age.

Isaiah

On occasion in Isaiah, *zāqēn* may be used in a more generic sense to mean 'old man', rather than the specific status of 'elder' that is seen a number of times in the book. One such occasion is 47:6, where Daughter Chaldea is chastised for making heavy the burden upon *zāqēn* 'the old'. Another is found in Third Isaiah's vision of the new age and portrayal of an idealized life cycle. No longer will an *ʿûl* 'infant' live only a few days or a *zāqēn* not fill up his days (65:20). The juxtaposition of *zāqēn* with the age-specific term *ʿûl* suggests that *zāqēn* is age related as well. The phrase that follows this line foretells that a *naʿar* 'youth' will live to be 100. Thus, while *zāqēn* and *naʿar* could be technical terms here, context suggests that they are simply generic terms, as *zāqēn* is in the earlier passage, 47:6. The imagery in 65:20 portrays an abolishing of premature death, which was probably quite a common hope at that time.

Other imagery includes the nouns *ziqnâ* and *śêbâ* in 46:4, where Yahweh promises the people that he will be their God even when they reach "old age" and "gray hair." These categories of old age are juxtaposed with infants "carried from the abdomen" and "lifted up from the womb"

---

118. See the listing in Cogan, *1 Kings*, 402.
119. See 2 Kgs 18:27 and Isa 36:12 (the *Qere* in both verses) as well as Isa 7:20. The *Qere* in the first two verses is also supported by several medieval manuscripts noted in BHS.

in the previous verse. The range of the categories, then, encompasses all people, young and old. A statement of this sort was surely reassuring to those who feared the uncertainty of old age in ancient Israel, a viewpoint expressed in Psalm 71. The opposing ends of this range may also intimate a vulnerability that the very young and the very old embody.

Jeremiah

In Jeremiah, we see the entirety of a population meristically denoted by the pairing of the elderly with the young men (*baḥûrîm* in 6:11 and 31:13 [in addition to *bětûlâ* 'virgin'] and *naʿar* in 51:22). Wolff sees in Jeremiah's words an indication of life-cycle terminology.[120] On the basis of Jer 51:22, he posits four divisions: (1) *naʿar*; (2) *bāḥûr* / *bětûlâ*; (3) *ʾîš* / *ʾiššâ*; and (4) *zāqēn*. On the basis of Jer 6:11, he posits five divisions: (1) *ʿôlāl*; (2) *bāḥûr*; (3) *ʾîš* / *ʾiššâ*; (4) *zāqēn*; and (5) *mělēʾ yāmîm* 'full of days'.[121] Both of these verses from Jeremiah appear within a context of judgment that is pronounced on an entire population.

Against Wolff, I note that in 6:11 *zāqēn* and *mělēʾ yāmîm* ('full of days') may not indicate a subdivided category of old age but may, rather, be synonyms of senectitude.[122] The previous pairs are not contrastive, as Holladay suggests.[123] Rather, they move from "child and youth" to "man and woman" to "old person and aged one." I suggest that each part of each pair is a rough synonym in terms of age. The first pair denotes youths who are not yet married; the second pair denotes a husband and wife (or, at the very least, persons above marriageable age); and the third pair denotes the elderly. Jer 51:22 includes the various ages of people, as noted above, but 51:23 includes shepherds, farmers, governors, and commanders. While Wolff may be correct that subdivisions of old age existed in Israel, Jer 51:22 simply seems to be citing a number of categories of people in Israel with respect to age and profession.

Ezekiel

Ezekiel contains only one reference to *zāqēn* that is not obviously referring to elders as a group of leaders. In 9:6, God orders the "executioners of the city" to slay without pity those who have sinned: *zāqēn bāḥûr ûbětûlâ wěṭap wěnāšîm* 'old man, young man, young woman, children, and women'. While this use of *zāqēn* may be a reference to old

---

120. Wolff, *Anthropology*, 120.
121. Ibid.
122. Ibid.
123. William L. Holladay, *Jeremiah 1* (Hermeneia; Philadelphia: Fortress, 1986) 215.

men, it is also possible that it is an honorific title. This single use is ambiguous and, therefore, cannot advance our examination of old age.

The Minor Prophets

In Hosea, we find a single reference to *śêbâ* 'gray hair' applied to Ephraim (7:9). The A line of the verse says, "Strangers consume his power, but he does not know it," while the B line reads, "Gray hair is sprinkled on him, but he does not know it." Because *śêbâ* is employed everywhere else in the Bible for gray hair, it seems quite natural to assume that it stands here for a distinct marker of age, when the energy of youth is sapped. This understanding fits the context quite nicely. However, there may be a double entendre here playing off the imagery of bread making that permeates Hosea 7. Shalom Paul has suggested that *śêbâ* here may refer to the gray hair seen in mold.[124] The idea of decay implicit in the biblical presentation of old age is indeed amplified if Paul's attempt to relate *śêbâ* to moldy bread is correct. In any case, this verse provides a negative portrayal of old age.[125]

Of the twelve minor prophets, the book of Joel contains the most references to the elderly. In 1:2, the prophet addresses the *zĕqēnîm* and "all the inhabitants of the land." Although *hazzĕqēnîm* may be used here as a general term for the leaders in the land, the meaning is ambiguous.[126] The term *zĕqēnîm* (without the article) is paired with "all the inhabitants of the land" again in 1:14 following the imperative 'gather' (*'ispû*). This is one of the few instances in which the anarthrous *zĕqēnîm* appears (other occurrences are Joel 2:16, Job 32:9, and Lam 5:14).[127] While it may be that these vocatives are simply indicating the leaders and then the rest of the people, precisely why these two terms are paired is unclear.

A command to gather the elders appears again in 2:16, yet the verb here is *qbṣ*. The reference to *zĕqēnîm* in 2:16 is closer to the usage in 3:1[2:28], where it is used in contrasting pairs to delineate groups according to age. In 2:16, *zĕqēnîm* are grouped with *ʿôlālîm* 'children' and *yônĕqê šādayim* 'nursing babes'. In 3:1, *zĕqēnîm* are paired with *baḥûrîm* 'young men,' who will "dream dreams" and "see visions," respectively, when Yahweh pours out his spirit. These pairings suggest that these words are not related to the honorific status that the term *zĕqēnîm*

---

124. Paul, "Image of the Oven," 119–20.
125. One could suggest that Paul's reading is the only way to understand the verse, to the exclusion of its reference to gray hair and, in so doing, preclude a negative reading of *śêbâ*. However, because this is the only possible reference to *śêbâ* as 'mold' in the Bible, this exclusive reading would have to account for too much contrary evidence.
126. Seesemann, "Die Ältesten im Alten Testament," 4.
127. Reviv, *The Elders in Ancient Israel*, 7.

clearly denotes elsewhere. Rather, they all seem to be generic and thus depicting age; these groupings are merely a way to speak of the totality of the people from young to old.

Psalms

The attainment of old age is often portrayed as a desire by the psalmists. Long life is couched as a blessing, something that the writers strive for and wish for both themselves and their loved ones. By contrast, a psalmist may request that the lives of his enemies be short or be cut short. The phrase *'ōrek yāmîm* 'length of days' and slight variations thereof are used to speak of the blessing of long life in the work of the psalmists. The king requests and receives *'ōrek yāmîm 'ôlām wā'ed* 'length of days forever and ever' (21:5), while the psalmist "dwells in the house of Yahweh *lĕ'ōrek yāmîm*" (23:6). A similar expression employing the Hiphil form of the verb *ysp* 'to add' is used in 61:7 to request that God "add to the days" of someone.

On one occasion, opponents are cursed by the psalmist with a short life. In Ps 55:24, men of blood and deceit are decreed to live only half their days (*lō' yeḥĕṣû yĕmêhēm*, literally, 'they shall not even halve their days').[128] Two psalmists use similar language to bemoan life cut short, be it their own life or that of the king. Ps 89:46 speaks of God's cutting short (Hiphil of *qṣr*) the Davidide's youth. In Ps 102:24, the psalmist complains (using the Piel of *qṣr*) that God has cut short his days, adding the parallel complaint that "he afflicted my strength."[129] Earlier in this psalm (v. 12), the psalmist describes his days as "stretched out like a shadow" and remarks in the parallel stich that "I am dried up like grass." The imagery of days that are stretched out like a shadow probably bespeaks old age and the approaching end of life. This is contrasted with God's eternity, which the psalmist observes in the following verse, declaring, "You [addressing God] are enthroned forever." The ephemeral nature of humanity's days is expressed with another botanical image in 103:15: "As for a human [*'ĕnôš*], his days are like grass, like a blossom that blooms in the field." The human life-span is established at 70 years, or 80, "if by reason of strength," according to Ps 90:10.

The terms *ziqnâ* 'old age' and *śêbâ* 'gray hair' are employed by the psalmist to stand for stages in life. The psalmist uses both terms in 71:18 to denote the last stage of life, until which he hopes to be blessed with God's presence. The term *śêbâ* is used one other time in 92:15, when the psalmist declares that the righteous "still produce fruit in *śêbâ*; they are

---

128. BDB 345b.
129. My translation, 'my strength', reflects the *Qere* over against the *Kethiv*'s 'his strength'.

always green and full of sap." This celebration of old age is reminiscent of the attitude of wisdom literature.

Because of its unique representation of the point of view of a senescent person, a closer examination of Psalm 71 is in order. Although the MT has no title, the LXX attests "of/for David" and adds the enigmatic phrase, "of the sons of Jonadab and of one of the first taken captive." The connection between these LXX additions and the old-age references in the psalm are not altogether clear, aside from the obvious facts that David is elsewhere portrayed in old age and that many psalms are attributed to him. Although Psalm 71 is a striking collection of individual fragments found in other psalms (Psalms 21 and 33, for example),[130] its indicators of the writer's concern for old age are not echoed in the other psalms. The psalmist desires not so much protection from enemies who can take his life as he does a guarantee against the threat of abandonment in old age (vv. 9 and 18).[131] M. Cogan has even suggested that the cry in v. 9, "Do not cast me off in the time of old age, or forsake me when my strength is spent," alludes to the threat of exposure enacted on the elderly in some of the world's cultures.[132] At the very least, this verse illustrates the fear among the elderly that they will be abandoned in the weakness that often attends senescence. The psalmist reflects on his life in v. 6 and on God's provision and instruction in v. 17; the latter verse evokes a wisdom theme. And in v. 15, the psalmist promises to be a witness to the mighty deeds of Yahweh, telling of many days spent under God's protection. Psalm 71 provides an interesting, if rare, portrayal of the concerns and anxieties of the elderly in this supplication to the deity on behalf of the aged in the community of Israel.

Wisdom Literature

The wisdom literature in the Hebrew Bible is important to our study because of the role that old age plays within wisdom circles. The wisdom texts of the Bible—Proverbs, Job, and Qoheleth[133]—present a varied picture of old age. On the one hand, Proverbs offers nothing but positive images of the aged. Long life is a reward for piety, and the elderly are to be respected because of the wisdom they possess. Job

---

130. Hans-Joachim Kraus, *Psalms 60–150* (trans. Hilton C. Oswald; Minneapolis: Augsburg Fortress, 1989) 71.

131. Artur Weiser, *The Psalms* (trans. Herbert Hartwell; Philadelphia: Westminster, 1976) 498–99.

132. M. Cogan, "A Technical Term for Exposure," *JNES* 27 (1968) 133.

133. James Crenshaw, ed., *Studies in Ancient Israelite Wisdom* (New York: KTAV, 1976) 5.

brings a critique to bear on this outlook and suggests that the aged are not always wise. Qoheleth brings a darker view of old age as a period of decline and celebrates youth wistfully but warns of its ephemeral qualities. I will examine each of these books individually and then assess their place within the wisdom traditions of the Hebrew Bible. For the sake of convenience, I have grouped them together even though they are separated in the Hebrew canon.

Job

In the narrative epilogue, Job is described as *zāqēn ûśĕbaʿ yāmîm* 'old and sated of days' when he dies, having seen four generations (42:16–17). Perhaps this is an attempt to connect Job to the patriarchs; Abraham is described the same way in Gen 25:8, as is Isaac in Gen 35:29. Other references to old age appear in Job 15:10 on the lips of Eliphaz, one of Job's "comforters," who says that the gray-haired (*śāb*) and the aged (*yāšîš*) are among them as they speak wisdom to Job. Here we see Eliphaz relying on the assumption that age denotes credibility. Eliphaz continues to bolster his claims by saying that the aged (of whom he speaks) are older than Job's father. In Job 8:8–10, we see further support for the association of old age and wisdom when Bildad (another "comforter") says,

> Inquire of the first generation, seek insight[134] of their fathers for discernment.
> For we are but born yesterday, so we do not know, and our days are but a shadow.
> Will they not impart teaching to you and from their minds bring forth wise words?

To this point, the picture of wisdom in Job is consistent with that of Proverbs. There is, however, an overturning of this assumption in the words of Elihu, who appears onstage in chap. 32. This new interlocutor remarks that he has thus far kept his peace because the other "comforters" were older than he (32:4). In 32:6–7, Elihu says, "I am *ṣāʿîr* 'younger' in days, and you all are *yĕšîšîm* 'aged ones', so I was afraid to speak my mind. I said, 'Let days speak and *rōb šānîm* 'one of many years' make wisdom known.'" To this point, Elihu, in keeping with the tradition, affirms the respect for old age. However, in 32:9, he says, "It is not the *rabbîm* 'great' who are wise and [not] the *zĕqēnîm* 'elderly' who perceive justice." It is possible here that the juxtaposition of *zĕqēnîm* and *rabbîm*

---

134. I have followed Marvin Pope, who suggests emending the MT's *kōnēn* to *bōnēn*. See Marvin Pope, *Job* (AB 15; Garden City, NY: Doubleday, 1965) 65.

may refer to leaders and elders without clear reference to the aged. Given the context of Elihu's comments in 32:6, however, where Elihu juxtaposes *ṣāʿîr* and *yĕšîšîm*, the reference in 32:9 appears to address relative age rather than to leadership status alone. Later in 35:33, Elihu says, "I will teach Job wisdom."

In Job 29, Job looks back at the time in his life when he was in his prime, as it were, calling it "the days of my autumn" (v. 4). Autumn is probably used as a figure for the prime of life because it is the harvest time, which symbolizes prosperity, as Pope notes.[135] At that time, says our protagonist, "*nĕʿārîm* 'youths' withdrew when they saw me, and *yĕšîšîm* 'aged ones' rose and stood" (v. 8). Of course, Job's primary concern is his reversal of fortune, yet the nuance of his lament is telling. Job is recalling a time when both youths and the aged respected him. In 30:1, Job notes that now the youths who once respected him are laughing at him.

One passage in Job may be interpreted as an indication that God or Shaddai is old. In 12:12, Job asserts that wisdom is among the *yĕšîšîm* 'aged ones' and insight among individuals who have lived long. In the following verse, he states, "With him are wisdom and might; to him belong counsel and insight." It is certain that what follows this verse are references to the deity. So we may safely assume that the antecedent of "him" in v. 13 is God. The proximity of these verses (12:12–13) may lead some to conclude that God is portrayed here with old-age imagery. Yet nothing here demands this conclusion, because the two verses may simply indicate that both the aged and God have wisdom. The two possessors of wisdom (that is, the aged and God) need not be related in any other way. The fact that they share one feature does not necessitate a sharing of others. In fact, later in this same chapter Job will say that God removes the *taʿam* 'judgment' of the *zĕqēnîm* 'elders' or, more likely, 'elderly'.[136] Job, furthermore, sets God apart from humanity's aging process by asking God, "Are your days like the days of man? Are your years like those of man?" That Job anticipates a negative response to this question is obvious from the context.

Proverbs

In the book of Proverbs, the few references to old-age imagery center mostly on the necessity of respect for the elderly and on long life as a

---

135. Pope, *Job*, 185. The word for autumn here is *ḥōrep*, which is related to the verbal root meaning 'to gather fruit'. See BDB 358a.

136. There is an interesting double entendre in this verse, because *taʿam* could also be rendered 'taste'. The decline of the sense of taste among the elderly is bemoaned by Barzillai in 2 Sam 19:35. See above, p. 32.

reward for the people of wisdom who fear Yahweh. *'Ōrek yāmîm* 'length of days/long life' is promised to those who heed the teachings of the wise in 3:2, and long life is said to be in the right hand of personified Wisdom in 3:16. In 3:2, *'ōrek yāmîm* is paired with *šĕnôt ḥayyîm* 'years of life', which are said to be added to individuals who keep the commandments. In 3:16, *'ōrek yāmîm* is paired with *'ōšer wĕkābôd* 'riches and honor', which are said to be in Lady Wisdom's left hand, thus indicating the value of long life.

Note that a similar grouping of "riches and honor" and "lengthening of days" (using the verbal form of *'ōrek*) appears in the story of Solomon's request of God in 1 Kgs 3:6–10. The wise king is given riches and honor because he did not request them (1 Kgs 3:11–14). God tells Solomon that his days will be lengthened if he is faithful to him. In the same vein is the saying that the fear of Yahweh 'prolongs life' (*tôsîp yāmîm*, literally, 'adds days') while the life of the wicked is cut short (Prov 10:27). Gray hair is employed to symbolize long life as *'ăṭeret tip'eret* 'a crown of splendor' in 16:31 and as *hādār* 'honor' in 20:29. In a manner so characteristic of Proverbs, the gray hair celebrated in 16:31 is achieved by following the path of righteousness. Related to this outward sign of old age is the acquisition of grandchildren, which is said to be *'ăṭeret zĕqēnîm* 'a crown of the aged' in 17:6.

Respect for elderly parents is commanded in 23:22, where the writer says, "Do not despise your mother when she is *zāqĕnâ* 'old'." Although old age is not expressly cited in them, other commands to respect one's parents are certainly related to this call for respect (19:26 and 20:20). Prov 19:26 forbids a man to drive his mother away. A similar concern for the welfare of mothers is seen in the Code of Hammurabi §§171–72, which allows sons to receive their deceased father's inheritance only if they provide for their mother.[137] The Egyptian "Instruction of Ani" says, "Give your mother a double portion of food as she did for you and carry her as she carried you. She had a heavy burden with you."[138] In Prov 19:26, the writer forbids doing violence to a father, perhaps in order to curb the abuse of elders when their care becomes increasingly burdensome. Again, Mesopotamian examples attest similar concerns. In a text documenting the dispersal of an estate in Nippur, the sons take an oath vowing to provide for their father that concludes with the line,

---

137. Another example of this law is seen in *Texts in the Iraq Museum* 4 27. See Marten Stol, "The Care of the Elderly in Mesopotamia in the Old Babylonian Period," in *The Care of the Elderly in the Ancient Near East* (ed. Marten Stol and Sven P. Vleeming; Leiden: Brill, 1998) 72.

138. Quoted in Schottroff, "Alter als Soziales Problem," 72 (my translation). See also *ANET* 420.

"Whoever does not support [his father], shall not exercise his right to the inheritance."[139]

Qoheleth

In Qoheleth, we encounter a more direct valuation of old age vis-à-vis youth. In many ways, it departs from what were probably conventional assumptions about age in Israel. These conventional assumptions are attested in the book of Job, where superior wisdom is believed to reside in the life experience of the aged. Similar attestations throughout the ancient Near East can be easily found.[140] In 4:13, Qoheleth says, "Better is a poor and wise youth than an old [*zāqēn*] and foolish king who will no longer take advice." In making his proverbial point, Qoheleth chooses imagery that is telling. Youth for Qoheleth is a time to take advantage of one's ability to enjoy life to its fullest. In 6:3, he claims that an abortion or untimely birth is preferable to one who has lived long (*šānîm rabbôt yihyeh*) but has not enjoyed the "good things" and has not attained a proper burial. This same sentiment is echoed in 6:6 where he concludes that, because all share the same fate, one should seize the day in youth, as it were—to squeeze all out of life that is possible. Doing so is preferable to a life of two millennia.

Qoheleth does not portray youth as an optimal age, however, because he maintains that the end of a thing is better than its beginning in 7:8. The "end" here probably refers to the fact that the thing in question has been tested and proved true or good, and so our writer probably has one's reputation in mind when he speaks of this "thing." Although having a reputation does not necessitate being old, the longer someone lives, the more tested and tried this reputation becomes, and thus an elderly person's good reputation in Qoheleth's estimation, is "better."[141] This point of view may be seen in 10:16, which pronounces woe to the land that has a *naʿar* 'youth' for a king and whose princes feast in the morning. The focus here seems to be on the naïveté of a *naʿar* who permits his courtiers to indulge themselves in the morning. Thus, although Qoheleth sees youth as a time of opportunity, his ambivalence is seen in his recognition of its limitations.

---

139. *Publications of the Babylonian Section* from the University of Pennsylvania 8/1 16. See Stol, "The Care of the Elderly," 71. Texts from Emar attest similar concerns. See John Huehnergard, "Biblical Notes on Some New Akkadian Texts from Emar (Syria)," *CBQ* 47 (1985) 430.

140. See James L. Crenshaw, "Youth and Old Age in Qoheleth" (*HAR* 10 [1986] 1 n. 3) for a detailed list of citations ranging from the Sumerian *Instructions of Suruppak* to the Egyptian *Instruction of Ptahhotep* and many others.

141. James Kugel, *The Idea of Biblical Poetry* (New Haven, CT: Yale University Press, 1981) 10.

The main text in Qoheleth that addresses old age and merits close attention in this study is 11:7–12:7. Commentators differ on how to group this set of verses, and its compositional history is debated as well.[142] Qoheleth may have borrowed an oral or written piece that described old age metaphorically and literally; or perhaps there were two sources: one that employed metaphor and another that was literal.[143] In any case, the final product is an interesting pastiche that has occasioned much debate. In what follows, I discuss briefly the interpretational history of 12:1–7, which serves as the crux for this section of Qoheleth; then I turn to these verses in detail, finally suggesting ways in which these data can be used to construct a picture of old age in Israel.

Interpretive Models for Qoheleth 12:1–7

Qoh 12:1–7 has been viewed by most scholars in one of three ways: literally, figuratively, or as a combination of the two. Early interpreters whose opinions are recorded in the targum, Mishnah, and Talmud took the verses to be an allegory. This sort of analysis is accepted even by some modern commentators for the first part of this section.[144] The references to astral bodies are assumed to be the eyes that dim with age, the trembling guards are the limbs that experience the tremors of old age, and the "grinders" are teeth that are lost. Those who look out the window are assumed to be the eyes, the closed doors are perhaps the ears, and the closing of the lips bespeaks ineffective speech. Perhaps the almond-tree blossoms refer to the white hair of the elderly.

However, the remaining images in v. 5 are difficult to bring into conformity with an allegorical grid. Some of them, such as the mourners in the street, the dust returning to the earth, and the breath returning to God, indeed seem to be literal. Some have suggested a metaphorical reading but differ over exactly what vehicle the metaphor presumes. For example, Christian Ginsburg suggested that this section describes an approaching rainstorm that is a metaphor for death.[145] C. L. Seow's eschatological reading, which is in some ways a return to patristic

---

142. See Michael Fox's article, "Frame Narrative and Composition in the Book of Qoheleth" (*HUCA* 48 [1977] 83–106), where he suggests that the "frame narrator" may in fact have written more than the passages at the beginning and the end that are usually regarded as bracketing the words of Qoheleth himself.

143. Choon-Leong Seow, *Ecclesiastes* (AB 18C; New York: Doubleday, 1997) 373.

144. Robert Gordis, *Koheleth: The Man and His World* (Texts and Studies 19; New York: The Jewish Theological Seminary, 1951) 328. See also Norbert Lohfink, *Qoheleth* (trans. Sean McEvenue; CC; Minneapolis: Fortress, 2003) 140.

145. Christian D. Ginsburg, *Coheleth, Commonly Called the Book of Ecclesiastes* (London: Longman, 1861) 457–69. Gordis discusses this possibility as well. See Gordis, *Koheleth*, 331.

interpretation, appears too closely linked with New Testament allusions and Christian sensibilities to be persuasive.[146]

Some scholars, such as Hagia Witzenrath, opt for a more literal reading of these lines, seeing in them the decline of a household when death approaches the elderly.[147] This perspective presumes the vehicle of the metaphor to be a house in decline. The various groups of people are literal individuals in the household compound, including guards and strong men, grinders of grain, and women looking through the lattice. This double grouping of two types of men and women in the compound may follow the lines of social status.[148] The "guards of the house" may have their counterpart, from the perspective of status, in the "grinders," a feminine participle. Likewise, the "men of strength" may be grouped with "the women who look out the window." Other women in the Bible who peer through a window certainly possess status: Sisera's mother (Judg 5:28), David's wife, Michal (2 Sam 6:16), and Jezebel (2 Kgs 9:30). The BHS stichometric presentation of this verse adopts this grouping, placing the former pairing on the right (3a and c) and the latter on the left (3b and d). The doors shutting and the sound of grinding diminishing refer to the lack of commerce, while the sound of birds refers to the absence of people. Verse 5 paints a general picture of neglect whereby the compound becomes inhabited with vegetation and insects. The broken wares of v. 6 are simply further indication of decline in the household.

Witzenrath maintains that nowhere in the Bible are features of a house used as a metaphor for individual body parts.[149] Outside the Bible, she cites the text of Ptahhoteph and dismisses its relevance because it employs direct allusions to body parts rather than figures of speech.[150] Witzenrath has also omitted from consideration an important Sumerian text that does in fact speak of body parts in a metaphorical manner—a text that we will discuss later.

A few interpreters suggest that the section has nothing to do with old age but, rather, describes the downfall of humanity or only the death of an individual.[151] John Sawyer's proposal that this text is a description

---

146. C. L. Seow, "Qoheleth's Eschatological Poem," *JBL* 118 (1999) 210.
147. Hagia Witzenrath, *Süß ist das Licht* (St. Ottilien: EOS, 1979) 45.
148. John F. A. Sawyer, "The Ruined House in Ecclesiastes 12: A Reconstruction of the Original Parable," *JBL* 94 (1975) 525.
149. She notes Job 4:19, 27:18; and Isa 38:12, where she suggests that these passages speak of the transitory nature (*Vergänglichkeit*) of life. Witzenrath, *Süß ist das Licht*, 47.
150. Ibid., 47.
151. Sawyer, "The Ruined House," 521; Graham S. Ogden, "Qoheleth XI 7–XII 8: Qoheleth's Summons to Enjoyment and Reflection," *VT* 34 (1984) 34.

of humanity's downfall is predicated on a few emendations and reading the Hebrew of Qoheleth as if it were postbiblical Hebrew.[152] Yet interestingly enough, even if one were to accept many of his emendations and mishnaic translations (which I do not) the text could still apply to old age. The same applies to Graham S. Ogden's argument that this section of Qoheleth only refers to death. Certainly the impending death of the elderly is a factor in old-age imagery. To say that this text only has death in mind, however, is to go beyond the plain sense of the verses.

Scholars who adopt a literal interpretation of these verses encounter other problems as well. The fact that a literal reading is, for the most part, possible in this passage is not surprising, because metaphor employs the literal world to speak figuratively of something else. The ability of a text to be read literally with few problems is no argument against reading it metaphorically. Attempts to categorize the pericope as either fully literal or fully allegorical fail to account for the stylistic variety among ancient authors. Fox notes that in the Sumerian text on old age there is some literal-metaphorical mixing: "my black mountain has produced white gypsum" refers metaphorically to the graying of the hair, while the statement that "my teeth [are] chewing strong things no longer" is obviously literal.[153] The weight of the interpretive tradition is solidly behind a figurative reading in these verses, a fact that is all too often dismissed by modern scholars. That said, I suggest along the lines of Fox's observations that Qoh 12:1–7 be read with an openness to both its metaphorical and its literal qualities.[154] Openness of this sort is the best way to reconstruct the general thrust of this section. In what follows, I examine the text verse by verse to provide a more detailed argument in support of this interpretive approach. I also include the last few verses of chap. 11 because of their relevance to understanding 12:1–7.

Analysis of Qoheleth 11:7–12:7

Seow understands the reference in Qoh 11:7 to eyes that see the sun as an idiom for being alive.[155] Seow cites Job 3:16; 33:28, 30; Ps 36:10; and 56:14, all of which speak of seeing light. However, none of these examples is an exact parallel, because none of them mentions "eyes" or "the sun." Assuming that all references to light in this section indicate a general idiom for "life" is too restrictive. Following this reasoning would

---

152. Sawyer, "The Ruined House," 524.
153. Michael V. Fox, "Aging and Death in Qoheleth 12," *JSOT* 42 (1988) 68. See B. Alster, *Studies in Sumerian Proverbs* (Copenhagen: Akademisk Forlag, 1975) 93.
154. Fox, "Aging and Death," 71.
155. Seow, *Ecclesiastes*, 369. Krüger takes the same position. See Thomas Krüger, *Qoheleth* (Hermeneia; Minneapolis: Fortress, 2004) 195.

lead to understanding the "days of darkness" to be death, something that Seow denies.[156] The general sense of the eyes' seeing the sun may be referring to life in general, yet I suggest that it is more fitting to read the image as a way to speak about eyesight and its potential loss in old age. At the very least we have here a double entendre. Note further that seeing with the eyes is what is commanded of the youth in 11:9b.

Commenting on Qoh 11:8, Gordis says that the "days of darkness" cannot refer to old age, "for there is no warrant that they will be many!"[157] He thinks that this is an expression for death.[158] However, if the "dark days" are supposed to refer to death, it is hard to see, as Krüger points out, why someone would be concerned about how long he will be dead.[159] As I noted above, the interpretation that light and darkness stand only for life and death is too confining. Krüger suggests that these "dark days" are past difficulties that the old man recalls as he reflects upon his life.[160] The many stories that mention failed eyesight in old age in the Bible (Isaac, Jacob, Eli, and the prophet Ahijah) suggest a more literal meaning. Both meanings may be intended here, implying that, if one lives long, his difficult days will multiply, along with the days in which it is possible that his eyesight may fade. At the very least, physical visual limitation in old age is part of the intended message.

Qoh 11:9 signifies a similar viewpoint, whereby the young are called to rejoice in their youth. However, a qualification follows this line that warns of God's judgment. Qoh 11:10 reminds the reader that youth and the "dawn of life" are "vanity/breath/fleeting."

The reference to "days of trouble" in 12:1 is assumed by many to be synonymous with old age.[161] The "days of your youth" here are juxtaposed with "days of evil [or misfortune]." The most natural way to read "days of evil/misfortune" is as the antithetical counterpart to youth.

The darkening of the heavenly bodies in 12:2 echoes the reference to darkness in 11:8 and within the context indicates the loss of vision in old age. Again, assuming that this darkening is only a circumlocution for death does not account for the imagery that follows, which evokes old-age decline.

In 12:3, the singular "day" is used in contrast to the "*days* of youth" and "*days* of trouble" in v. 1, which may lend credence to interpreting this day as the day of death, because death occurs at a specific time.

---

156. Seow, *Ecclesiastes*, 369.
157. Gordis, *Koheleth*, 324.
158. Ibid.
159. Krüger, *Qoheleth*, 196.
160. Ibid.
161. Gordis, *Koheleth*, 331.

However, even an individual with a casual knowledge of Hebrew is aware that *yôm* can refer to more than a single day (that is, *bĕyôm* can simply mean "at the time of," in a general sense).[162] The switch from plural to singular is likely stylistic.

Seow also says that the verb *zwʿ* in v. 3 should not be understood as signifying trembling as an effect of old age, because the verb denotes frightened behavior elsewhere. However, the verb is only attested three times in Biblical Hebrew (including our verse) and twice in Biblical Aramaic.[163] Furthermore, Seow's point does not take into account the way metaphor is employed. Can Qoheleth not describe a guard as "shaking from fear" in order to create a metaphor for an old-age tremor? This verb is a nice complement to the image of bending low in the next stich. Because *ʿwt* can denote the idea of twisting and bending, its use is a poignant way to speak of old-age contracture: arms and legs becoming twisted and gnarled in a contracted position. Both verbs on the literal level bespeak undesirable attributes in the individual to whom the verb applies—guards and men of status. The grinders in this verse are probably teeth, which are grammatically feminine in Hebrew.

Because the participle *hārōʾôt* is feminine, the metaphor of people who look out the windows (*ʾărubbôt*) in v. 3 should have a grammatically feminine referent. I have already noted the literal interpretation that equates the windows with noble women peering into the street, such as Sisera's mother, Michal, and Jezebel. Yet in every occurrence of someone's looking through a window in the Bible, the word for window is *ḥallôn*. In fact, the only architectural reference to an *ʾărubbâ* is found in Hos 13:3, where the word describes an opening in a house from which smoke escapes.[164] If the 'window' in Qoh 12:3 were to be understood literally, I would expect *ḥallôn* to be used.[165] Instead, I suggest that the imagery is used to describe the eyes, which are also gramatically feminine in Hebrew. The verb *ḥšk* 'to darken' is used of the dimming of the eyes in Lam 5:17 and Ps 69:24.

---

162. Num 3:1 refers to Moses' time on Sinai as a "day," and Ps 18:1 uses "day" to refer to the time when God gave David rest from his enemies.

163. The Hebrew uses are Esth 5:9 and Hab 2:7 (Pilpel), and the Aramaic citations are Dan 5:19 and 6:27.

164. The other seven uses of *ʾărubbâ* in the Hebrew Bible are found in Gen 7:11; 8:2; 2 Kgs 7:2, 19; Isa 24:18; 60:8; Mal 3:10. The common use of this word in the phrase "windows of heaven" (Gen 7:11; 8:2; 2 Kgs 7:2, 19; Mal 3:10) is further indication that an *ʾărubbâ* is an opening overhead.

165. The use of *ʾărubbâ* in Aramaic is important to this discussion. Jastrow defines *ʾărubbâ* as "an aperature in the roof looking to the ground floor" and says it is distinct from *ḥallôn*. Marcus Jastrow, *A Dictionary of the Targumum, the Talmud Babli and Yerushalmi, and the Midrashic Literature* (New York: Pardes, 1950) 116a.

The doors closing from the street are probably a reference to the ears, because the noun "sound" is used in the following two stichoi. Once again, this image works on a more literal level, marking the cessation of active commerce in the house of the elderly. This carries over to the next stich, where the sound of grinding, which refers to chewing or to a literal grinding of grain, has become faint. In v. 4c, however, the multivalence is suspended. The double entendres that precede, referring both to body parts and courtyard activity, are not present here, so far as I can tell. Verse 4c–d focuses on the courtyard imagery. The cessation of activity in the courtyard attracts birds, the sound of which is now heard when the elderly person rises in the morning. Assuming that the aged person wakes *at the sound* of the birds (that is, the birds awaken the person) is not necessary here. Some who posit a metaphor suggest that this line refers to the light sleeping habits of the elderly.[166] One could easily counter that the elderly often experience a hearing loss that might offset any chance of being awakened early by the chirping of birds. Although we may expect a different verb for "awaken" in Hebrew,[167] the verb *qûm* can refer to rising after one has slept (for example, in Ruth 3:14).

The "daughters of the song" in the next phrase probably refer simply to the women (servants or family) who sang in the courtyard of the compound. That these women are "low" or "quiet" is in opposition to the sound of birds in the previous stich. The bustle of a thriving house in which human singing was heard is replaced by the sound of singing birds.

The fear of heights and terrors on the way bespeaks the loss of courage among the elderly, who can no longer control their surroundings. The loss of bravery resonates with the trembling "guards" and "cowering" strong men in v. 3, and I suggest that the unwillingness to tread the path or climb to the heights echoes the closing of the doors in v. 4. The abstract idea noted here in the metaphors is impeded ambulation.

Verse 5c–e resumes the metaphor of old age, yet the precise references of each of these phrases remain enigmatic. The easiest perhaps is the "almond blossoming" in v. 5c. A text-critical problem with the verb merits brief discussion. The *Qere* of v. 5c suggests that the verb *ynʾṣ* be emended to *ynṣ* from the verb *nṣṣ* 'to blossom' on analogy with Song 6:11 and 7:13. This emendation changes the translation from 'he spurns the almond tree' to 'the almond tree blossoms'. That the MT needs emendation is indicated by the usage of *nʾṣ* 'to spurn' elsewhere. In the 24 times it is used, its object is often the deity (Yahweh in Num 14:11,

---

166. Gordis, *Koheleth*, 334. He cites the targum and the Talmud as well.
167. Seow, "Qoheleth's Eschatological Poem," 218.

23; 16:30; Deut 31:20; 2 Sam 12:14; Ps 10:3; Elohim in Ps 10:13; Elyon in Ps 107:11; the Holy One of Israel in Isa 1:4). The object can also be the offering given to Yahweh (1 Sam 2:17), his name (Ps 74:10, 18; Isa 52:5), his word (Isa 5:24, Jer 23:17), and his city (Isa 60:14). On occasion, the object of this verb is the advice/discipline of a father (Prov 5:12, 15:5) or of a deity (Ps 107:11) or personified Wisdom (Prov 1:30). A few times, it is used of Yahweh to demonstrate his rejection of king and priest (Lam 2:6) or his people in general (Deut 32:19; Jer 14:21, 33:24), but it is never used of plants, either as object or as subject. As noted earlier, the white blossoms of the almond tree serve as a poetic reference to the graying of the hair in the elderly.[168]

The next two images are more difficult to interpret. Rashi and Ibn Ezra say that the locust in v. 5 is a circumlocution for the penis.[169] This is probably based on the understanding of the next stich as a reference to an aphrodisiac, as we will see in a moment. Seow suggests that the "grasshopper" may be a reference to a locust tree in Palestine, commonly called "St. John's Bread," known for its drooping and stunted trunk.[170] As a metaphor for the stooped nature of the elderly, this connection is attractive. However, I also suggest that the reference to the grasshopper dragging himself along may simply refer to the gait of an elderly person. The grasshopper in this scenario does not refer to a specific body part; rather, the focus is on the way a grasshopper carries itself.[171] Otto Zöckler cites Luther, Geier, and Vaihinger, who suggest that the locust refers to the crooked or bent skeleton or spinal column of a man in old age.[172] The Dt form of verbs can have an estimative nuance, conveying a sense of "show oneself as X" where X is the meaning of the verbal root in the Qal stem.[173] So here the form *yiśtabbēl* may convey the idea of the grasshopper "showing himself as burdened."

Gordis interprets the targum's translation of *wětāpēr hā'ăbîyônâ* as "you will cease from sexual intercourse."[174] The word *hā'ăbîyônâ* is assumed to be the caperberry bush, which may have been used as an

---

168. Gordis, *Koheleth*, 335. He notes that the blossom is originally pink but turns white within a month.
169. Ibid.
170. Seow, "Qoheleth's Eschatological Poem," 222.
171. Otto Zöckler, *Ecclesiastes* (trans. William Wells, expanded Tayler Lewis; New York: Scribners, 1870) 157. Zöckler is cited by Gordis, *Koheleth*, 335.
172. Zöckler, *Ecclesiastes*, 157.
173. E. Kautzsch, ed., *Gesenius' Hebrew Grammar* (hereafter GKC; Oxford: Clarendon, 1910) §54e. See also Ronald J. Williams, *Hebrew Syntax: An Outline* (Toronto: University of Toronto Press, 1996) §155.
174. Gordis, *Koheleth*, 336. He suggests reading *mškb'* 'intercourse' for the targum's *mškn'*.

aphrodisiac.¹⁷⁵ The verb *tāpēr* is parsed as a Hiphil of *prr* 'to make ineffective'.¹⁷⁶ This phrase would thus bespeak diminished libido among the elderly, a common phenomenon. Interpreters have worked backward from this stance to assume that the grasshopper in the previous stich must stand for something sexual. Yet, as noted above, the grasshopper more likely refers to the gait of the elderly.

In vv. 5–6, our author steps out of the world of metaphor to ground the verses in a clear reference to death, when the human enters his eternal home and the mourners come. Verse 6 takes up the metaphor again, but now the subject is death. In the initial phrase, the MT's *Kethiv yērāḥēq* (from *rḥq* 'to be remote') is quite unlikely. It would be translated 'the silver cord *is not remote*,' yet the *Qere yērātēq* (from *rtq* 'to bind') is not totally satisfactory either. Symmachus, the Syriac, and the Vulgate emend the text with the verb *ntq* 'to break down', which fits the context and is the best solution.

Pots may have been smashed at Israelite funerals, as they are at some funerals today.¹⁷⁷ Broken pots have been found in funerary contexts, and their placement indicates that the pieces were deliberately arranged there after the bowl was smashed.¹⁷⁸ A pot may have been a fitting metaphor for the body, because they both were believed to be made of clay, if Gen 2:7 indicates a prevalent assumption about humanity's being the quintessence of dust.¹⁷⁹ Smashing the pottery would then be a fitting symbolic gesture, marking the return of the body to the dust from whence it came, which is mentioned in the next verse. That breath returns to God who gave it is another aspect of the death metaphor here. Just as Gen 2:7 provides a context for the dust allusion, so also does it contain the idea that breath from God animates the clay of humans.

---

175. Gordis assumes that this word is derived from the root *ʾbh* meaning 'to desire', which, because of spirantization of the *bet* in late Hebrew, is blended with the root *ʾwh* 'to desire' (ibid., 335–36).

176. Aquila's translation assumes that the MT's *tāpēr* is actually *tipreh* from *prh* 'to be fruitful' and so indicates that the caperberries are on the increase. The remaining LXX texts, however, are reading the form found in the MT, which is from the root *prr* 'to break, frustrate'. See BDB 830a.

177. Seow, *Ecclesiastes*, 381.

178. Ibid.

179. Other biblical texts speaking of humans as mere dust are Gen 18:27 and Ps 103:14. Synonyms of *ʿāpār* 'dust' such as *ʾădāmâ* 'dirt' (Gen 3:19, 23) and *dakkāʾ* 'fine dust' (Ps 90:3) are also used of human origin and essence. This sort of notion is seen even in Mesopotamia where, in the Old Babylonian text "Creation of Man by the Mother Goddess," humans are made from clay (lines 15 and 23). The Assyrian version of this text, lines 14–20, also attest the same idea. See *ANET* 99–100. In the *Epic of Gilgamesh*, the goddess Aruru creates Enkidu using a pinch of clay (tablet I, line 101, in the standard version). See also Hesiod's *Theogony* 570–72, where Hephaestus makes womankind from clay.

Qoh 11:7–12:7 is unique among the biblical texts in its attention to the body's decline in old age. While the book of Song of Songs is not immediately applicable to the imagery of old age in the Hebrew Bible, it provides an interesting counterpoint to Qoheleth's poem. Like Qoh 11:7–12:7, Song of Songs is centered on a description of the body—the youthful nubile bodies of the two lovers. If my interpretation of the features in Qoh 11:7–12:7 are correct (the general picture of the trembling guards referring to old-age tremor and the bent strong men referring to limb contracture [Qoh 12:3]), then the picture of the male in Song 5:14–15 portrays a vivid contrast. His arms are rounded gold, his body is ivory work, and his legs are alabaster columns—portraying the picture of health and strength. More specifically, instead of the "grinders ceasing" as an indication of lost teeth, the female lover's teeth are "like a flock of shorn ewes that ascend from the washing, all of which bear twins" (Song 4:2 and 6:6). The reference to bearing twins is probably an allusion to the symmetry of her teeth, something that may have been quite rare and thus all the more appreciated.[180]

The wisdom books of the Hebrew Bible clearly present a multifaceted view of old age. Proverbs provides a rather Deuteronomistic view of old age, whereby old age is the reward for pious living. The phrase *'ōrek yāmîm* 'long life' is akin to the expression "to lengthen days" (using a verbal form of the word *'ōrek*) often seen in Dtn and Dtr². It is the kind of outlook that one would expect to find in children's lessons, encouraging young people to keep the commandments so that they will not experience an early death.

Qoheleth and Job certainly have a different perspective. The epilogue (Job 42:17) speaks of Job's achieving old age and being "sated of days," as were the patriarchs. The poetry of Job also assumes that wisdom attends old age (8:8 and 12:12). Yet, as in so many other ways, Job differs from Proverbs in its willingness to question the lessons taught to the children, as it were. Even so, as Murphy points out, "Job does not cancel out the book of Proverbs. It is in a dialectical movement with it."[181] Qoheleth reminds his audience that youth is preferable to old age, because in youth one may enjoy the pleasures of life. However, this advantage is only relative because, as he so often says, all is futile.[182] The depiction of old age in 12:1–7 is not the kind of assessment that the collectors of Proverbs would make. It forces the reader/hearer to face the inescapable reality of the approach of old age and its accompanying decline.

---

180. Marvin Pope, *Song of Songs* (AB 7C; New York: Doubleday, 1977) 462.
181. Roland Murphy, "Wisdom in the OT," in *Anchor Bible Dictionary* (hereafter *ABD*; ed. David Noel Freedman; New York: Doubleday, 1992) 6:926.
182. Crenshaw, "Youth and Old Age," 10.

Ruth

In the story of Ruth, the vulnerable predicament of old age is clearly demonstrated in the plight of the Israelite Naomi, wife of Elimelech. After losing her husband as well as her two sons, Naomi faced a bleak future even under the best circumstances. Simmons has demonstrated a marked disadvantage for elderly women in societies worldwide in which farming and herding are the primary source of sustenance.[183] Naomi was a sojourner in Moab and as such was facing a rather tenuous existence in her old age. We hear her own cry of hopelessness when she said, "I am old" in 1:12 and immediately associated this state with the inability to bear children. As we have seen before, the theme of barrenness and childlessness in old age is reminiscent of the patriarchal narratives of Abraham and Sarah. Naomi chose to return to Bethlehem upon hearing that the famine there had subsided, and so she made the journey accompanied only by Ruth, her Moabite daughter-in-law. The pain of her loss and the sting of her concomitant vulnerability as a widow without an heir is readily apparent in her request to be addressed as a "bitter one" with whom Shaddai had dealt bitterly. Again the story presumes a vulnerable existence for aged individuals, especially elderly widows without children.

Even so, upon arrival in her hometown, Naomi seeks a way to overturn her misfortune by playing matchmaker for Ruth. Here we see old age portrayed with wisdom and insight as Naomi positions her daughter-in-law to meet a potential suitor. In 2:19, Naomi immediately recognizes that Ruth has been favored when she sees the amount of grain that Ruth brings home after a day of gleaning. After Ruth tells her mother-in-law the name of the man who has treated her favorably, Naomi begins to plot a more specific way to assure a successful courtship (2:22). The encounter at the threshing floor is meticulously planned by the elderly Naomi, who not only knows where Boaz will be that night (3:2) but also how to exploit the opportunity to full advantage. Her suggestions to Ruth achieve the desired end, producing a match and an heir who becomes a "nourisher of her old age [*śêbâ*]" in 4:15. Naomi's portrayal as an aged woman, aside from the obvious disadvantage of her vulnerability, is overwhelmingly positive because she uses her experience and wisdom to provide for herself in old age and for her daughter-in-law's future.

It is possible that Boaz also evinces characteristics of old age. The Babylonian Talmud suggests that Boaz was both elderly and a widow-

---

183. Simmons, *Role of the Aged*, 47. In his study, women in societies of collectors, hunters, and fishers faired better than old men.

er.[184] In fact, Rabbi Isaac says that Boaz's wife had passed away about the same time that Naomi and Ruth returned from Moab. The Talmud's reconstruction is probably derived from the two references in Ruth that could lead to a conclusion of this sort about Boaz. First, he refers to Ruth as "my daughter" in 2:8, the same form of address that Naomi uses in addressing her in 1:11. The second indication of Boaz's age comes during the encounter at the threshing floor, where he discovered that the mysterious stranger at his side in the middle of the night was Ruth. He praises her for not going after the *baḥûrîm*, whether poor or rich (3:10). The term *bāḥûr* is often juxtaposed with *zāqēn* 'old, elder' and its synonyms (Prov 20:29, Ezek 9:6, Lam 5:14, Jer 31:13). So here it probably refers to a young man whom Ruth might be inclined to marry.[185] Whether this verse implies that Boaz is not a *bāḥûr* because of his age or his status, or whether this is an indication of anything about Boaz is a debated point. At the very least, we may surmise that the *baḥûrîm* Boaz speaks of are young relative to him. The tractate's portrayal of Boaz as an old man, however, may have been an attempt to make the scene at the threshing floor appear less questionable sexually. Indeed the picture of an elderly wise man speaking to a youthful Ruth as a father figure would preclude a racier interpretation of the meeting.[186] Along a similar line as the Talmud, the *Targum of Ruth* supplements the phrase "going after the *baḥûrîm*" with "to commit fornication with them." Although it does seem likely that Boaz is providing some indication of his age when he speaks of the behavior that Ruth has resisted, the question cannot be answered.

Although Boaz's age cannot be established with certainty, the fact of Naomi's old age provides the reader with insight into the view of old age in Israel. The combination of childlessness and widowhood was a predicament likely feared by many in the ancient world. The existential pain of not having progeny was only exacerbated by the socioeconomic nightmare that awaited childless widows, who could not support themselves. Concerns for care in the afterlife may have worsened the situation further.[187] A predicament of this sort provides the anxiety-ridden backdrop for the story of Ruth that permits the heroic deeds of Ruth and Boaz to shine forth.

---

184. *B. B. Bat.* 91a.
185. Kirsten Nielsen, *Ruth* (trans. Edward Broadbridge; Louisville, KY: Westminster John Knox, 1997) 76.
186. Jack Sasson, *Ruth* (2nd ed.; Biblical Seminar; Sheffield: JSOT Press, 1989) 86.
187. Brichto, "Kin, Cult, Land, and Afterlife," 31.

Lamentations

In Lamentations, a number of images are employed to portray the misery of Jerusalem in the day of its destruction. Within these pictures appear young and old alike, depicted as suffering the devastation. Young and old are grouped together to indicate the totality of Jerusalem's inhabitants (in 5:14, *zĕqēnîm* 'old men' are paired with *baḥûrîm* 'young men', and in 2:21, *zāqēn* and *naʿar* are together in the dust of the city). In 2:10, the *zĕqēnîm* of daughter Zion are paired with the virgins (*bĕtûlôt*) of Jerusalem. Here the reference to *zĕqēnîm* probably has the more general meaning of "old men" since they are paired with "young women." Both are sitting on the ground in the traditional position of mourning.[188] Related to the portrayal of old age is the image of the widow that is used to depict the city of Jerusalem in 1:1 and the mothers of the city in 5:3. The vulnerability and need to which the elderly are subject are encapsulated in the status of the widow.

Daniel

Daniel is a pivotal book in the development of old-age imagery in the Hebrew Bible because of its portrayal of Yahweh as the "Ancient of Days" (7:9, 13, 22). This is the first occurrence of an explicit portrayal of Yahweh with old-age attributes. I reserve my treatment of Daniel 7 for chap. 4 of this book.

Ezra–Nehemiah

The books of Ezra and Nehemiah offer a few references to old age that are worthy of note. Regarding the general category of age, Levites who were 20 and older were given oversight of the Temple of Yahweh in Ezra 3:8, establishing a likely threshold at which the community marked the transition of a Levite (and, I suggest, all men) from youth to mature adult. A number of times, *zĕqēnîm* is used to denote leaders of the community. There is one occasion, however, in Ezra 3:12 where it is probably used adjectivally, in the phrase *rāʾšê hāʾābōt hazzĕqēnîm* 'the elderly heads of the fathers'. It is indeed true that *hazzĕqēnîm* may constitute 'the elders' in addition to the 'heads of the fathers' in this phrase.[189] The grammar of the MT, however, suggests that the word is being used adjectivally, because this group is said to remember the original temple—a fact that would, in Ezra's day, demand old age. These elderly men mourned

---

188. See references to mourning while sitting on the ground in Ps 137:1.
189. This reading is supported in the Lucianic tradition of the LXX, which adds a copula between 'heads of fathers' and 'elders'.

the condition of the Second Temple because it paled in comparison with the First, an assessment that only they are equipped to make.

1–2 Chronicles

Old-age references are sparse in the books of Chronicles. David is described with the phrase *zāqēn wĕśābāʿ yāmîm* 'he was old and he was sated of days' when he sets up Solomon on his throne (1 Chr 23:1). In 1 Chr 29:28, David is said to die *bĕśêbâ ṭôbâ* 'in a good old age' and *śĕbaʿ yāmîm* 'sated of days'. Unlike the parallel account of this power transfer in the DH, the Chronicler in no way intimates the senility that is hinted at in the DH's account. In fact, the Chronicler portrays David amassing the supplies for the temple in his old age and making preparations for its completion by Solomon, whom David describes as *naʿar* and *rak* 'young and inexperienced' (1 Chr 22:5, 29:1). In this account David, the elder statesman, is presiding over the power transfer with forward-looking wisdom and preparation on behalf of his youthful and, literally, "tender" son. According to the Chronicler, these youthful attributes are also applied to Solomon's son by Abijah, who recalls the son of Solomon as *naʿar* and *rak lēbāb* 'tender of heart' (2 Chr 13:7). In 2 Chr 1:11, Solomon is rewarded because he requested wisdom from God rather than riches and *yāmîm rabbîm* 'many days', understood as "long life." Here again, a high premium is placed on living long, as seen in other parts of the Bible. In the next verse, God tells Solomon that because he has not requested riches and honor, he will be given them as well. Yet no mention is made of long life, perhaps because the Chronicler wants to avoid mentioning the idolatrous ways of Solomon in his old age, as recounted in 1 Kgs 11:4.

In 2 Chr 24:15, the priest Jehoiada is said to have 'grown old and sated of days' (*wayyizqan . . . wayyiśbaʿ yāmîm*) achieving the age of 130 before he died. In his time, this priest had preserved the Davidic line from the scheming Athaliah and established Joash on the throne. The Chronicler does not exploit the longevity of Jehoiada to inspire orthodox Yahwism, however. He is no doubt aware of the tension here with the untimely end of the faithful Josiah.

Two other books in the Hebrew Bible, Esther and Song of Songs, yield limited contributions to this study. According to Esth 3:13, orders were sent to kill all Jews from *naʿar weʿad zāqēn* 'youth and up to old man' and *ṭap wĕnāšîm* 'children and women'. This set of terms may include groupings of social or honorific status, but age ranges might also have been intended. In any case, the groupings merely indicate the totality of Jews. The Song of Songs is a celebration of love between two young lovers. Thus, it associates virility and passion with youth, as is seen in other parts of the Hebrew Bible. Though it does not paint a negative picture of old age, placing the love poetry on the lips of two young lovers and describing their bodies as they are in youth perhaps tacitly suggests that old age and passionate love are not readily associated. Admittedly this picture is an inference, and so the contribution of the Song to this study is quite limited.

Conclusion

The Hebrew Bible's assessment of old age is multifaceted, as this chapter has demonstrated. The legal texts of the Pentateuch enjoin respect for the elderly and mandatory cessation of manual labor for the aged, while the narrative texts portray actions not in keeping with sensibilities of this sort. Lot and Isaac are duped by family members in old age. Infirmity often attends the later years of many biblical personages. These problems range from infertility to blindness, circulatory problems, and the loss of sensory perception. However, old age is also a time to pass on wisdom and dispense blessings.

Chapter 2

The Ugaritic Evidence

As we turn now to examining the view of old age at Ugarit, it is important to note that reconstructing the culture and world view of Ugarit using the Ugaritic tablets is a rather difficult enterprise. First, many of the tablets are quite fragmentary. Although there is much to examine among the main three Ugaritic narrative texts, these stories are incomplete and hard to follow in some places. Their poor state of preservation makes it difficult to extract information from the literary sources on any sociological topic. Even if the texts were perfectly preserved, however, the examination of old age in the Ugaritic tablets would still be hampered by the fact that many of the figures in these sources are deities. The portrayal of old age among the gods of the Ugaritic pantheon does not necessarily reflect the realities faced by Ugarit's mortal population. Some scholars have indeed suggested that the literary texts can indicate nothing about the culture in which they were written.[1] Certainly, narrative texts are more ambiguous sources for determining the thought patterns of a culture than, say, legal codes, to cite a genre that strives for univocal expression and seeks to avoid ambiguity. We have already seen above, in our readings of Judges 19 (the Levite and his concubine) and 1 Kings 1–2 (David's possible senility) some of the difficulties that attend literary interpretation. However, to say that these texts can tell us nothing about the culture of Ugarit is extreme.[2]

Admittedly, literary texts alone cannot be used to reconstruct the cultural norms of an ancient city with certainty.[3] At best, we can marshal

---

1. Parker assumes as much when he cites the work of R. Finnegan, *Oral Poetry: Its Nature, Significance, and Social Context* (Cambridge: Cambridge University Press, 1977) 265. See Simon Parker, *The Pre-Biblical Narrative Tradition* (SBLRBS 24; Atlanta: Scholars Press, 1989) 218.

2. J. David Schloen, *The House of the Father as Fact and Symbol: Patrimonialism in Ugarit and the Ancient Near East* (Studies in the Archaeology and History of the Levant 2; Winona Lake, IN: Eisenbrauns, 2001) 352. Schloen uses his patrimonial model to interpret architectural features and administrative texts in ways that palpably disprove Parker's statement.

3. Mildred Seltzer notes the challenges posed by looking at the view of aging in a particular work of literature and trying to determine to what extent the author's work is idiosyncratic and to what extent it reflects a more general societal picture. See her essay "When Fields Collide or a View from Gerontology," in *Old Age in Greek*

the evidence pertinent to the question, form tentative statements about how old age was probably perceived in Ugaritic culture, and test and refine these statements with all the testimony that we can coax from ancient evidence.[4] Our own human experience with old age as well as evidence from other modern cultures can certainly inform our assessment of these ancient sources. In this chapter, the bulk of the data under review is epigraphic, taken from the Ugaritic tablets unearthed at Ras Shamra and its environs. Yet both the Ras Shamra excavations and others sites have also yielded anepigraphic sources that contain iconographic depictions of old age and youth. Both types of data yield a constellation of portrayals that can provide a glimpse into the way old age was conceived in the ancient kingdom of Ugarit.

Epigraphic Sources

El, the "Father of Years"

Any study of old age in the Ugaritic corpus must begin with El, the high god of the Ugaritic pantheon. That El was considered to be an aged god is quite certain. On numerous occasions in the Baal and Aqhat epics, El's gray hair and gray beard are mentioned. His epithet *ab šnm*, also employed in the Baal and Aqhat narratives, has been plausibly interpreted as *ʾabu šanîma* 'father of years'.[5]

---

and Latin Literature (ed. Thomas M. Falkner and Judith de Luce; Albany, NY: SUNY Press, 1989) 222.

4. Schloen speaks of this testimony as "murky refractions . . . of mundane social realities." See J. David Schloen, *The Patrimonial Household in the Kingdom of Ugarit: A Weberian Analysis of Ancient Near Eastern Society* (Ph.D. diss., Harvard University, 1995) 399.

5. F. M. Cross, *Canaanite Myth and Hebrew Epic* (Cambridge: Harvard University Press, 1973) 16. The citations for El's epithet are KTU 1.1 III 24; 1.2 I 10; 1.4 IV 24; 1.6 I 36; 1.17 VI 49. The noun *šnt* 'year' in Ugaritic is normally pluralized as *šnt* because it is considered grammatically feminine. Some scholars, such as Cyrus Gordon, have concluded from the grammar that *šnm* in El's epithet is actually a divine name. See Cyrus Gordon, "El, Father of Šnm," *JNES* 35 (1976) 262. Nicholas Wyatt thinks that *šnm* is a translation of the Kassite goddess Šumāliya. See N. Wyatt, "The Story of Dinah and Shechem," *UF* 22 (1990) 447. Pardee argues that Ugaritic *šnm* must be kept distinct from the Kassite deity. See Dennis Pardee, "Tukamuna Wa Šunama," *UF* 20 (1988) 197. A. Jirku says *šnm* is a divine name also attested in the Amarna letters. See A. Jirku, "Šnm (Schunama) der Sohn des Gottes ʾIl," *ZAW* 82 (1970) 279. A more plausible solution is given by Pope, who connects *šnm* with the Arabic verb *saniya* 'to become high, exalted in rank', citing Prov 24:21. See Marvin Pope, *El in the Ugaritic Texts* (Leiden: Brill, 1955) 33. Oldenburg also employed an Arabic cognate 'to gleam' and rendered the phrase, "Father of Luminaries." See Ulf Oldenburg, *The Conflict between El and Baʿal in Canaanite Religion* (Leiden: Brill, 1969) 17. Eissfeldt suggested that the root for *šnm* is *šny* 'to change', and he derives from this the translation 'mor-

El is celebrated for his wisdom, and this quality is directly associated with his old age. On three occasions in the story of Baal, El's decree is called wise: once by the goddess Anat and twice by Athirat. After the high god has granted Anat the request that she made on behalf of Baal, Anat says, *thmk . il . hkm [.] hkmk ʿm . ʿlm* 'your decree, O El, is wise, your wisdom is eternal' (1.3 V 30). Her response, in this particular context, is probably not meant to convey a deep respect for him, because she had threatened to "make his gray beard run with blood" just a few lines earlier. It may simply be her way of saying, "You are wise to do as I say!" Even so, Anat's response would be playing on the legendary wisdom of the elderly god. Athirat seems to be more sincere in the accolades of wisdom that she bestows on her mate. She, like Anat, comes to El requesting a house for Baal. Her words are virtually identical to those of Anat, saying, "Your decree, O El, is wise, you are wise unto eternity" (1.4 IV 41).[6] Yet unlike Anat, Athirat speaks her words of flattery before she makes her request. When Athirat's petition is granted (1.4 V 1-2) she says, *rbt . Ilm . l hkmt šbt . dqnk . l tsrk* 'You are great O El, indeed you are wise. The gray hair of your beard surely advises you'.[7] Note how her words connect wisdom and greatness with the icon of old age, the gray hair of his beard.

El's reputation for wisdom is also attested in a line from the text of Kirta (1.16 IV 2). Unfortunately, the first 16 lines of the column in question are missing.[8] It is difficult to determine, therefore, to whom these words are directed. In any case, someone says to someone, *hkmt . ktr . ltp[n]* 'You are wise like Bull the Gentle'. That 'Bull the Gentle'

---

tals'. See Otto Eissfeldt, *El im Ugaritischen Pantheon* (Berlin: Akademie, 1951) 31. Yet why "change" would be a locution for humans as mortals in not obvious. KTU 1.65 suggests that *tkmn* and *šnm* are sons of El, and thus associating *šnm* with a goddess is specious. (The reading *tkmn* is actually an emendation of *trmn*, likely a scribal error because the cuneiform signs *k* and *r* are relatively similar in form.) Gordon's argument from the grammar is also weak because in Hebrew *šānâ* can take the plural *šĕnôt* (fem.) or *šānîm* (masc.). Against Jirku, *šunama* in EA 250:43 is more likely a geographical name, as Moran suggests. See William Moran, *The Amarna Letters* (Baltimore: Johns Hopkins University Press, 1992) 303. Cross explains El's epithet *ab šnm* as a frozen formula that may reflect a dialectal feature within Ugaritic. See Cross, *Canaanite Myth*, 16 n. 24. Because we know that El's senescence is secure from other statements about him, Cross's suggestion is the most plausible. 'Father of Years' is the translation used by Simon Parker (Aqhat) as well as Mark Smith (Baal) in Simon B. Parker, ed., *Ugaritic Narrative Poetry* (SBLWAW 9; Atlanta: Scholars Press, 1997); for their translations, see pp. 62 and 92, respectively.

6. Instead of *hkmk ʿm . ʿlm*, Athirat says, *hkmt ʿm . ʿlm*.

7. Both verbs here are stative in the suffix conjugation with an asseverative *l* with the second form.

8. Parker, ed., *Ugaritic Narrative Poetry*, 36.

refers to El is quite obvious, because this expression combines two of his well-attested titles (for "Bull," see 1.1 III 26 and 1.2 I 33; for "compassionate," see 1.1 IV 13, 18). Further proof of this fact is found in the first preserved line of the column, which is slightly damaged at the beginning but ends with the form *kil* 'like El'. Even though the statement regarding El's wisdom here is not explicitly related to his old age, as it was in the Baal text, this line from Kirta also illustrates the legendary status of El's wisdom. In fact, *ḥkm* 'to be wise' is used only of El in the three main narrative texts in Ugaritic.[9] The narrative portrayals that associate old age and wisdom intersect with similar assumptions held the world over.[10] In light of these intersecting attestations that associate old age and wisdom, we would expect these qualities to be linked in the real world of Ugarit.

Physical weakness and frailty are other attributes of old age that are indicated a number of times in these narrative texts from Ugarit. In the story of Aqhat, the goddess Anat is spurned by Aqhat, the young man who refuses to give her his bow (1.17 VI). The last two lines of 1.17 VI as well as the first ten lines of 1.18 I are quite fragmentary, although it appears that Anat is complaining to El about Aqhat's insolence. She then threatens El (1.18 I 11–12) and we learn with certainty that it is Anat who is reviling El in line 20, when her insult is answered by the high god. Anat's threat is closely related to one of the icons of old age, El's gray beard. The lines read: *ašhlk* [. *šbtk . dmm*] / *šb*[*t . dq*]*nk . mmʿm* 'I will make your gray beard run with blood, the gray of your beard with gore'.[11] Clearly in this context, we see that Anat's anger demonstrates little regard for El and his seniority. El's response is apparently calm acceptance because he says nothing that appears to be inflammatory or obviously denigrating to Anat.[12] The picture here seems to be that of

---

9. The only other attestation of this root is the form *ḥkmt*, which appears on a rather fragmentary text (KTU 1.129 4) where the form *bʿl* appears in the next line. However, because the text is so badly broken, it is impossible to conclude that the two words are related.

10. This was certainly true in the antebellum United States. See D. Gutmann, *The Human Elder in Nature, Culture, and Society* (Boulder, CO: Westview, 1997) 240. Simmons notes that many Native Americans viewed old men as repositories of wisdom. See Leo W. Simmons, *The Role of the Aged in Primitive Society* (New Haven, CT: Yale University Press, 1945) 68.

11. The restoration is based on two virtually identical lines from 1.3 V 2 and 1.3 V 24–25. The contents of these two texts and their relevance to the threat here in Aqhat are discussed below.

12. Jo Ann Hackett, "Rehabilitating Hagar: Fragments of an Epic Pattern," in *Gender and Difference* (ed. Peggy Day; Minneapolis: Fortress, 1989) 19.

a wise elder figure who understands hot-tempered youths.[13] As I suggested in the first chapter, when discussing Sarah's confrontation of Abraham in Genesis 16, Gutmann's observation that older men tend to become more passive is helpful in understanding the docile behavior of the elder male in this scenario.[14] These ancient writers attest this pattern, using it in their stories, depicting aged male deities. After the aged El responds to Anat, the maiden goddess departs without further comment.

A similar encounter between Anat and El appears in the third tablet of the Baal text. Anat first plans to threaten El in the language she uses in the story of Aqhat (1.18 I 11-12) and then speaks to him directly in 1.3 V 24-25. Because I want to focus on a number of details in 1.3 V 1-2, I am reproducing the two lines here with a translation.

| [xxx a]mṣḥ.nn . k imr . l arṣ | . . . I will pull him like a lamb to the ground |
| [ašhl]k . šbth . dmm šb[t . dqnh | I will make his gray hair run with blood |

I want to examine the second line first and note its parallels elsewhere. I reproduce them here for ease of comparison.

1.18 I 11-12	ašhlk [. šbtk . dmm] / šb[t . dq]nk . mmʿm.
1.3 V 2	[ašhl]k . šbth . dmm . šbt . dqnh.
1.3 V 24-25	ašhlk . šbtk [. dmm] / šbt . dqnk . mmʿm.

First of all, note the wording of the threat that she actually speaks in lines 24-25. The partial reconstruction and the addition of *mmʿm* 'gore' at the end of the line notwithstanding, the phrases are virtually identical.[15] Comparison with the lines in 1.18 I 11-12 above is striking as well, again despite the lacuna. In the context of 1.3, Anat is threatening El because her brother Baal does not have a house, as do "the gods" and "the sons of Athirat." Five lines later, however, Anat is praising El for his wisdom, as I noted above. El has told her in the interim that, among the goddesses she is unique, and he seems to be open to her request in line 28. Again, Gutmann's thesis concerning aged-male docility is buttressed by El's passive disposition in this text. Despite El's seeming pliant

---

13. Hackett has suggested that there may be an epic pattern that explains the similarity between the scene here and the scene in Genesis where Sarah accosts Abraham, as well as a similar scene in the *Epic of Gilgamesh*, where Ishtar confronts Anu. See ibid., 12-24.

14. D. Gutmann, *Reclaimed Powers: Toward a New Psychology of Men and Women in Later Life* (New York: Basic Books, 1987) 182.

15. It is possible that *mmʿm* could be present after *dqnh*, because the text is damaged at the beginning of line 3.

acceptance and Anat's violent rhetoric, the threat does not immediately achieve the results desired by Anat, because we see Athirat later in the story asking El to carry out Anat's request (1.4 IV 50–51).

Another facet of 1.3 V 1–2 that I want to discuss is related to these violent threats toward the elderly El seen in the first line. I am treating this separately from line 2, discussed in the previous paragraph, because of its imagery, which compares El with a lamb. Anat's plans begin with the line [a]mṣḥ .nn . kimr . larṣ 'I will pull him [El] to the ground like a lamb'. Initially the statement's tone comes as no surprise to the reader who is accustomed to Anat's proclivity to spout violent rhetoric. However, a closer look at the imagery she uses may indicate something about El that would be quite natural, given his senescence. To Anat, El's agedness implies physical weakness, even though her actions indicate her acceptance of El's political power, as it were. That is, the fact that she must go to El to make her request, violent threat though it be, is a tacit admission of his power over her. This fact notwithstanding, Anat seems to exploit the perceived physical weakness of El to undermine his authority over her. Here we see an assumption of senescent physical weakness in the narrative world of the Baal text that mirrors the weakness of old age in the real world. It is also possible that the lamb's light-colored coat makes the lamb a fitting comparison with El, the gray-bearded deity. This is especially true given the way that Anat centers her threat on El's grizzled facial hair.

Although the god El is clearly portrayed with some of the vulnerability that is associated with old age among mortals, he is no *deus otiosus*. In a few places in the Ugaritic tablets, El is portrayed as a lusty old man. The first instance of this sort is found in KTU 1.4 IV 23–24, where Athirat has come to visit El. In lines 38–39, El asks her, *hm . yd . il mlk / yḥssk . ahbt .ṯr . t'rrk* 'Does the hand of El arouse you, the love of Bull stir you?' It is well documented that the word *yd* 'hand' in Ugaritic is occasionally a circumlocution for penis.[16] In the lines that follow El's amorous overtures, Athirat showers him with accolades of his wisdom but does not accept his offers. She immediately turns to her request that a house be provided for Baal, whom she proclaims king. Exactly how this exchange is to be related to the overall story of Baal is unclear. But it does provide an indication of El's persistent passions, which form the chief subject of another famous text from Ras Shamra.

---

16. See KTU 1.23 33–34, where the deity's "hand" is said to grow long as the sea. See Gregorio del Olmo Lete and J. Sanmartín, *A Dictionary of the Ugaritic Language in the Alphabetic Tradition* (trans. W. G. E. Watson; Leiden: Brill, 2003 [hereafter, *DUL*]) 953.

Another text that merits our attention is KTU 1.23, a perplexing text that has received much attention by commentators. Although the text is fragmentary, it is clear that El is depicted coupling with and impregnating two women, who give birth to deities. The two women with whom he couples are called *mštʿltm*. The meaning of the word *mštʿltm* has received much attention. The sentence in which it appears reads: *yqḥ . il . mštʿltm mštʿltm l riš agn* 'El takes the *mštʿltm*, the *mštʿltm* from the top of the *agn*' (lines 35–36). The form *mštʿltm* has been parsed as a Št (causative stem) participle from the verb *ʿly* 'to ascend'. Thus Watson suggests that *mštʿltm* refers to women who draw water in an *agn* 'bowl', which they would carry on their head (*l riš*) a well-known custom in the Near East.[17] So for Watson, the action is causative, "bringing up," and the -t infix conveys a somewhat reflexive sense of putting what is brought up on the head.

Similarly, Pardee accepts Watson's parsing but suggests that the women are making an offering to El because the causative of the verb *ʿly* is used in ritual texts for the act of presenting a gift to a deity.[18] Mark Smith has suggested that -t infix forms almost always have to do with bodily function and do not always convey the explicit reflexive-reciprocal sense that is often assumed.[19] In the sexually charged context of this text, Smith's observations are particularly intriguing. Del Olmo Lete suggests that *mštʿltm* are necromancers, presumably from the idea of raising the departed spirits.[20] Yet, as Watson points out, it is not clear why necromancers should appear in this text.[21] De Moor has suggested that the meaning of the word is 'girl acrobat'.[22] Others have assumed the *š* to be a component of the root. Cross, for example, assumes that *mštʿltm* is related to the Hebrew word *šōʿal* 'hollow of the hand' and so translates the phrase 'two handfuls to the top of the bowl'.[23]

---

17. Wilfred G. E. Watson, "Ugaritic and Mesopotamian Literary Texts," *UF* 9 (1977) 281.

18. Dennis Pardee, "Dawn and Dusk" in *The Context of Scripture*, vol. 1: *Canonical Compositions from the Biblical World* (ed. William W. Hallo; Leiden: Brill, 1997) 280 n. 44.

19. Mark S. Smith, *The Rituals and Myths of the Feast of the Goodly Gods of KTU/CAT 1.23: Royal Constructions of Oppositions, Intersection, Integration, and Domination* (Resources for Biblical Study 51; Atlanta: Society of Biblical Literature, 2006) 77.

20. Gregorio del Olmo Lete, *Interpretación de la mitología cananea: Estudios de semántica ugarítica* (Fuentes de la Ciencia Bíblica 2; Valencia: Institución San Jerónimo, 1984) 143.

21. W. G. E. Watson, "Review of Gregorio del Olmo Lete, *Interpretación de la mitología cananea. Estudios de semántica ugarítica*," *AuOr* 5 (1987) 164.

22. J. C. de Moor, *An Anthology of Religious Texts from Ugarit* (NISABA Religious Texts in Translation 16; Leiden: Brill, 1987) 123.

23. Cross, *Canaanite Myth*, 22.

Pope connects *mštʿltm* to the Arabic *šʿl* 'to burn', suggesting that *agn* is from the Indo-European word *agni* 'fire' and so renders the phrase 'torches taken from the top of the fire'.[24] Lewis adopts Pope's conclusion in his translation, rendering *mštʿltm* as 'brands' and *agn* as 'firestand'.[25] Indeed, Pope's assessment has much to commend it. The children that are born of this union between El and the *mštʿltm* are Dusk and Dawn, stages of the sun's cycle. Pope notes that the iconography of Kronos, reproduced in his article in a footnote, shows the god holding two torches with a firepot on a stand at his feet.[26] The use of fire and heat to denote sexual activity fits nicely within this context as well. Later, in line 56, the word *ḥmḥmt* 'pregnancy' is used, a word related to the verbal root *ḥmm* 'to heat up'.[27] Despite the differing opinions on the etymology and translation of *mštʿltm* and *agn*, there is virtual agreement that the *mštʿltm* are the two women whom El impregnates later on in the story. In line 39, they are called *aṯtm* 'women', and they give birth at the end of the extant text.

For our purposes, 1.23 is important because it portrays El as a lusty god who is able to sire children. Lines 51–52 read, *bm . nšq . w hr . bḥbq . ḥmḥmt tqt[nṣn w] tldn šḥr wšlm* 'with a kiss, conception, with an embrace, pregnant heat. The two are in labor pain and give birth to Dawn and Dusk'. It seems logical to assume that the activity that precedes lines 51–52 precipitates these pregnancies and subsequent births.[28]

Debate has raged around the exact state of El's virility in this text. The euphemistic use of *yd* 'hand', *ḫṭ* 'scepter', and *mṭ* 'staff' for the deity's penis and its erect or flaccid condition are at the center of the controversy. The source of contention is the verb *nḫt*, which appears four times in this text (lines 37, 40, 43, and 47). I reproduce them here for clarity.

37	*il . ḫṭh . nḫt . il . ymnn . mṭ . ydh*
40	*nḫtm . ḫṭk . mmnnm . mṭ . ydk*
43–44	*nḫtm . ḫṭk . mmnnm . mṭ . ydk*
47	*nḫtm . ḫṭk . mmnnm . mṭ . ydk*

Each time, the subject of this verb is *ḫṭ* 'scepter', and each time, this subject is in poetic parallel with *yd* 'hand'. Tropper has argued that Ak-

---

24. Marvin H. Pope, "Ups and Downs in El's Amours," *UF* 11 (1979) 701.
25. In Simon Parker, ed., *Ugaritic Narrative Poetry*, 210.
26. Pope, "Ups and Downs," 702 n. 6. Pope has reproduced a line drawing of the scene.
27. *DUL* 363.
28. This is Lewis's conclusion. See his comments in Simon Parker, ed., *Ugaritic Narrative Poetry*, 206.

kadian *nahātu* 'to become low' is related to Ugaritic *nḫt*.²⁹ The verb *nḫt* is used by the two women to describe El's *membrum virile*, and Pope has suggested that El was impotent.³⁰ The suggestion is partly rooted in Pope's assumption that El is becoming the otiose god who is being replaced by the younger Baal.³¹ This position is heavily colored by Pope's attempt to connect this story to Hesiod's *Theogony* and Homer's *Iliad*, which depict rivalries between old and young gods.³² Pope suggests that El's impotence is cured by the ritual in the text.³³

Other scholars offer alternatives to Pope. Cross renders *nḫt* 'stretched'³⁴ and del Olmo Lete and Sanmartín present 'to reach or to put at the disposal of'.³⁵ The form that is parallel with *nḫt* on three occasions (lines 40, 44, and 47) is *mmnnm*, appearing each time as *mmnnm . mṯ ydk*, and referring to the 'staff of [El's] hand'. Cross explains the form *mmnnm* in light of the form *ymnn . mṯ . ydh* in line 37. Cross at one time suggested that the form here should be identified as a denominative verb from *yamīn* 'right hand', meaning "to draw with the right hand."³⁶ Pope says this is impossible and posits the root *mnn* as the basis for his translation 'jaded, tired', based on an Arabic cognate.³⁷ However, as Good points out, the Arabic *munnatun* means 'strength'.³⁸ Cross has subsequently abandoned his original suggestion, adopting Pope's posited root *mnn*, though he suggests a meaning 'to strain', from which the secondary root 'to weary' (from straining) is derived.³⁹

When we look at this text as a whole, the only other verb that is used to describe the "hand of El" is *'rk* 'to lengthen'. His "hand" lengthens like the sea and like the flood in lines 33–34, following hard upon his

---

29. Josef Tropper, "Akkadisch *nuḫḫutu* und die Repräsentation des Phonems /ḫ/ im Akkadischen," *ZA* 85 (1995) 66.
30. Pope, "Ups and Downs in El's Amours," 705.
31. Idem, *El in the Ugaritic Texts*, 103. See also Oldenburg, *The Confllict between El and Baal*, 146. This position continues to be supported by Mark Smith. See Mark S. Smith, *The Memoirs of God* (Minneapolis: Fortress, 2004) 93.
32. Pope (*El in the Ugaritic Texts*, 29) suggests that El's decline is analogous to Kronos (identified as El) who is banished by his sons Zeus, Hades, and Poseidon, corresponding to Baal, Mot, and Yam.
33. Ibid., 41. Segert assumes the same. See Stanislav Segert, "An Ugaritic Text Related to the Fertility Cult (*KTU* 1.23)," in *Archaeology and Fertility Cult in the Ancient Mediterranean* (ed. Anthony Bonanno; Amsterdam: Grüner, 1986) 218.
34. Cross, *Canaanite Myth*, 23.
35. *DUL* 628.
36. Cross, *Canaanite Myth*, 23 n. 58. He cites 1 Chr 12:2 as evidence.
37. Pope, "Ups and Downs," 706.
38. Robert M. Good, "Hebrew and Ugaritic nḫt," *UF* 17 (1986) 156.
39. Saul M. Olyan, *Asherah and the Cult of Yahweh in Israel* (SBLMS 34; Atlanta: Scholars Press, 1988) 42.

coupling with the two women. All the references to his "hand" drooping or becoming weary follow in lines 37, 40, 43–44, and 47. In each of these four instances regarding his "hand," there is mention of a bird being cooked on coals (38–39, 41, 44, 48). Some have suggested this procedure of killing a bird and roasting it over coals is designed to cure El's impotence.[40] There are Mesopotamian potency incantations that involve killing and preparing a bird.[41] After the fourth occasion of roasting the bird, there is mention of kissing, conception, embrace, and giving birth (lines 49–52). Precise etymology for the two verbs notwithstanding, the most economical understanding is that El's penis is erect at first but becomes less so and, through some action regarding a roasted bird, again becomes sufficiently erect so as to impregnate the women.

Before I draw conclusions in this section on KTU 1.23, there is one other important matter to discuss: El's age in this story. The vast majority of scholars who have commented on this text, including Cross, Pope, and Segert, assume El to be old, as is the case in the other Ugaritic texts.[42] However, Smith, departing from his teachers on this point, suggests that El is in fact a young deity in this context and goes on to suggest that KTU 1.23 is an earlier story about El in the prime of life.[43] Smith says that this story has El impregnating women and having children, a rather different picture from El in the Baal text, where he has adult children but no babies or infants. Smith also cites van Selms, who says that El plays a more active role in 1.23 than in the *Baal Cycle*.[44]

Smith's conclusions, however, go beyond what these texts can bear. First of all, establishing relative chronologies of stories in the Ugaritic corpus is fraught with difficulty. This is especially true of 1.23, a text that is difficult to interpret and integrate into the larger narrative world of Baal, Kirta, and Aqhat. Furthermore, to conclude on the basis of El's impregnating two women that this story portrays El at an earlier time is to base a conclusion on evidence that is simply far too inadequate. Similarly, van Selms's conclusions about El's more active state in 1.23

---

40. Pope, *El in the Ugaritic Texts*, 41. See also André Caquot, Maurice Sznycer, and Andrée Herdner, *Textes ougaritiques, Tome I: Mythes et légends* (Paris: Cerf, 1974) 374 note d.

41. These are the ŠÀ.ZI.GA therapeutic rituals in Robert Biggs, *ŠÀ.ZI.GA: Ancient Mesopotamian Potency Incantations* (Locust Valley, NY: Augustin, 1967) 56–57, cited in Mark Smith, *The Rituals and Myths*, 87.

42. Cross, *Canaanite Myth*, 24; Pope, *El in the Ugaritic Texts*, 40; Segert, "An Ugaritic Text," 218.

43. Mark Smith, *The Rituals and Myths*, 88.

44. Ibid., 74. He is citing A. van Selms, "Yammu's Dethronement of Baal: An Attempt to Reconstruct Texts UT 129, 137 and 68," *UF* 2 (1970) 252.

vis-à-vis his portrayal in the Baal text strikes me as rather subjective. El functions as the chief god in the Baal text, the highest authority to which other deities appeal. He has a rather active role in these stories. How, precisely, one would gauge levels of El's vigor in these texts is not clear to me, in any case. The apparent juxtaposition of El's hand as "lengthened" and "drooping/weary" is more at home in the context of El's senescence in my estimation. The fact that his problem with a flaccid penis is addressed four times in the text seems to me better suited to the experience of an elderly male. This is also why I believe Pope to be right when he disagrees with Albright's suggestion that El is experiencing postcoital detumescence.[45] El's senescence provides the more logical backdrop for erectile dysfunction in the story in a way that a more youthful version of El would not. The motif of an elderly man impregnating women in his old age, furthermore, is hardly an uncommon theme in the world of West Semitic lore.

That KTU 1.23 does give a glimpse of the elderly El is the most likely conclusion when all is considered. Cross, Pope, and Segert rightly noted this, and the narrative world of the text virtually demands it. To be sure, El is no where explicitly referred to as old in 1.23. Smith's suggestion of a youthful El and his concomitant assumption about the relative chronology of this story are indeed possible but not likely, in my estimation. El is the same senescent deity we see elsewhere in the Ugaritic texts. Though he seems to demonstrate the impotence so common among elderly men, he is able through his actions with these two women to overcome this obstacle and impregnate both of them. In this text, the portrayal of El is as a lusty god who is still sexually active despite the ups and downs in his amours.

Old Age and Mortals in Ugaritic Narrative

Danel

The *Legend of Aqhat* provides an interesting, though subtle glimpse into senescent physical weakness in what appears to be an ideal of human old age at Ugarit. On four occasions on the first tablet of the Aqhat story (1.17, of which I translate I 26–33 below) Danel speaks of his longing for a son.

nṣb . skn . ilibh . b qdš	to set up a stela for his ancestor in the sanctuary,
ztr . ʿmh . l arṣ . mšṣu . qṭrh	a sign of his family, to rescue his smoke from the underworld

---

45. Pope, *El in the Ugaritic Texts*, 40.

l ʿpr . ḏmr . aṯrh . bq . lt	to protect his steps from the dust, to close the mouth of
niṣh . gršˍ . d . ʿšy . lnh	his reviler, to drive away them who annoy him,
aḥd . ydh . b škrn . mʿmsh	to grasp his hand when he is drunk, to support him
[k]šbʿ . yn . spu . ksmh . bt . bʿl	when he is sated of wine, to eat his portion in Baal's house
[w] mnth . bt . il . ṯh . ggh . b ym	and his part in El's house, to plaster his roof on the day of
[ṭl]ṭ . rḥs . npsh . b ym . rṯ	mud, to wash his things on the day of dirt.

The refrain appears again in column I lines 45–49, but the last half is not preserved. Two more variations of this refrain appear in column II of this tablet. The third occurrence, 1.17 II 1–8, is at the top of column II, but the first line is too damaged to read. The extant text begins with *l z*, and the remainder of the line is restored on the basis of the other two, *mutatis mutandis*. The rest of the section is identical in both word selection and word order with the reading on column I, except that the line *spu . ksmh . bt . bʿl w mnth . bt . il* has been transposed with the line *aḥd . ydh . b škrn . mʿmsh kšbʿ . yn*. The fourth occurrence of this refrain, 1.17 II 16–23, is again identical in word selection and word order, with the exception of the omission of the line *l arṣ . mšṣu . qṭrh*. This omission was surely a scribal lapse owing to haplography of *homoioarkton*, when the writer wrote the *l* in *l arṣ* and then skipped to the *l* in *l ʿpr*.[46]

The abstract notion behind this refrain is a parent's desire for a son who can care for him when he reaches an age at which he needs care.[47] Danel is nowhere portrayed explicitly as old, and the concerns set forth in this refrain are oriented toward the future. Thus, we gain a glimpse of what were certainly some of the anxieties of the elderly at Ugarit. It is likely, based on our conclusions in chap. 1, that by the time a man had a son who could do the things mentioned in these lines, he would already be considered old. The refrain indicates a concern for cultic duties in the sanctuary, including setting up a stela and engaging in cultic meals there. The stela for the *ilib* 'ancestral spirit'[48] would preserve the

---

46. M. J. Boda, "Ideal Sonship in Ugarit," *UF* 25 (1993) 11.
47. Some have suggested that these lines tell of the duties of a son for his father after the father has passed away. See, for example, Meindert Dijkstra and J. C. de Moor, "Problematical Passages in the Legend of Aqhâtu," *UF* 7 (1975) 177. The references to drunkenness and roof-mending clearly obviate such a hypothesis. See John F. Healey, "The *Pietas* of an Ideal Son in Ugarit," *UF* 11 (1979) 354.
48. The term *ilib* is not a specific deity or "god of the father" but, rather, the spirit of the departed ancestor. See Karel van der Toorn, "Ilib and the 'God of the

memory of the dearly departed and would also probably have served the proleptic purpose of reminding the son to care for his father when he passed away. That is, a son who provides for the ancestral spirits now will likely ensure that these provisions will continue into the next generation. Eating the portions in the sanctuary may be a further indication of the concern for this type of care extended to the dead, which may, as Brichto has noted, say something about the idea of an afterlife.[49] Concern for opponents and protection from them are present here as well, along with anxiety over physical possessions and habitation.

The two stichoi that refer to assistance given to the father when he is drunk are not the only places where these exact concerns are found in the Ugaritic tablets. KTU 1.114 depicts El giving a party complete with food and drink. In line 16, we learn that El has become inebriated, in language that is quite reminiscent of the refrain from Aqhat: yšt . y[n] . ʿd šbʿ . trṯ . ʿd škr 'He [El] drinks wine until sated, new wine until drunk'. Both verbal roots, šbʿ 'to be sated' and škr 'to be drunk', appear in both texts. The connections continue in lines 18–19, where two deities, Thkmn and Shnm, support El in his intoxicated state.[50] The verbal form is yʿmsn.nn from the root ʿms 'to support', which is the same root used in the refrain for the support given to the father. Line 21 reads ql . il . km mt / il . kyrdm . arṣ 'El falls like a dead man, El, like one who descends to the earth'. The death language here possibly evokes the frailty of old age when death looms near. The common theme expressed in these texts suggests a prevailing concern among many of the aging people in Ugarit: will there be anyone there for me when, in my waning years, I am too drunk to make my way? There may be a tacit admission that the aged have a reduced tolerance for strong drink, yet I do not mean to imply that all individuals at Ugarit anticipated spending their old age in a state of inebriation. That this theme appears four times in the Aqhat story and once again in a separate text, however, suggests that this was a common concern for people approaching old age.

Father,'" *UF* 25 (1993) 386. The term appears in KTU 1.109 11–14 with other deities to whom offerings are to be made. Yet this in no way proves that *ilib* is a single deity. It is more likely that this offering was made to each person's departed kinsman.

49. H. C. Brichto, "Kin, Cult, Land and Afterlife: A Biblical Complex," *HUCA* 44 (1973) 31–35.

50. RS 24.440 is a mug from Ugarit depicting a bearded figure, seated, and holding an upraised flask, who has been identified with El. Another unidentified figure is also holding a rhyton and perhaps a flask as well. See the photograph and the hand drawing in C. F.-A. Schaeffer, "Nouveaux témoignages du culte de El et de Baal à Ras Shamra–Ugarit et ailleurs en Syrie-Palestine," *Syria* 43 (1966) 3. I will comment further on this depiction later in this chapter.

Kirta

Although Kirta is nowhere explicitly portrayed as old, the end of the extant text depicts a scene perhaps with a background fraught with concern about the king's old age. I suggest that Kirta (as a father of eight children who were lost and yet as someone who has adult children at the end of the extant story) is at the stage in life when at the very least he is quickly approaching old age. The end of the last tablet may be an epic type-scene of power transfer from an older king to his son. Thus, the narrative depiction of Kirta's life is the foundational evidence for the assumption regarding his age at the end of the story.

To see the picture of Kirta in his later years, we begin with column VI of the last tablet (1.16), which opens with Shataqat healing Kirta's sickness. In lines 23–24, Kirta has returned to his throne. Yet in the very next line, Kirta's son Yassib begins to plot his takeover of his father's throne. This disjointedness has been explained by Parker as the beginning of a new story that was linked to the preceding episode because it contains a reference to Kirta's sickness.[51] The audience is privy to the inner thoughts of Yassib as he plans his confrontation with Kirta. He immediately carries out these private plans and accosts Kirta with numerous reasons why he should abdicate the throne in deference to Yassib. To his father he intends to say (lines 30–38):[52]

30 When raiders come, you talk;
    when invaders come, you are idle.
    You let your hand fall to inaction.
    You do not render judgment for the widow.
    You do not render justice for the disadvantaged.
35 Like a sister is the bed of sickness,
    the couch of disease is a companion.
    Descend from being king and I will rule,
38 from your dominion and I will sit on it.

What he actually says to him (lines 43–53) however, is slightly expanded (expansion in italics):

43 When raiders come, you talk;
    when invaders come, you are idle.
    You let your hand fall to inaction.
    You do not render judgment for the widow.
    You do not render justice for the disadvantaged.

---

51. Simon Parker, *The Pre-Biblical Narrative Tradition*, 199.
52. Both translations that follow are mine.

48   *You do not expel those who work against the poor.*
     You do not feed the orphan before you.
     At your back is the widow.
     Like a sister is the bed of sickness,
     the couch of disease is a companion.
52   Descend from being king and I will rule,
     from your dominion and I will sit on it.

What Yassib means when he refers to sickness and weakness is not clear, especially in light of Kirta's recent recovery, narrated on the same tablet. Although Yassib may not have known of the recovery, this seems unlikely in that Kirta is described as sitting on his throne and no longer on his bed when Yassib begins to plot his machinations. There are some indications here that Yassib's complaints are perhaps rooted in the effect of age on the king's behavior. He begins by saying that Kirta merely talks when raiders raid. The meaning of these two lines has been widely debated.[53]

F. Renfroe, whose suggestion I have adopted here, offers the most likely rendition of the lines within the context of Yassib's complaint to Kirta.[54] In the first line of this section, Renfroe understands the word, *ġz*, to be a cognate of the Arabic verb *ġzw* 'to raid, attack' and argues that the verb *dbr* in the same line denotes speaking, as it does in other Semitic languages.[55] In the next line, *w ġrm ttwy*, which I translated 'when raiders come, you are idle', the form *ġrm* is to be related to the Arabic verb *ġwr* 'to raid, plunder', and *ttwy* is connected to the Arabic *twy* 'to remain'.[56] The temporal meaning of *k-* in the first stich governs both phrases. Thus, Yassib accuses Kirta of giving mere lip service to security.

The complaint that Kirta has let his hand fall to inactivity may be a subtle reference to waning virility, because *yd* 'hand' can also refer to penis.[57] The word *ġlt*, rendered in my translation 'inactivity', likely comes from the verb *ġly*, which denotes the action of withering, applied to plants in Aqhat (1.19 I 31) and Baal (1.6 V 18).[58] The verb also refers to lowering, which is what the gods do with their heads in the Baal

---

53. See M. Dietrich and O. Loretz, "Kerets Krankenheit und Amtsunfähigkeit," *UF* 17 (1986) 123–27, for a compilation of suggested translations.
54. F. Renfroe, "The Foibles of a Feeble Monarch," *UF* 22 (1990) 282–83.
55. *DUL* 264 lists such a meaning for *dbr* in KTU 2.71 14; 2.72 18; and 1.82 8.
56. Renfroe, "The Foibles of a Feeble Monarch," 283.
57. See KTU 1.4 IV 23 and 1.23 33, 34 (2x), 35 for the euphemistic use of "hand."
58. The Aqhat text is broken in a critical location that would indicate exactly what droops or wilts here, but the parallel verb *ḥrb* 'to dry out' and the location of this action at a threshing floor seem to support this conclusion. The Baal text is also slightly damaged in this line. See *DUL* 321 for the reconstruction assumed here: *ʿlk pht ġly b šdm* 'on account of you I have seen withering in the fields'.

story (1.2 I 23–24). The suggestion that this line is a double entendre is strengthened by the range of the verbal action standing behind the noun ģlt, which could easily apply to impotence. Senescent impotence is a common feature among males and is reminiscent of the elderly King David. If I am right in claiming that the foundations of these accusations are rooted in old-age frailty, then what is assumed of David in 1 Kings 1 could also apply here. That is, my suggestion that David's physical impotence is assumed to indicate political impotence could apply to Kirta here in precisely the same manner. This hypothesis fits the context nicely.

KTU 1.2 I, lines 35–36/50–52 offer some interesting possibilities in this regard as well. The bicolon begins: *km . aḫt . ʿrš . mdw* 'like a sister [or sisters] is the sick bed'. This sick bed is paralleled by *ʿrš . zbln* 'disease bed' in the next stich, introduced with the word *anšt* 'companion'. However, some have understood *anšt* as a verbal form meaning 'to fall ill, sick from rage' from the verb *ʾnš*.[59] This is probably the meaning of *anšt* in the Baal text (1.3 V 27). However, the parallelism here makes it more likely that *anšt* is a noun that finds its parallel in *aḫt*, a suggestion strengthened by the -*t* ending marking both as feminine. As the temporal *k* governs both phrases in the first line, so too here the comparative *km* governs both of these lines. The sense of the two lines is probably an indication of how much time Kirta has spent in bed because of infirmity. Some would no doubt see a sexual connotation in this reference to *aḫt*.[60] This inference is probably not warranted, as Walls has argued[61] and, in any case, it is not necessary to make the substantive point that Kirta has been confined to his bed for a long period of time. Again, as with the biblical David, Kirta's physical ailment is assumed to be grounds for usurpation of his throne.

Although the precise meaning of Yassib's accusations against his father may elude us, it is clear that Yassib wants Kirta to step down so as

---

59. *DUL* 83. J. C. de Moor and K. Spronk make the unlikely suggestion that *anšt* is a stative verbal form meaning 'you are a companion' parallel with *aḫt*, also understood as a stative verbal form meaning 'you are a brother'. See their article, "Problematical Passages in the Legend of Kirtu (II)," *UF* 14 (1982) 190.

60. See, for example, Marvin Pope, *Song of Songs* (AB 7C; New York: Doubleday, 1977) 657, where he cites ancient Near Eastern evidence to indicate the sexual connotation of "sister" in Egyptian and Mesopotamian love poetry as a parallel to the term used in the Song of Songs. Admittedly, the association of *aḫt* with "couch" is conceivably suggestive of a sexual topos.

61. Neal H. Walls, *The Goddess Anat in Ugaritic Myth* (SBLDS 135; Atlanta: Scholars Press, 1992) 90. Walls points out that when Baal and Anat are called brother and sister, such terminology may be quite literal or "may indicate their similar natures as aggressive warriors."

to permit him to take over the throne. Again, that Kirta is considered old is not explicitly confirmed in the extant text. Yet when we combine the tenor of Yassib's accusation with the story's own chronology, the likelihood of Kirta's elderly status increases. Note that, in the story's timeline, at the point when Yassib confronts Kirta, the monarch has previously fathered eight children who died and now has adult children. Here our firm evidence ends and speculation begins. It is tempting to import the old-age features from the biblical story of David, when he faced a similar threat from his son Adonijah. Perhaps an epic type-scene informs both accounts of transfers of power from an older monarch to his son. Certainly the internal evidence of the *Legend of Kirta* itself justifies our reading of Kirta as an aged man in the last scene of the extant tale.

RS 20.239

Aside from the narrative Ugaritic texts, there is only one document that may give us some insight into the elderly in this ancient kingdom. It is a letter, designated RS 20.239, written in Akkadian from someone named Mada'e to the ruler (*sākinu*) presumably of Ugarit.[62] In this text, the elders (*šībūtu*) of the city of Rakba are called to enter the temple (*bīt ilim*) to take an oath about some cattle that are to be sold. Five people are mentioned in this group, three of whom are close relations. This does not mean, contra Vita, that elders in the Kingdom of Ugarit were all part of a single family.[63] The exact nature of the case in which they testify is not detailed in this letter. This lone Akkadian letter constitutes all that is known of elders in the nonliterary texts known from Ugarit. It should be noted that the ambiguity of the term "elders" in Israel—as a marker of old age or of status—likely obtained also in Ugarit. As in the case of Israel, therefore, we may not assume that "elders" in that ancient city were considered "old."

---

62. Jean Nougayrol et al., *Ugaritica V* (Mission de Ras Shamra 16; Paris: Imprimerie Nationale, 1968) 141 no. 52. This conclusion is based on the provenance of the tablet. The title *sākinu* was used of a number of officials and did not have a standard or fixed meaning. See Michael Heltzer, *The Internal Organization of the Kingdom of Ugarit* (Wiesbaden: Reichert, 1982) 142.

63. Juan-Pablo Vita, "The Society of Ugarit," in *Handbook of Ugaritic Studies* (ed. W. G. E. Watson and N. Wyatt; Leiden: Brill, 1999) 483. It seems that Vita is basing his conclusions on M. Heltzer, *The Rural Community in Ancient Ugarit* (Wiesbaden: Reichert, 1976) 79. Heltzer also intimates such a position, but he warns that this text is the only evidence. Heltzer has indeed overstated the case by saying, "But the characteristic feature is that the eldership was distributed *among members of one family* and high ranking officials" (emphasis mine). Vita apparently accepts the italicized portion above as paradigmatic for the entire kingdom.

Thus, within the texts unearthed from ancient Ugarit we are able to see a glimpse of a few features associated with old age. The refrain in Aqhat that describes an ideal of old age and the threats by Anat against El suggest a feeling of vulnerability among the aged. The association of wisdom with old age seen in the portrayal of El mirrors what is sometimes seen in the Hebrew Bible and other texts from the ancient Near East. El's virility, alluded to in the Baal text and dramatized in KTU 1.23, may be an attempt to gainsay the presumed impotence of elderly men. Unfortunately, the remaining narrative texts, letters, legal texts, and economic texts reveal little to expand our understanding of old age among the people of Ugarit.

Iconographic Sources

Images of El

To a limited degree, the iconography of El illustrates his old age. The limitations in this regard stem from the lack of clear identifications of figures in Levantine iconography, especially when compared with the iconography of Mesopotamia and Egypt.[64] Admittedly, there is a danger of circular reasoning in relating the Ugaritic textual evidence to the often unlabeled figures depicted in Canaanite art. I do not claim that these identifications of El are certain, but there is a strong correlation between the literary depictions of El and some of the images excavated at Ras Shamra and elsewhere.

One likely depiction of El is found on a stela (RS 8.295) depicting two male figures, one standing and one seated on a throne with his feet on a stool.[65] The enthroned figure has a beard and a horned cap and has his right hand extended to the one standing, while his left hand is held up with his palm facing outward. A winged disk appears between the two figures. For a number of reasons, it has been suggested that the seated figure is El.[66] On several occasions in the texts, for example, El is portrayed with his feet on a footstool. The beard is also indicative of El as evinced in numerous texts. In fact, beards are quite rare on deities of the Levant, unlike their Mesopotamian and Egyptian counterparts.[67] The presence of a beard both on the seated figure on this stela and in

---

64. Nicholas Wyatt, "The Stela of the Seated God from Ugarit," *UF* 15 (1983) 271.

65. This statue was first discussed by C. F.-A. Schaeffer, "Le stèle de l'hommage du dieu El(?)," *Syria* 18 (1937) 128–34. A photograph of the original and a hand drawing of it can be found in Marguerite Yon, ed., *Arts et industries de la pierre* (RSO 6; Lyon: Maison de l'Orient, 1991) 336.

66. Wyatt, "The Stela of the Seated God," 277.

67. Ibid., 275.

the epigraphic depiction of El is strong evidence that the seated figure is the Canaanite high god. Likewise, the horns on his cap are bovine in form (unlike, say, a ram's horns) appropriate for El, whose sobriquet is "Bull."

Excavations at Megiddo unearthed a Late Bronze Age fortress-temple. Within this compound, a bronze statuette of a seated male deity was found. Facial features of the deity were highlighted by black inlay, probably bitumen, which emphasized a moustache and beard.[68] Stager has suggested that this temple was dedicated to the god El.[69]

A strikingly similar depiction was unearthed at a Punic site in Sousse. This relief portrays a bearded figure sitting on a cherub throne with his right hand raised and grasping an upright staff in his left.[70] He has a tall conical hat, and he is facing a standing figure with its right hand raised. A winged sun disk appears between them on what appears to be the roof of the structure in which they appear. Cintas assumed that the enthroned figure was Baal, even though the relief bears no inscription.[71] He admitted that this Punic relief is connected to prototypes unearthed in the Levant.[72] The depiction has too much in common with that of El in RS 8.295 to justify the "Baal of Sousse" label that Cintas gave it.

Another bearded figure, assumed to be El, was unearthed at Ugarit (RS 88.070). This figure, approximately 25 cm in height and 12 cm in width is seated on a high-backed throne.[73] Sockets are all that remain of the arms and eyes, indicating that these missing parts were constructed of a different material, as Yon and Gachet have noted.[74] However, the feet of the seated figure rest on what appears to be either a stool or an extension of the throne.

A similar seated bearded figure is seen in RS 24.440, a gray pottery mug with pinkish slip and brown glaze. Depicted on the side of the mug is a male bearded figure seated on a chair, grasping an object that appears to be a goblet being held at face level. Facing him is another male bearded figure standing with one arm raised to shoulder height and the

---

68. Lawrence E. Stager, "The Fortress-Temple at Shechem and the 'House of El, Lord of the Covenant,'" in *Realia Dei: Essays in Archaeology and Biblical Interpretation* (ed. Prescott H. Williams Jr. and Theodore Hiebert; Atlanta: Scholars, 1999) 236.

69. Ibid., 235.

70. See P. Cintas, "Le Sanctuaire punique de Sousse," *Revue Africaine* 91 (1947) 14. The hand drawing is on p. 14, and the photograph is a plate on the facing page. Cross, *Canaanite Myth*, 35.

71. Cintas, "Le Sanctuaire punique," 16.

72. Ibid., 16–17.

73. Marguerite Yon and Jacqueline Gachet, "Une statuette du dieu El à Ougarit," *Syria* 66 (1989) 349. For a photograph of the statue, see Marguerite Yon, *The City of Ugarit at Tell Ras Shamra* (Winona Lake, IN: Eisenbrauns, 2006) 130, fig. 13.

74. Yon and Gachet, "Une statuette du dieu El," 349.

other arm extended forward with a jug in his hand. Between the two men is a table, upon which appears a large bowl. Yon has suggested that the seated figure is the god El.[75] Its archaeological provenance being the house of the priest may strengthen her suggestion that this mug depicts a deity. Another facet of this depiction is the footstool upon which the seated male rests his feet. Pope noticed this feature and connected it with El.[76] If the item he holds in his hand is a goblet, we may suggest that the seated figure is portrayed as drinking. I noted earlier in my discussion of KTU 1.114 16 that El is portrayed as drinking to satiety. The combination of a seated bearded figure before whom someone stands and the posture of drinking linked with the story from 1.114 suggests that the most likely Ugaritic personage being depicted is El.

Worthy of note is a numismatic depiction among the so-called Yehud coins of a bearded figure seated on a winged disk with a bird resting on his hand. It has been suggested that this portrait may be a syncretized Yahweh figure.[77] Because this coin is unique, it is difficult to determine its subject with any degree of certainty. Nevertheless, the beard and the winged disk or perhaps throne provide some interesting overlap with the similar depictions of El cited earlier.

To be added here is the "Job Stela," dated to the reign of Ramesses II (13th cent. B.C.E.) which seems to depict El. A hieroglyphic inscription, *ʾi-rʒ-kʒ-n-i-dʒ-pʒ-n*, is understood by some as a transcription of Northwest Semitic *ʾil qny ṣpn* 'Ilu, Creator/Owner of Zaphon'.[78] Although there is debate over whether Egyptian *kʒ* can represent Semitic *q*, the mention of Il and Zaphon strongly suggest that this stela bears another iconographic representation of Canaanite El. Unfortunately, the stela, found in the Transjordan, has since been lost, and all that is available for analysis is a hand-drawn facsimile.[79] The crown on the figure to the left does

---

75. Yon, *The City of Ugarit*, 147. The photo and restored drawing appear on p. 146.

76. Marvin H. Pope, "Scene on the Drinking Mug from Ugarit," in *Near Eastern Studies in Honor of W. F. Albright* (ed. Hans Goedicke; Baltimore: Johns Hopkins University Press, 1971) 404.

77. Baruch Kanael, "Ancient Jewish Coins and Their Historical Importance," *BA* 26 (1963) 41. The inscription above the seated figure was originally read as *yahu*. Sukenik was the first to suggest that it be read as *yhd*. See E. L. Sukenik, "Paralipomena Palestinensia," *Journal of the Palestine Oriental Society* 14 (1934) 180.

78. Johannes C. de Moor, *The Rise of Yahwism: The Roots of Israelite Monotheism* (Leuven: Leuven University Press, 1990) 126. See also Izak Cornelius, *The Iconography of the Canaanite Gods Reshef and Baʿal* (OBO 140; Fribourg: Universitätsverlag / Göttingen: Vandenhoeck & Ruprecht, 1994) 145.

79. See Hugo Gressmann, *Altorientlishce Bilder zum Alten Testament* (Berlin: de Gruyter, 1927) pl. 45 no. 103.

not appear to be Egyptian, despite the hieroglyphic inscription.[80]

Attribute Animals of El and Baal

One more facet of El's iconographic depiction is of particular interest for this study, which is the question of his age in relation to the age of Baal. In part 2 of this book, I will demonstrate that the difference in age between these two deities is crucial for our analysis of the evidence for Yahweh's relative age in the biblical sources. The difference in age between Baal and El is vividly illustrated by the fact that, although both gods are depicted with bovine imagery, Baal is associated with a young bull calf, while El is associated with an adult bull. To be sure, the distinction in these relative ages does not mark El as "old" per se. The adult bull used for El conveys his relative age vis-à-vis the young bull used for Baal. Daniel Fleming has noted this graphic depiction of the relative ages of El and Baal.[81] Othmar Keel and Christoph Uehlinger do not, however, recognize this distinction between El's bull and Baal's bull calf, a distinction that, I will argue, is quite clear in most cases. I will show that the iconography, supported by textual data, demonstrates the age distinction between the Ugaritic gods El and Baal by associating El with an adult bull and Baal with a bull calf. This relative age distinction demonstrated by the evidence will serve as a framework for the arguments about the relative age of Yahweh that will be advanced in part 2.

Keel and Uehlinger have conclusively established the pattern whereby a deity is, in older iconographic representations, portrayed with an animal that is later used by itself to represent the deity with which it was originally paired.[82] In the older representations, the deity is often depicted as standing on the back of the animal. Keel and Uehlinger refer to these beasts as "attribute animals." Thorough examination of the numerous iconographic representations of deities has yielded some fascinating results regarding the depiction of El and Baal. That El is associated with the depiction of a bull is to be expected on the basis of the Ugaritic texts, because "bull" is one of his main epithets. As I have indicated earlier in this chapter, El is depicted with a horned helmet in RS 8.295, which is an iconographic parallel to his well-attested epithet. Baal's iconography, while not as clearly portrayed at El's, nevertheless demonstrates a noticeable pattern. When considering Baal's

---

80. Cornelius, *Iconography of the Canaanite Gods*, 145. See also Gressmann (*Altorientalische Bilder*, 36) who also says that the iconography is not Egyptian but is either Semitic or Hittite.

81. Daniel E. Fleming, "If El Is a Bull, Who Is a Calf? Reflections on Religion in Second Millennium Syria Palestine," *ErIsr* 26 (F. M. Cross Volume; 1999) 25.

82. Othmar Keel and Christoph Uehlinger, *Gods, Goddesses, and Images of God in Ancient Israel* (trans. Thomas H. Trapp; Minneapolis: Fortress, 1998) 141.

iconographic depiction, please note that I am including Hadad within this purview, given Baal and Hadad's virtual synonymity in Late Bronze Age contexts, as many scholars have noted.[83] While Baal is never given the epithet 'bull calf' (*ʿgl*) in the texts, the iconography and some of the textual evidence do suggest that this young bovine was his attribute animal. Neal Walls states that "Baal is never portrayed as a bull in Ugaritic sources, nor is he associated with cows in other Ugaritic contexts."[84] Walls apparently does not think that the attribute animal stands for the deity with which it is associated.[85] Yet Keel and Uehlinger have made a clear and cogent case for the function of attribute animals in Canaanite iconography.

Before looking at the specific examples, I think it is important to establish the criteria I will use for delineating between an adult bull, which I will argue will be standing for El, and a bull calf, which I will suggest will be the counterpart for Baal. In their original German text, Keel and Uehlinger refer to the animal of both El and Baal as a *Stier*; Baal's animal is not distinguished as a *Kalb*.[86] In many of the cases where this iconography appears, there are sufficient signs to distinguish an adult bull and young bull calf. The three most notable signs of a bull calf are spindly legs; smaller, less-pronounced horns; and a thinner, less-pronounced trunk. The best example of the use of all these criteria is the bull calf unearthed at Ashkelon, which I will discuss later. Some of the examples of a bull calf appear with a deity. Because youthfulness and wings are associated with Baal in the LB age, the items that portray a youthful male figure with no beard and a short loincloth probably portray a representation of Baal.[87] In each case that follows, I will point out the presence of these criteria in order to argue for the distinction that I am positing between these two attribute animals.

An old Syrian hematite cylinder seal from Megiddo, discovered outside a clear stratigraphic context, depicts a storm god wearing a loincloth and a high, pointed head covering, and wielding a club in his left hand and an ax in his right.[88] Keel and Uehlinger note that there is a rope in his right hand, with which he holds a bull calf that is lying

---

83. Alberto R. W. Green, *The Storm-God in the Ancient Near East* (Biblical and Judaic Studies from UCSD 8; Winona Lake, IN: Eisenbrauns, 2003) 175. See also Mark Smith, *The Early History of God* (San Francisco: Harper & Row, 1990) 13.

84. Walls, *The Goddess Anat*, 122.

85. Ibid., n. 46. In all fairness to Walls, I should note that his book was published during the same year that Keel and Uehlinger published their original German work.

86. Othmar Keel and Christoph Uehlinger, *Göttinnen, Götter und Gottessymbole* (Quaestiones disputatae 134; Freiburg: Herder, 1992) 462.

87. Idem, *Gods, Goddesses, and Images of God*, 195.

88. Ibid., 37. A clear photo of this seal appears in Barbara Parker, "Cylinder Seals from Palestine," *Iraq* 11 (1949) 34, seal no. 15.

down.⁸⁹ The drawing that they cite does not portray the rope connected to the right hand of the standing figure or to the calf's neck beside him.⁹⁰ On the left-hand side, two persons face the center with their left arms raised. The one closest to the center is a nude female with a flowing robe attached to her shoulders and extending behind her. The other figure on the left appears to be a female as well, but this is by no means certain. This figure is holding an Egyptian symbol for life in its right hand and appears to have some sort of headdress.⁹¹

A second male appears to the left of the calf, but his identity is difficult to determine because his head is not clearly portrayed by the seal. His left hand is raised like the two figures on the left, and he is facing toward them. Between him and the naked female appear three bull heads looking straight-on. These three heads appear to be the center of attention, because every person on the seal is facing toward them. The heads of the bulls are appreciably larger than the head of the calf, who is lying down to the right. Keel and Uehlinger assume this unidentified male to be a ruler and fellow-worshiper with the two women.⁹² If the three figures are in a stance of worship, they must be directing their adoration to the three bull heads. The diminished size of the calf lying down suggests that it is not an adult bull. Could this seal display the iconography of the bull calf with the Baal figure depicted beside the attribute animal for El, the adult bull?

Another hematite seal unearthed at Gaza depicts what could be a bull calf at the feet of a striding figure who bears the marks of Baal—a short skirt and a lightning bolt or tree in his raised hand. The bovine figure at his feet has been identified as a miniature bull at the end of a leash.⁹³ Although the precise date of the seal is unknown, Parker suggests the Hyksos period (16th cent. B.C.E.).⁹⁴

Yet another hematite seal depicts what appear to be two deities facing each other. The figure on the left bears marks of Baal—a striding male with a lightning bolt or perhaps a tree in his raised right hand. The other figure in the seal appears on the left with a full-length robe. The Baal figure appears with his right foot on the back of a small horned animal. Although the seal's iconography is elementary, the animal could

---

89. This is an example where Keel and Uehlinger call this figure a "bull" (*Stier* in the German original). It is quite clear that its size suggests a calf. See Keel and Uehlinger, *Gods, Goddesses, and Images of God*, 37.
90. Ibid., 40, fig. 30.
91. Ibid., 39.
92. Ibid.
93. B. Parker, "Cylinder Seals," 7. The photo of this seal, marked as no. 8, appears on p. 34 of Parker's article.
94. Ibid., 7.

be identified plausibly as a bull calf. Parker suggests that the miniature bull is seated.[95] The photo, however, does not demonstrate this clearly, because the animal's legs are obscured.

Schaeffer also published a hematite seal unearthed in Syria that depicts two bovine animals striding before a standing figure who bears the characteristics of Baal.[96] The two animals are clearly horned, and the front legs of each are folded back under the body so that the two appear to be either lying down or in the process of leaping. Each animal has a hump on its back, and both are of identical size, which is knee-high to the striding deity. Their diminutive size may suggest the image of a bull calf. That their necks and trunks are not terribly thick may also suggest a calf.

As I noted above, the clearest example of the bull calf depiction is the figurine unearthed at Ashkelon, along with its miniature ceramic shrine, in the storeroom of a sanctuary and dating to 1550 B.C.E.[97] Stager initially associated this bull calf with either Baal or El.[98] However, later he and King concluded that the calf was to be associated with Baal.[99] The spindly legs, the smaller trunk, and horns no higher than the ears clearly mark this animal as a bull calf.

In the top register of the Taanach cult stand, a winged sun disk is portrayed on the back of what some have called a bull calf.[100] The lack of horns on the animal, however, obviates clear analysis. Keel and Uehlinger suggest that, because bovines are always portrayed with horns during this period, the beast is a horse, an attribute animal of Anat/Astarte.[101] Yet it is possible that the horns are not prominently displayed precisely in order to indicate the calf-like features of the animal. Ruth Hestrin notes that the identification of it as a horse is not likely because there is no mane.[102] She too suggests that this is a young bull,

---

95. Ibid., 6. The photo of the seal (no. 2) appears on p. 33.
96. C. F.-A. Schaeffer, *Ugaritica II* (Paris: Geuthner, 1949) 40.
97. Lawrence Stager, "When Canaanites and Philistines Ruled Ashkelon," *BAR* 17/2 (1991) 24. Keel and Uehlinger admit that this figure may be a bull or a bull calf. See Keel and Uehlinger, *Gods, Goddesses, and Images of God*, 37 n. 12.
98. Lawrence E. Stager, *Ashkelon Discovered* (Washington, DC: Biblical Archaeology Society, 1991) 6.
99. Philip King and Lawrence Stager, *Life in Biblical Israel* (Louisville: Westminster John Knox, 2001) 173, illustration 84.
100. Ibid., 343–44. Mark Smith assumes the figure to be a bull calf as well. See Smith, *The Early History of God*, 20.
101. Keel and Uehlinger, *Gods, Goddesses, and Images of God*, 158.
102. Ruth Hestrin, "The Cult Stand from Ta'anach and Its Religious Background," in *Phoenicia and the East Mediterranean in the First Millennium B.C.* (ed. E. Lipiński; Studia Phoenicia 5; Leuven: Peeters, 1987) 67 n. 7.

the symbol of the god Baal.[103] Keel and Uehlinger note that horses are rarely depicted with manes in Iron-Age terra-cottas.[104] So it seems that a clear identification of this animal is simply impossible at this juncture. If King, Stager, and Hestrin are correct, the cult stand attests a young bull that would further my thesis.[105]

While the parallel between textual epithets and iconographic depictions clearly matches El with adult bovine characteristics, the Ugaritic texts do not explicitly use ʿgl 'bull calf' to portray Baal. In KTU 1.3 III 44, Anat claims that she has destroyed ʿgl il ʿtk, perhaps to be rendered 'Rebel, the calf of El'.[106] Although it is uncertain exactly who the 'calf of El' is, it is quite clear that Anat is not claiming to have destroyed Baal, her brother. In KTU 1.5 V 4–5, we have the line [ ]t . npš . ʿgl / [ ]nk, preceded by the title aliyn in line 1, where the text is badly damaged. These lines are followed by a first-person speech that is apparently addressed to Baal. While it is possible that the calf here may refer to Baal, who is banished to the underworld, the damaged text prevents certainty. That "calf" here may be a reference to Baal may be supported a few lines later on the same tablet when he makes love to a ʿglt 'heifer' (line 18), which has often been assumed to be Anat.[107] Irrespective of who this heifer actually is, if indeed we are to discern a goddess here, which is by no means conclusive,[108] for our purposes the ʿgl-ʿglt connection is intriguing.

---

103. Ibid, 75.
104. Keel and Uehlinger, *Gods, Goddesses, and Images of God*, 158.
105. There are a few examples from the ancient Near East that associate a storm god with an adult bull. An undated stela from Arslan Tash has a storm god on the back of a bull, perhaps a bull calf. Note that the horns are relatively small, and the trunk of the animal is not fully pronounced, as it would be on an adult bull. A second example is unstratified from Tell Ahmar. The bull here looks fully developed, and the deity is holding a three-pronged implement bearing a resemblance to a lightning bolt. The best counterexample is an 8th–7th-century stela labeled Aleppo National Museum 2459 and depicts what is clearly an adult bull, upon which is depicted a deity holding a three-pronged lightning bolt. Note that in this stela the animal's trunk is fully pronounced, unlike the Arslan Tash example. The back of the stela is covered with Hittite hieroglyphs. These three examples are discussed and displayed in James B. Pritchard, *The Ancient Near East in Pictures* (2nd ed. with supplement; Princeton: Princeton University Press, 1969) 501, 531, 500, respectively. These three examples come from regions well north of Ugarit. It may be that the distinction I am positing for the attribute animals of Baal and El was blurred in northern Syria, perhaps due to influence from the iconography used of the Hittite storm god.
106. S. Parker, *The Pre-Biblical Narrative Tradition*, 111.
107. John Gray, *The Legacy of Canaan* (2nd ed.; Leiden: Brill, 1965) 445. De Moor shares the same opinion. See de Moor, *Anthology of Religious Texts*, 186.
108. Walls, *The Goddess Anat*, 123–24.

My suggestion is, of course, based heavily on the distinction between bovine developmental stages indicated in the words ʿglt 'heifer' (female bovine that has not birthed a calf) and arḫ 'cow'.[109] If one assumes that a heifer is not sexually mature, the mating of an ʿgl may be questioned as well. Yet, even if these hypothetical inconsistencies are valid, in the narrative world of myth where deities ride the clouds, writers could escape such cavil. Thus, there are a few texts that seem to associate Baal with bull calves, as in the anepigraphic sources, while no extant evidence suggests that Baal was ever portrayed as a bull.[110] In part 2 of this study, I will return to the topic of the relative ages of El and Baal at Ugarit to make an argument about the relative aging of Yahweh in ancient Israel.

Conclusion

This chapter has provided an overview of the picture of old age at Ugarit. The data were culled from the epigraphic and iconographic sources. We looked at El, the chief god of the Canaanite pantheon, who is often portrayed with old-age imagery in the literary sources as well as the iconography from Ugarit. We noted other references in the texts to old-age concerns seen in the stories of Aqhat and Kirta, and we discussed briefly the attribute animals of El and Baal as indicators of relative age among the two deities.

The picture of old age at Ugarit is in many ways similar to that of the Hebrew Bible. Senescence has its good and bad sides. As the father of years, El portrays the patriarchal paterfamilias of sorts for the pantheon. He is the wise counselor acknowledged by Anat, his impetuous daughter, and he is able to bring a seasoned ameliorating sensibility to volatile threats from her. El also constitutes the authority to whom the other deities must appeal. His strength is depicted in the bull, his attribute animal. El enjoys a healthy and active libido, as seen in KTU 1.23, even to the point of siring children in his senescence, paralleling the patriarchs in the biblical narratives.

However, El is also the deity to whom threats of violence are made, threats that exploit weakness. This is seen in Anat's threats of bodily harm to him. Decline is also portrayed in the story of El's banquet, where he is depicted as a drunken, staggering oaf who cannot control

---

109. The use of these two terms bears out this distinction. Where a calf is present along with its mother (1.6 II 6; 1.10 III 1; 1.15 I 5), the latter is referred to as arḫ. Although some would suggest that Anat as the arḫ bʿl would be an exception here, because this goddess is not a mother, Walls has shown this assumption to be specious. See Walls, *The Goddess Anat*, 124.

110. A. H. W. Curtis, "Some Observations on 'Bull' Terminology in the Ugaritic Texts and the Old Testament," *Oudtestamentische Studiën* 26 (1990) 25.

his bodily functions. A similar concern for this state is seen in Aqhat by his father, Danel. The story of Kirta also shows old-age vulnerability at the end of the story, when Kirta is accosted for his frailty by his son Yassib, who wants the throne. In short, the picture of old age mirrors the depiction we see in biblical Israel. It is a time of good and ill.

Part 2

AGING Yahweh

Chapter 3

Why Yahweh Is Not Old

Now that we have a sense of the ways in which old age was viewed in biblical Israel and Ugarit, we turn our attention to two basic questions that will constitute the subject of the next two chapters. The questions are prompted by the depiction of Yahweh in Daniel 7 as "Ancient of Days" with "hair like wool." The first question is: Why was Yahweh not portrayed explicitly with old-age imagery through most of Israel's history? The second is: Why did the Maccabean-period author of Daniel 7 adopt the imagery of old age to portray Yahweh as the "Ancient of Days"? I address the first of these questions in this chapter. I begin by examining how the biblical tradition generally conceives of Yahweh as "eternal" but not "old." I then demonstrate that the biblical tradition frequently uses imagery associated with El and Baal to depict Yahweh. Building on my conclusions about the use of attribute animals in the iconography of El and Baal at Ugarit, I argue that ancient Israelites preferred to associate Yahweh with the bull calf of Baal and not with the bull of El. This indicates that for most of Israel's history the preference for bull calf iconography paralleled the assumption that Yahweh was a youthful God. Finally, I note a few other factors that probably contributed to the Israelite resistance to portraying Yahweh as aged.

Yahweh: Eternal, Not Elderly

There are few specific terms for stages of the human life cycle in Biblical Hebrew. Rather, these stages are generally defined by references to marriage, parenthood, and the physical presence of facial hair and its subsequent graying. References of this sort are never used of Israel's deity. Despite the extrabiblical evidence that may suggest that some Israelites believed that Yahweh had a consort (that is, Asherah),[1] marriage to a feminine deity is not imagined for Israel's God in the Hebrew Bible. Of course, the Bible includes many metaphorical uses of spousal imagery that portray Yahweh as the husband of Israel, bespeaking his love and covenant commitment to his people (Hos 2:21–22). However, nothing analogous to the divine-marriage texts of the ancient Near East

---

1. Saul M. Olyan, *Asherah and the Cult of Yahweh in Israel* (SBLMS 34; Atlanta: Scholars Press, 1988) 33.

appear in the Hebrew Bible. The same is true in many ways for parentage. Again, the metaphorical imagery of fatherhood is present, especially in later texts, as we will see in the next chapter. This imagery also includes the language of adoption applied to the Davidic kings, which I will also address in the next chapter. Despite these frequent references to Yahweh as a metaphorical or adoptive father, it is important to note that Yahweh never sires another divine being or impregnates a human woman in any extant text. To be sure, this circumstance is to be explained by more than an Israelite resistance to portraying Yahweh within the human life cycle. But even so, the fact remains that he is not portrayed thus. I even suggest that this is why Yahweh, despite all the anthropomorphic depictions that mention a number of his body parts, is never said to have a beard or gray hair in a pre-Maccabean text. These outward manifestations of age, which can also serve as markers of age-related status, are not used to depict Israel's God. By avoiding age-related imagery, the biblical tradition prevents Yahweh from entering the human life cycle and thus preserves his eternality.

A few scholars have assumed that Yahweh is, in fact, portrayed with senescent imagery outside Daniel 7, yet the passages they cite may be read as a description of Yahweh's eternality, not his "biological" age. Paul Mosca admits that there is no precise parallel to the "Ancient of Days," but he suggests that the phrase evokes titles such as ʾăbî ʿad 'eternal father' in Isa 9:5, ʾĕlōhê ʿôlām 'eternal God' in Isa 40:28, and *melek ʿôlām* 'eternal king' in Jer 10:10.[2] James Crenshaw says that Isa 46:4 is "a depiction of God as the Ancient of Days cradling the people of Israel like a babe."[3] However, this verse speaks of the senescence of the people, not God.

Mark Smith cites Ps 90:2, 102:28; Job 36:26; Isa 40:28, 57:15; and Hab 3:6 in support of his contention that "Yhwh is described as the aged patriarchal god."[4] Ps 102:28 and Job 36:26 speak of Yahweh's years being *lōʾ yittāmmû* 'without end' and *lōʾ ḥēqer* 'unfathomable', respectively. The word ʿôlām 'eternity' plays a significant role in these texts that are putatively illustrative of Yahweh's old age. Hab 3:6 speaks of the hills and of Yahweh's ways in construct with the word ʿôlām, but it says nothing about Yahweh himself. Isa 40:28 speaks of Yahweh as ʾĕlōhê ʿôlām, and Ps 90:2 says, "You are God *mēʿôlām ʿad ʿôlām*." The word ʿad, a synonym of ʿôlām, is used in a similar manner in Isa 57:15, where God is called *šōkēn ʿad* 'inhabiter of eternity'. In addition to these texts, Smith

---

2. Paul G. Mosca, "Ugarit and Daniel 7: A Missing Link," *Bib* 67 (1986) 501 n. 25.
3. James L. Crenshaw, "Youth and Old Age in Qoheleth," *HAR* 10 (1986) 12.
4. Mark Smith, *The Early History of God* (San Francisco: Harper & Row, 1990) 9.

translates the phrase *ʾĕlōhê qedem* in Deut 33:27 as "the ancient god" but later renders it 'the eternal God'.[5] Smith seems to think that these terms are interchangeable.

In a similar manner, Cross points to some inscriptional evidence (Mine M inscription no. 358) that reads *ʾl d ʿlm*, which he translates 'El the Ancient One' or 'El, Lord of Eternity'.[6] He associates this with the biblical reference to *yhwh ʾēl ʿôlām* in Gen 21:33. Even though Cross renders *ʿlm* 'ancient' and 'eternal', suggesting that they are synonymous, the difference between the two is significant. I suspect that Cross's equation of the terms is dependent on the depiction of El as old in other contexts, especially in the Ugaritic narrative sources and that Cross has assumed that El's age is indicated by this epithet. El is clearly portrayed as old, but his epithet *ʾl d ʿlm* does not necessitate this depiction, and thus the use of this epithet for Yahweh in the Hebrew Bible cannot be taken as an indicator of Yahweh's age.[7]

Furthermore, a closer examination of *ʿôlām* and especially *mēʿôlām* reveals that these forms are not meant to indicate age within a human life cycle. Neither is used to describe people who are otherwise marked with old-age features in the Bible. In fact, the only occurrence of *mēʿôlām* used of people in the Hebrew Bible is Gen 6:4, where it is used to describe the offspring of the sons of God and daughters of men. They are described as *haggibbōrîm ʾăšer mēʿôlām* 'mighty men who are from long ago'. Who these beings actually were is not clarified in the text, and precisely what it means that they were *mēʿôlām* is not explained either. Even so, the use of *mēʿôlām* here surely does not refer to their age. The context here as well as the general use of *mēʿôlām* indicate a meaning of 'a long time ago'.[8] This is the meaning in the Mesha Stela, where the men of Gad are said to have lived in the land of ʿAtaroth *mʿlm* (KAI 181, line 10).[9] Thus, when this form is applied to Yahweh, be it in an epithet such as *ʾĕlōhê ʿôlām* or *melek ʿôlām*, or in a phrase saying that he is God *mēʿôlām ʿad ʿôlām*, the word *ʿôlām* expresses duration and eternality

---

5. Ibid., 21.

6. F. M. Cross, *Canaanite Myth and Hebrew Epic* (Cambridge: Harvard University Press, 1973) 19.

7. Cross (ibid., 25) also seems to assume that the refractions of El, which he lists as Baal Hamon, Kronos, and Saturnus, are all described with senescence adjectives (*gerontis*, *senex*, and *saeculo*) that derive from the epithet *ʿlm*, given to El. Again, however, these adjectives could be based on the imagery used of El rather than the epithet *ʿlm*, which could be simply understood as 'eternal', as Cross suggests earlier.

8. See the discussion by H. D. Preuss, "*ʿôlām*," *TDOT* 10:533–34.

9. H. Donner and W. Röllig, *Kanaanäische und Aramäische Inschriften* (hereafter KAI; 2nd ed.; Wiesbaden: Harrassowitz, 1969) 33.

rather than age. The same is true for the word ʿad, which is also used to speak of eternity. I suspect that the confusion arises in part from the English rendering 'of *old*' in many translations of these two words. The word 'eternal' should be preferred in translating these verses, in order to indicate the meaning of the Hebrew ʿôlām unambiguously. Yahweh, therefore, can be the eternal king, the eternal God, and have years that are unfathomable or without end, but still not be considered old. Admittedly, this sort of notion of God's eternality may have played a role in the eventual portrayal of God with old age imagery in later writings. However, God's *eternal* nature does not necessitate that he be *elderly*. In fact, one could argue that these texts suggest that he is ageless.

Yahweh as a Selective Conflation of El and Baal

When we examine thoroughly the imagery used of Yahweh in the Hebrew Bible, we find that it includes features drawn from the sets of attributes associated with El and Baal, respectively.[10] The similarities between these three deities allowed for what Jan Assmann calls "translatability," the practice of equating disparate deities whose mythical narratives and theocosmological speculations share several points of contact.[11] I want to avoid the assumption, however, that El and Baal are absolute types that are antithetical to one another. These two deities are examples of the way gods were portrayed in ancient Ugarit. While there were surely other portrayals of deities that may have influenced the biblical writers, extant attestations are limited. The upshot of these limited data is that the features attested of El and Baal often garner the most attention when scholars seek antecedents for Yahweh's portrayal.

In this section, I first note features that El and Yahweh possess exclusively as well as a few that they share with other deities in the Ugaritic texts. Then I examine the few features shared between Baal and Yahweh. Finally, I discuss why Yahweh shares the attribute animal of Baal rather than that of El. These shared features will include titles such as *judge, creator, king,* and *warrior* and descriptive words such as *compassionate* and *cloud rider*. I will also look at the choice of domicile as a point of contact between the deities. The purpose of these comparisons is to provide a broader context in which divine imagery used of Yahweh in the Bible can be seen in El and Baal. I will use this contextual foundation to elucidate the way in which the relative age of these deities plays a role in the way that Israelites portrayed Yahweh.

---

10. Cross, *Canaanite Myth*, 186. See also Mark Smith, *The Early History of God*, xxiii.

11. Jan Assmann, *Moses the Egyptian* (Cambridge: Harvard Univ. Press, 1997) 45.

Features Shared by Yahweh and El

The fact that Yahweh is portrayed with many of the same characteristics as El, apart from old age, is quite clear.[12] One of the titles that is applied to Yahweh and El is *judge*. The Canaanite high god seems to be described thus in KTU 1.128 15, where the phrase *il dn* appears in a Hurrian invocation hymn to El. The term *dn* in this Hurrian text has long been noted to be a Semitic loanword.[13] Cross translates the phrase 'El the Judge'.[14] Craigie suggests that this text may demonstrate a syncretized El who has taken on the role of judge seen in the Hurrian deity Mitra.[15] KTU 1.108 reads *il . yṯb . b ʿṯtrt il ṯpẓ . b hdrʿy*, which Cross translates "ʾEl sits enthroned with Astarte, ʾEl sits as judge with Haddu his shepherd'.[16] These lines (2–4) from 1.108 have received much attention, and there is not a consensus regarding the translation.[17] Although the word 'judge' in this line is not in dispute, Pope has suggested that *il* is a generic 'god' rather than the proper name, 'El'.[18] That the proper name *Kothar* appears in line 5 suggests otherwise, however. So El is, on occasion, imagined as a judge. Yet caution is in order here, because other deities are given the title *judge*. The most obvious example here is Yamm, who is also known as *ṯpṭ . nhr* 'Judge River'. Baal also receives the title *judge* from Anat, who declares to El in 1.3 V 32, *mlkn . aliyn . bʿl . ṯpṭn* 'Our king is Almighty Baal, [he is] our judge'. Athirat utters the same line to El in 1.4 IV 44. The personal name *ṯpṭbʿl* also appears at Ugarit.[19] That these other deities bear the title of *judge* prevents drawing an exclusive connection between El and Yahweh.

Yahweh is depicted as a judge in a number of texts. He is called *šōpēṭ* in Gen 18:25; Judg 11:27 (Yahweh); Ps 7:12 (*ʾĕlōhîm*), 75:8 (*ʾĕlōhîm*); and

---

12. M. Pope, *El in the Ugaritic Texts* (Leiden: Brill, 1955) 34.

13. Emmanuel Laroche, "Documents en langue hourrite provenant de Ras Shamra," in Jean Nougayrol et al., *Ugaritica V* (Paris: Imprimerie Nationale, 1968) 515.

14. Cross, *Canaanite Myth*, 39. Laroche has "El du jugement." See Laroche, "Documents en langue hourrite," 515.

15. Peter C. Craigie, "EL BRT. EL DN (RS 24.278, 14–15)," *UF* 5 (1973) 278.

16. Frank Moore Cross, "The 'Olden Gods' in Ancient Near Eastern Creation Myths and in Israel," *From Epic to Canon* (Baltimore: Johns Hopkins University Press, 1998) 76. The form *ṯpẓ* is an allophonic variation of *ṯpṭ* (*DUL* 926).

17. I discuss this dispute in chap. 4.

18. Marvin H. Pope, "The Cult of the Dead at Ugarit," in *Ugarit in Retrospect: Fifty Years of Ugarit and Ugaritic* (ed. Gordon D. Young; Winona Lake, IN: Eisenbrauns, 1981) 172.

19. Sergio Ribichini and Paolo Xella, "Problemi di onomastica ugaritica: Il caso dei teofori," *Studi Epigrafici e Linguistici* 8 (1991) 160.

Job 23:7.[20] The term *dayyān* is employed for God in Ps 68:8 (*ʾĕlōhîm*). David calls Yahweh a *dayyān* in 1 Sam 24:16 and invokes God to judge (*yišpōṭ*) between him and Saul in 1 Sam 24:13, 16 (*yišpĕṭēnî*). Two personal names from the Bible, Jehoshaphat (2 Sam 8:16, 20:24; 1 Kgs 22:42; 1 Chr 18:15) and Shephatiah (2 Sam 3:4, Jer 38:1, 1 Chr 3:3) support a similar depiction of Yahweh.[21] Onomastic evidence from epigraphic sources lends support here as well, attesting the names *ydnyhw* and *šptyhw*.[22] In light of the use of the title *judge* for a number of gods at Ugarit, it is likely that Yahweh's similar portrayal demonstrates an overlap with the general notion of a deity's being a judge. Thus, in this sense the specific connection to El is again not exclusive.

Although the evidence is not overwhelming, El is depicted, like YAHWEH, as a creator. The main text that portrays El as creator is KTU 1.3 V 9, which is a damaged line reconstructed in KTU as [*t*]*bu . ddm . qny*[*. w*] *adn .*[*bn i*]*lm* 'She (Anat) enters the tent of the Creator and Lord of the sons of gods'. El is obviously the referent of the epithets in this context. Perhaps to be included here is the Hittite myth *Ilkunirsa*, the title of which has been convincingly argued to be a Hittite transliterational rendering of *il qny arṣ* 'El, Creator of the Earth'.[23] In similar fashion, YAHWEH is called "creator" in the Hebrew Bible (Gen 14:19, *qōnēh šāmayim wāʾāreṣ*;[24] Deut 32:6, *qāneka*; Isa 40:28, 43:15, *bōrēʾ*; Job 31:15, *ʿōśēnî* 'my maker'). The 8th-century Phoenician inscription from Karatepe describes El as *qn ʾrṣ* 'creator of earth'.[25] A Jerusalem jar inscription dated to the 8th–7th century attests *mkyhw qn ʾrṣ*, which seems to

---

20. The Job citation contains the Masoretic pointing *miššōpĕṭî* 'from my judge'. The versions interpret the form as *mišpāṭî* 'my judgment'.

21. Jehoshaphat is used of a member of David's court (2 Sam 8:16), an administrator in Solomon's court (1 Kgs 4:3, 17), and a Judahite king (1 Kgs 22:41–42). Shephatiah is used of David's fifth son (2 Sam 3:4), a Benjaminite warrior (1 Chr 12:6), a Simeonite leader (1 Chr 27:16), King Jehoshaphat's son (2 Chr 21:2), a court official of King Zedekiah (Jer 38:1), a returnee with Zerubbabel (Ezra 2:4, 57; 8:8; Neh 7:59), a Benjaminite who settled in Jerusalem after the exile (1 Chr 9:8), and a Judahite who also settled in Jerusalem (Neh 11:4).

22. See Yohanan Aharoni, *Arad Inscriptions* (Jerusalem: Israel Exploration Society, 1981) no. 27, line 4. See also Jeaneane D. Fowler, *Theophoric Personal Names in Ancient Hebrew* (JSOTSup 49; Sheffield: JSOT Press, 1988) 341. Ibid., 363. Bordreuil and Lemaire date this scarab to the end of the 8th or from the beginning of the 7th century B.C.E. See Pierre Bordreuil and André Lemaire, "Nouveaux sceaux hébreux, araméens et ammonites," *Sem* 26 (1976) 51.

23. Cross, *Canaanite Myth*, 16.

24. Some have suggested that the title *ʾēl ʿelyōn* in Gen 14:19 complicates the picture because *ʿelyōn* is an epithet of Baal. See Rolf Rendtorff, "El, Baʿal und Jahwe," *ZAW* 78 (1966) 290.

25. See KAI 26A III 18, with commentary in KAI 2:37.

associate *yhw* with *qn 'rṣ*, although the preceding line is unreadable.[26] Avigad suggests that the name El is to be restored just before *qn 'rṣ*.[27]

Another similarity between Yahweh and El is their choice of domicile. Both El and Yahweh are said to live in a tent. Yahweh says as much to David in 2 Sam 7:6: "I have not lived in a house from the day I brought the Israelites up from Egypt to this day. I will be one who makes his way in a tent and in a tabernacle." The tent shrine used to house Israel's palladium, the ark of the covenant, is also telling.[28] El's dwelling is called a *dd*, which is parallel with *qrš* in 1.2 III 5; 1.3 V 7-8; 1.4 IV 23-24; 1.5 VI [reconstructed]; 1.6 I 34-35; 1.17 VI 48-49; and with *ahl* in 1.15 III 18. Clifford has argued that 'tent' is the best understanding of *dd*, and his case has persuaded others as well.[29] The parallel word *qrš* has also received due attention. The same word is used in Biblical Hebrew to describe the supports for the tabernacle. Cross notes that the Hittite tale of *Ilkunirsa* describes El's abode with GIŠ.ZA.LAM.GAR which denotes the Akkadian *kuštāru* 'tent'.[30] When the evidence from *Ilkunirsa* is combined with the cognate *qereš* from Biblical Hebrew, the meaning 'tent' for Ugaritic *qrš* is the most likely definition.[31]

Both deities are also said to be compassionate. El is often called *ltpn il dpid* in the three major narrative texts from Ugarit (KTU 1.1 III 22; 1.1 IV 13, 18; 1.4 II 10; 1.4 III 31; 1.4 IV 58; 1.5 VI 11; 1.6 I 49; 1.6 III 4, 10, 14; 1.6 VI 39; 1.15 II 14; 1.16 IV 9; 1.16 V 10, 23; 1.18 I 15).[32] The epithet has traditionally been translated 'kind El, the compassionate', based on Arabic cognates. *Ltpn* can be compared to *laṭīf* 'friendly' and

---

26. Sandra Gogel lists this inscription as Jerusalem Jar Inscription 1. See Sandra Gogel, *A Grammar of Epigraphic Hebrew* (Resources for Biblical Study 23; Atlanta: Scholars Press, 1998) 409.

27. Nahman Avigad, *Discovering Jerusalem* (Nashville: Thomas Nelson, 1980) 41.

28. See Cross, *Canaanite Myth*, 242.

29. Richard J. Clifford, *The Cosmic Mountain in Canaan and in the Old Testament* (HSM 4; Cambridge: Harvard University Press, 1972) 52-53. Cross (*Canaanite Myth*, 55) is in agreement with Clifford. Yet see *DUL* 285, for the suggestion 'cave, grotto'. See also F. Renfroe, *Arabic-Ugaritic Lexical Studies* (Abhandlungen zur Literature Alt-Syrien-Palästinas 5; Münster: Ugarit-Verlag, 1992) 97-102, where he suggests 'encampment'. Cyrus Gordon, *Ugaritic Textbook* (hereafter *UT*; AnOr 38; rev. ed.; Rome: Pontifical Biblical Institute, 1998) §721 has 'territory, premises'.

30. CAD K 601. See also Cross, *Canaanite Myth*, 72; and Mark Smith, *The Ugaritic Baal Cycle* (Leiden: Brill, 1994) 189. Yet see *DUL* 712 which suggests the more generic 'residence, private room'.

31. M. Smith (*Ugaritic Baal Cycle*, 189) says *qrš* is most likely a reference to El's tent, even though he also maintains that *dd* is more likely to be 'mountain'. The numerous occasions on which these terms are paired in the Ugaritic texts, however, make this unlikely.

32. For *ltpn* alone as El's epithet, see KTU 1.1 II 18; 1.1 III 6; 1.6 IV 11.

pid to *fu'ād* 'friendly'.³³ This long-held consensus has come unraveled of late, however. Healey suggested that *ltpn* was El's proper name, and so the phrase should be rendered '*Laṭīpān*, the Perceptive God', connecting *pid* with the more common meaning of Arabic *fu'ād* as 'clever'.³⁴ Tropper and Hayajneh take Healey's work a step further, showing the relevance of this new translation for understanding the Ugaritic texts and even for understanding the portrayal of Mesopotamian deities.³⁵ Although they suggest a radical departure from the traditional rendering of this epithet, Tropper and Hayajneh are quick to add that

> es versteht sich freilich von selbst, dass diese neue Interpretation der Epitheta Els der traditionellen Interpretation nicht wirklich konträr gegenübersteht. Die Scharfsinnigkeit Es [*sic*, for "Els"] schließt in keiner Weise aus, dass dieser Gott den Menschen gegenüber zugleich auch freundlich und gütig gesinnt sein kann. In den ugaritischen Epitheta Els hat sich dieser Charakterzug jedoch nicht niedergeschlagen.³⁶

Despite this insightful linguistic corrective, there are a number of examples of El portrayed as a merciful god. The Kirta story certainly depicts El in this way as the god who answers Kirta's prayer and heals him from his sickness. El's patience with Anat in the Aqhat story also contributes to this general portrayal of El as a god of compassion. Likewise Yahweh is called a merciful and gracious God (Exod 34:6; Ps 78:38, 86:15, 111:4, 136:1–26, 145:8; Joel 2:13; Jonah 4:2).

Yahweh and El are both referred to as king. El is given this royal title in KTU 1.3 V 36; 1.4 IV 24, 38, 48; 1.6 I 36; and 1.17 VI 49. The personal name *ilmlk* is attested in Ugaritic (KTU 1.4 VIII 49; 1.6 VI 54; 1.16 VI 59; 1.17 VI 56; 4.115 9; 4.133 2; 4.165 13; 4.261 10; 4.382 28; 4.607 16; 4.616 2; 4.659 8; and 5.18 9) and the Akkadian of Ugarit (RS 18.20 15; 19.70 8; and 17.288 27). Yahweh is given the title 'king' in Deut 33:5; Ps 24:10, 47:9; Isa 33:22; Mal 1:14; and Dan 3:33.³⁷ This royal title is, however, bestowed on other ancient Near Eastern deities. Baal is also said to rule as king (KTU 1.2 IV 10; 1.3 V 32; and 1.4 IV 43) though in this same text El is also called "king," as noted above, and El is still in a position

---

33. *DUL* 507.

34. J. F. Healey, "The Kindly and Merciful God: On Some Semitic Divine Epithets," in '*Und Mose schrieb dieses Lied auf': Studien zum Alten Testament und zum Alten Orient. Festschrift Oswald Loretz* (ed. M. Dietrich and I. Kottsieper; AOAT 250; Münster: Ugarit-Verlag, 1998) 350.

35. Josef Tropper and Hani Hayajneh, "El, der scharfsinnige und verständige Gott: Ugaritisch *ltpn il d pid* im Licht der arabischen Lexeme *lāṭīf* und *fu'ād*," *Or* 72 (2003) 179.

36. Ibid., 177.

37. Marjo Christina Annette Korpel, *A Rift in the Clouds* (Münster: Ugarit-Verlag, 1990) 284.

to confer kingship in the story when Baal is presumed dead. A similar situation obtains in the Egyptian pantheon, whereby Amun-Re is called king, while other gods could also be so designated in a kind of vassal kingship.[38] Because a common feature of this sort is too general to assume that Yahweh's kingship is merely a feature of El, this shared characteristic is not as illustrative of the pattern as are some of the others.

Shared features between Yahweh and El can also be seen in a different kind of evidence. The theophoric component "-el" in the name *Israel* attested in the 13th-century Merneptah Stela, for example, preserves the notion that Israel's God was called El from its earliest stages.[39] An inscription from about 700 B.C.E. from Khirbet Beit Lei assumes that El and Yahweh are the same.[40] Cross reads inscription B in this collection as *nqh yh 'l hnn nqh yh yhwh* 'Absolve [us] O merciful God! Absolve [us] O Yahweh'.[41] That "El" is rarely used in the Hebrew Bible as a reference to a non-Israelite deity is also an "extraordinary datum."[42] The absence of any polemic against a god named El in the Hebrew Bible supports this thesis as well.[43] This fact is in stark contrast to the anti-Baal polemic seen in a number of parts of the Hebrew Bible (e.g., Judg 6:31, 1 Kgs 18:27, and Hos 2:19).

Features Shared by Yahweh and Baal

While there are numerous points of contact between the imageries used of Yahweh and El, Yahweh and Baal share many features as well. Yahweh is portrayed "riding the clouds" in Deut 33:26; Ps 68:5, 34; and 104:3. Baal is called *rkb ʿrpt* 'cloud rider' in a number of locations, including KTU 1.2 IV 8, 29; 1.3 II 40; 1.3 III 38; 1.3 IV 4; 1.4 III 11, 18; 1.4 V 60; 1.5 II 7; 1.19 I 43–44; 1.10 I 7; 1.10 III 36; and 1.92 40.

---

38. J. C. de Moor, *The Rise of Yahwism* (Leuven: Leuven University Press, 1990) 101.

39. M. Smith, *The Memoirs of God* (Minneapolis: Fortress, 2004) 26.

40. O. Keel and C. Uehlinger, *Gods, Goddesses, and Images of God in Ancient Israel* (trans. T. H. Trapp; Minneapolis: Fortress, 1998) 311.

41. Frank M. Cross, "The Cave Inscriptions from Khirbet Beit Lei," in *Near Eastern Archeology in the Twentieth Century: Essays in Honor of Nelson Glueck* (ed. J. A. Sanders; Garden City, NY: Doubleday, 1970) 302. Lemaire does not reconstruct the presence of *'l* before *hnn*, however. André Lemaire, "Prières en temps de crise: Les inscriptions de Khirbet Beit Lei," *RB* 83 (1976) 560. Cross's reading is retained in F. W. Dobbs-Allsopp et al., *Hebrew Inscriptions: Texts from the Biblical Period of the Monarchy with Concordance* (New Haven, CT: Yale University Press, 2005) 131.

42. Cross, *Canaanite Myth*, 44.

43. M. Smith, *The Early History of God*, 8. See also Otto Eisfeldt, "El and Yahweh," *JSS* 1 (1956) 26. An exception is seen in Isa 43:10c, where Yahweh says, *lĕpānay lōʾ nôṣar ʾēl* 'before me, no god was made'; and, again, in Isa 43:12, where he says, "I am God [*ʾēl*]," perhaps conveying a play on words with the notion of god and the divine name El.

This particular feature will prove important in my discussion of Daniel 7 in chap. 4. Just as they share the cloud-rider imagery, Yahweh and Baal are both said to have a voice like thunder. Yahweh gives forth his voice, which moves over the waters, breaks the cedars of Lebanon, and shakes the wilderness of Kadesh (Ps 29:3–9). Baal gives forth his voice from the clouds in 1.4 V 8, and his voice "shakes the earth" in 1.4 VII 31. His voice is also noted in the rains in 1.19 I 46, perhaps suggesting thunder. Yet Yahweh's voice is also described as *qôl děmāmâ daqqâ* 'a still small voice' (KJV) or 'the sound of sheer silence' (NRSV, 1 Kgs 19:12) perhaps indicating, as Cogan suggests, "that this is the desired mode of discourse between the prophet and the divine presence."[44] This departure from the parallel with Baal may serve a polemical purpose in the anti-Baal context of 1 Kings 18–19.[45]

The warrior motif so prevalent in depictions of Yahweh is mostly paralleled in descriptions of Baal. The Ugaritic texts present Baal in combat with Yamm (KTU 1.2 IV 15–35) and Mot (1.6 VI 20–31). When we widen our view of the evidence to include anepigraphic sources, the iconography demonstrates Baal's martial portrayal as well. The parade example is the so-called *Baal au foudre* stela, which depicts the youthful god with a club in one hand and a spear in the other.[46] An epithet such as Yahweh *ṣěbā'ōt* 'Yahweh of hosts' portrays a similar image of the deity as warrior.[47] Divine warrior imagery used of Yahweh is also quite common (Exodus 15; Deut 33:2–5, 26–29; Josh 10:12–13; Judges 5; 2 Sam 22:7–18; Psalm 68; and Hab 3:3–15).[48]

Yet El's warrior traits have been noticed by Miller in the work of Sakkunyaton,[49] where Kronos, the refraction of El within the Greek milieu, battles his father, Uranos.[50] The personal name *ilmhr* 'El is a warrior' is attested in Ugaritic in a list of people and their armaments

---

44. M. Cogan, *1 Kings* (AB 10; New York: Doubleday, 2001) 453.
45. Cross, *Canaanite Myth*, 194.
46. What this spear represents is debated. Early assessments (Schaeffer et al.) assumed it was a lightning bolt, while more recent iconographers suggest it is a plant or tree. See I. Cornelius, *Iconography of the Canaanite Gods Reshef and Baʿal* (OBO 140; Göttingen: Vandenhoeck & Ruprecht / Fribourg: Universitätsverlag, 1994) 137. Other iconographic depictions of Baal picture him holding what appears to be a lightning bolt. Yet some of these examples, however, may also be a stylized tree similar to the one here. See ibid., 141. In any case the depiction of this object, whether it be lightning or a tree, and the stance of the deity suggests martial imagery.
47. Cross argues that this name was originally an El epithet that meant 'he who creates heavenly armies'. See Cross, *Canaanite Myth*, 71.
48. These are the poetic texts cited in Patrick Miller, *The Divine Warrior in Early Israel* (HSM 5; Cambridge: Harvard University Press, 1973) 52.
49. Idem, "El the Warrior," *HTR* 60 (1967) 411.
50. Idem, *The Divine Warrior*, 51.

(KTU 4.63 I 9). The same name appears in 4.631 18 in a record of a land transfer and in 4.775 10 in a list of people and their animals.[51] A similar name is also attested in the Akkadian texts of Ugarit: DINGIR. UR.SAG (logogram for 'divine warrior/hero') in RS 11.839 21; 16.126B+ ii 41; 16.145 5, 10; and 27.053 9.[52]

Similar names are used with 'Baal' as an element. The name, or perhaps title *mhr b'l* 'soldier Baal' is used in KTU 1.22 I 8 in parallel with *mhr ʿnt* 'soldier Anat'. While El demonstrates some martial characteristics, the majority of Yahweh's warrior imagery is paralleled by the imagery of Baal. Thus, the few references to El's warrior status notwithstanding, it is clear that Yahweh's depiction as a warrior finds a greater number of parallels in the portrayal of Baal.[53]

The Bull Calf as Attribute Animal of Baal and Yahweh

In chap. 2, I demonstrated on the basis of epigraphic and iconographic evidence that it is quite likely that the attribute animal of El was the bull, while the attribute animal of Baal was the bull calf. While the biblical representation of Yahweh draws freely on elements of the Canaanite portrayals of both El and Baal, it seems that in the Israelite imagination, Yahweh was associated exclusively with the attribute animal of Baal, the bull calf. This association is extremely telling, because it indicates that, although ancient Israelites attributed qualities of both El and Baal to their God, they preferred to think of Yahweh as a young warrior, like Baal, and not as an aged deity.

Some scholars have argued that Yahweh, like El, is depicted with bull imagery in the epithet *ʾăbîr yaʿăqōb* (Gen 49:24; Isa 1:24; 49:26; 60:16; Ps 132:2, 5).[54] A personal name with a similar structure, *ʾbryhw*, is attested epigraphically.[55] Those who see Yahweh as the 'bull of Jacob' repoint the word *ʾăbîr* 'mighty one' as *ʾabbîr* 'bull'. However, it is unlikely that the word should be transcribed with a double *bet*, based on

---

51. *Land transfer*: Miller, "El the Warrior," 426. This occurrence is the only one cited by Miller.

List of people and their animals: all of these text citations can be found in *DUL* 57–58.

52. Citations from John Huehnergard, *The Akkadian of Ugarit* (HSS 34; Atlanta: Scholars Press, 1989) 410. For the meaning of *qarrādu* (UR.SAG), see CAD Q 140–44.

53. The parallels can only be pressed so far. After all, despite being portrayed with warrior imagery, Baal is said to die, which is never said of Yahweh.

54. Miller, "El the Warrior," 421. Korpel suggests that the Masoretes have deliberately omitted the *dageš* in the *bet* in all six texts in order to avoid associating Yahweh with a bull. See Korpel, *A Rift in the Clouds*, 533.

55. Fowler, *Theophoric Personal Names*, 334.

the comparative evidence available from Akkadian syllabic spellings of Northwest Semitic words.[56]

The LXX tradition of these six biblical texts also supports the assertion that the meaning is not 'bull'. The word *dunastēs* 'sovereign' is used for *'ābîr* in Gen 49:24, and a participle of the verb *ischuein* is used in Isa 1:24. The word *ischus* 'power, might' is employed in Isa 49:26, and *theos* 'God' is used in Ps 132:2, 5, and Isa 60:16. In addition to the biblical evidence, there is no Ugaritic text that refers to El as *ibr*, the reflex of the Hebrew word *'ābîr*.[57] The title *'ābîr* given to Yahweh should thus be translated 'mighty one', as it is in most English translations.[58] Bovine imagery is indeed employed to depict Yahweh, but as we will see in a moment, the biblical evidence shows that it is the bull calf imagery that dominates, rather than the adult bull.[59]

While the Hebrew Bible prohibits the use of images to represent Yahweh, two biblical episodes indicate that those who might have portrayed Yahweh with an attribute animal chose the *'ēgel* 'bull calf'. Aaron is said to have constructed a golden bull calf in the wilderness (Exod 32:4; Deut 9:16, 21; Neh 9:18; Ps 106:19). King Jeroboam I of Israel is condemned in the DH for installing bull calves (*'ăgālîm*) at the cultic sites of Dan and Bethel (1 Kgs 12:28, 32). Hosea also alludes to the use of bull calf images in Israelite worship (8:5–6, 13:2).

Although most of these biblical texts are polemically charged, I am not convinced that the term *calf* is used to denote the small stature of the image at these cult sites as Zevit argues.[60] Neither am I persuaded

---

56. John Huehnergard, *Ugaritic Vocabulary in Syllabic Transcription* (HSS 32; Atlanta: Scholars Press, 1987) 269 n. 11. Huehnergard notes that *ibrn*, when linked with names, appears as *i-bi-ra-nv*, never with the geminated *b*, and so is more likely 'strong'.

57. M. Köckert, "Mighty One of Jacob," in *Dictionary of Deities and Demons in the Bible* (ed. Karel van der Toorn, Bob Becking, and Pieter W. van der Horst; Leiden: Brill, 1999) 573.

58. Harry Torczyner, "אביר kein Stierbild," *ZAW* 39 (1921) 300. Fowler renders the name *'bryhw* on the seal as 'Yahweh is strong'. See Fowler, *Theophoric Personal Names*, 87.

59. Num 23:22 and 24:8 read "God [El] was the one who brought them out of Egypt; his [eminence] is like the eminence of a wild bull." The animal used in the comparison is a *rě'ēm* 'wild bull'. In this poem (vv. 18–24), note that El is the name of the deity on every occasion except one: v. 21c, "Yahweh his God is with him." Whether the "eminence of a wild bull" is supposed to be applied to Israel or God (El) is not certain. See Martin Noth, *Numbers* (trans. James D. Martin; OTL; Philadelphia: Westminster, 1968) 187. If the phrase applies to the deity, it is interesting to note the connection between God (El) here and the bull imagery.

60. Ziony Zevit, *The Religions of Ancient Israel: A Synthesis of Parallactic Approaches* (New York: Continuum, 2001) 448 n. 22.

that *calf* is used as a derogatory term to refer to the images that were actually adult bulls at these sites. The silver-plated calf unearthed at Ashkelon is a clear example of the use of a calf in a cultic setting. It is therefore more likely that, when the biblical writers refer to the calves at these sites, the bovine term is not polemic denigration but, rather, an appropriate designation for the images.

We may safely conclude that the calves that Jeroboam I established at Dan and Bethel were most likely portraying the attribute animal of Yahweh, upon which he could stand.[61] Portrayal of Yahweh's beast was probably permissible before the anti-Baal polemic of the 9th century B.C.E, as seems to be indicated in the absence of any explicit condemnation of the bovine images either in 1 Kings 13, when the Judahite prophet predicts the destruction of the cult site of Bethel, or in the Elijah-Elisha narratives.[62] This sort of portrayal is consistent with Keel and Uehlinger's thesis that over time these "attribute animals" became the symbol of the particular deity, coinciding with the tendency in Iron Age I Israel to avoid anthropomorphic depictions of deities.[63]

The significance of the use of a bull calf as an attribute animal for Yahweh is its connection to a similar portrayal of Baal in his iconography. That these two deities share the same attribute animal indicates that the portrayal of Yahweh in this regard is employing Baal attributes rather than attributes of El. Because youthful and aged depictions of the same deity are incompatible, Yahweh was associated with the bull calf rather than the bull, which would have connoted the mature traits of El. As Fleming has argued, it is no mere coincidence that Yahweh is connected to bull calf imagery in the Hebrew Bible and not to the adult bull.[64] Yahweh's relative youth is conveyed in the literary sources and even encoded in the iconography of "unorthodox" Yahwism.

Further support for Israelite resistance to associating Yahweh with the elderly El comes from onomastic evidence. De Moor notes that biblical personal names associated with the early Iron I period reflect the notion that Yahweh and El were one and the same.[65] Over time, however, the percentage of El names decreased, and de Moor interprets this decrease as marking the transformation from a "Yhwh/El religion

---

61. P. King and L. Stager, *Life in Biblical Israel* (Louisville, KY: Westminster John Knox, 2001) 343. See also Cross, *Canaanite Myth*, 73.
62. Ibid., 75.
63. Keel and Uehlinger, *Gods, Goddesses, and Images of God*, 141.
64. D. E. Fleming, "If El Is a Bull, Who Is a Calf? Reflections on Religion in Second-Millennium Syria Palestine," *ErIsr* 26 (Cross Volume; 1999) 24.
65. De Moor, *The Rise of Yahwism*, 10.

to a purely Yʜᴡʜ religion."⁶⁶ This conclusion may be straining the evidence, as Keel and Uehlinger suggest.⁶⁷

The reduction in El names may, however, indicate a differentiation between the two deities at this time, a distinction that may include a recognition of the relative age of each of these deities. It may have been that Yahweh's youthfulness, paralleled by Baal's, was perceived as incompatible with the legendary senescence of El. The word *youthfulness* is, of course, a relative term. Because Baal is not referred to with the kind of explicit old-age imagery used of El, one can speak of Baal's relative youthfulness vis-à-vis El. This onomastic evidence may show a growing divide in the perceptions of the people between the elderly El and the more youthful Yahweh. The desire of ancient Israelites to associate Yahweh with the relatively youthful Baal probably led them to reject the El characteristics that explicitly denoted his age.

Yahweh versus the "Other Gods"

Although there is ample overlap between the portrayal of Israel's God and the Ugaritic depiction of El and Baal, Yahweh is certainly more than the sum of their parts. Assuming that Yahweh is merely "El + Baal" fails to account for the rich diversity of imagery used of Israel's God and the theological matrix from which his portrayal derives. For all the overlap between these three deities, Yahweh retains his distinctiveness from the Canaanite gods. It would be simplistic to posit a single cause—namely, the selection of the bull calf as Yahweh's attribute animal—for the absence of old-age imagery from most biblical portrayals of Yahweh. Thus, I conclude this chapter by pointing out that Israelite concern for Yahweh's distinctiveness probably contributed to keeping Israel's God relatively young.

There is profound ambivalence in Israel's attitude toward the cultures that surrounded it. On the one hand, as we have already noted, Israelites were amenable to portraying their God with a compilation of images used of Baal and El in the Ugaritic texts. Yet on the other hand, this acceptance of the portrayal of other gods was circumscribed. A parade example here is the sexual exploits of ancient Near Eastern gods, which are nowhere attributed to Yahweh. He is never imagined as lustful because he has no need.⁶⁸ According to the Hebrew Bible, he has no consort, although external inscriptional evidence is certainly sug-

---

66. Ibid., 11.
67. Keel and Uehlinger, *Gods, Goddesses, and Images of God*, 207 n. 31.
68. Korpel, *A Rift in the Clouds*, 626.

gestive.[69] Unlike El who is on occasion a reveler given to excess, Yahweh is never imagined as inebriated in the Hebrew Bible.[70]

Yahweh's southern provenance and his role in the exodus tradition are some of his unique features vis-à-vis the Ugaritic gods.[71] Yahweh is said to be from Sinai (Deut 33:2, Judg 5:5, Ps 68:9) Paran (Deut 33:2, Hab 3:3) Edom (Judg 5:4) and Teiman (Hab 3:3 and Kuntillet Ajrud 15:7[72]). Another discontinuity between Yahweh and the two Ugaritic deities is the lack of a theogony in Israel's traditions. Israel's God is not birthed from other gods, and he is not imagined as an explicit product of any union or creation. Theogonies abound in Israel's ancient Near Eastern environment, from Egypt to Mesopotamia. The absence of narratives of this sort in Israel's tradition is telling.[73] Even when he is depicted as a father, the focus is not on portraying Yahweh as an ancestor or progenitor but, rather, as a merciful and kind caregiver.[74] The God of the Hebrew Bible simply is, and his origins are not explained. This is probably why Yahweh is not described in terms of the human life cycle in most of the biblical tradition, anthropomorphisms notwithstanding: to do so would imply that he has a beginning and, conceivably, an end.

---

69. For evidence of a consort for Yahweh, see Meindert Dijkstra, "I Have Blessed You by Yhwh of Samaria and His Asherah: Texts with Religious Elements from the Soil Archive of Ancient Israel," in *Only One God? Monotheism in Ancient Israel and the Veneration of the Goddess Asherah* (ed. Bob Becking et al.; Biblical Seminar 77; London: Sheffield Academic Press, 2001) 44. See also Olyan, *Asherah and the Cult of Yahweh*, 74. For a counterpoint, see Judith M. Hadley, *The Cult of Asherah in Ancient Israel and Judah* (Cambridge: Cambridge University Press, 2000) 124.

70. Yahweh is imagined as feasting on occasion. See Isa 25:6.

71. M. Smith, *The Early History of God*, 3. Elsewhere, Smith suggests that this southern connection may indicate an early association of Yahweh with the Ugaritic Athtar that was later obscured, along with the astral features that Yahweh supposedly shared with Athtar, by the assimilation of Baal and Yahweh. This seems to me to be too speculative, and Smith's suggestion has the added liability of being based on a supposed conflict between Baal and Athtar reflected in Athtar's inability to take the throne in the wake of Baal's death in the Baal story (KTU 1.6 I 63). See Mark Smith, "When the Heavens Darkened: Yahweh, El, and the Divine Astral Family in Iron Age II Judah," in *Symbiosis, Symbolism and the Power of the Past: Canaan, Ancient Israel, and Their Neighbors from the Late Bronze Age through Roman Palaestina* (ed. W. G. Dever and S. Gitin; Winona Lake, IN: Eisenbrauns, 2003) 272–74.

72. The numbering for the Kuntillet Ajrud text is taken from Gogel, *A Grammar of Epigraphic Hebrew*, 414.

73. The absence of these narratives in Israel's traditions may also be an attempt to prevent Yahweh from being considered an "olden god" who was relegated to the netherworld after being bested by younger gods. This feature is present in much of ancient Near Eastern mythology. See Cross, "The 'Olden Gods,'" 75. Yet caution is in order, because the Ugaritic tablets attest no theogony in Ugaritic culture either.

74. Joachim Jeremias, *Abba: Studien zur Neutestamentlichen Theologie und Zeitgeschichte* (Göttingen: Vandenhoeck & Ruprecht, 1966) 16.

One final explanation for the absence of old-age imagery in Yahweh's portrayal is worthy of note. In chaps. 1 and 2, I noted a few places where old age is portrayed as a time of weakness and vulnerability. In the Hebrew Bible, this is seen in the deception of aged individuals such as Lot by his daughters (Gen 19:31–35) and Isaac by his wife and son (Gen 27:5–29). Among the Ugaritic texts, KTU 1.114 describes how the aged El is flanked by Thkmn and Shnm, who assist him in his inebriated state. As I noted in these respective chapters, portrayals of old people as weak do not give the complete picture of the place of the elderly in Israelite and Ugaritic culture. However, the fact that this sort of weakness is a recurring element in portrayals of old age may assist in explaining the relative youth of Israel's God. Israel's God, figured as a divine warrior, could not be imagined as weak and vulnerable, and so his imagery did not include the social and biological markers of old age.

Chapter 4

Yahweh Comes of Age

Now that I have demonstrated that Yahweh was not explicitly portrayed with old-age imagery in most of Israel's history, it is necessary to examine the overturning of this tradition. In this chapter, I address the pivotal transformation that takes place in Daniel 7, where the epithet "Ancient of Days" is applied to Yahweh for the first time. Several issues must be addressed in this chapter as I attempt to account for this new portrayal of Israel's God. First, I review the date of Daniel 7's composition, as well as the old-age imagery it contains and an important text-critical issue. The date of this text will prove critical in understanding the backdrop of the transformation that takes place in Daniel 7, and the text-critical issue has foundational bearing on the episode involving the Ancient of Days. Second, I will argue that Yahweh's aging can best be explained along two developmental trajectories in Israel's history. The first trajectory is the renewed influence of Canaanite mythology in the development of the vision described in Daniel 7, allowing Yahweh to acquire a senescent epithet and concomitant imagery. I will demonstrate how the relationship between the "one like a son of man" and the "Ancient of Days" mirrors the relationship between Baal and El as portrayed in Ugaritic narrative poetry. The second trajectory is the growing tendency in later biblical traditions to depict Yahweh as a father, taking into account the tension on this point between the canonized traditions and the onomastic evidence. Finally, I consider whether Hellenization affected the process whereby the relatively young God was transformed into an elderly paternal figure.

Daniel 7: Preliminary Matters

While the author of Daniel 7 is all but lost to us, the details of the text he handed down contain enough allusions to social units and historical events that it is possible to establish an approximate date of composition. Dating Daniel 7 is crucial to explaining the transformation in thinking that permitted Yahweh to be depicted with explicit old-age imagery. This date of composition has been hotly debated. The traditional view holds that a historical figure named Daniel wrote it in the 6th century

B.C.E., but critical scholars have suggested a much later date.¹ Gammie suggests that Daniel 2, 5, and 7:1–18 constitute the original stage of the book, which he then dates to the 3rd century B.C.E.² Most scholars, however, place the date of Daniel 7 just before the Maccabean revolt, slightly before 167 B.C.E.³ Features of the vision can be correlated with events and personages from the reign of Antiochus IV. The "little horn," for example, is usually assumed to be Antiochus IV himself.⁴ Others have sought philological grounds to argue for a 2nd-century B.C.E. date.⁵ While some of the individual arguments for a Maccabean date may not be as strong as others, a 2nd-century B.C.E. date for Daniel 7 best accounts for the data as a whole.⁶ Positing this late date for this chapter allows a longer time for development in Israel's tradition and raises the question whether certain circumstances in the 2nd century B.C.E. precipitated this new portrayal of the deity in the postexilic community. I will take this up below when I consider the influence of Hellenization on the transformation I am positing.

Before looking at the details of the text of Daniel 7, I should present a brief synopsis of the account. Daniel 7 begins with a dream that Daniel had in which the four winds were stirring up the great sea, out of which came four beasts. These creatures are described in detail and then thrones appear, and a figure referred to as "Ancient of Days" takes his seat and is served by thousands. It is a courtroom scene that ends with one of the beasts slain and the others stripped of their dominion. It is at this point in the vision that "one like a son of man" appears with the clouds of heaven. He comes to the one called "Ancient of Days" and is given everlasting dominion. Daniel is then given the dream's inter-

---

1. Collins notes that the conservative position of 6th-century provenance was held by some in the 19th century. See John J. Collins, *Daniel* (Hermeneia; Minneapolis: Fortress, 1993) 27. One is hard-pressed to find a scholar within the last 50 years who holds traditional views. Even scholars who hold to unity of authorship admit a Maccabean date of composition. See H. H. Rowley, *Darius the Mede and the Four World Empires in the Book of Daniel* (Cardiff: University of Wales Press, 1959) 175–76; and R. H. Charles, *A Critical and Exegetical Commentary on the Book of Daniel* (Oxford: Clarendon, 1929) xxxviii.

2. John G. Gammie, "The Classification, Stages of Growth, and Changing Intentions in the Book of Daniel," *JBL* 95 (1976) 202. See also James A. Montgomery, *The Book of Daniel* (ICC; Edinburgh: T. & T. Clark, 1979) 59.

3. John E. Goldingay, *Daniel* (WBC 30; Dallas: Word, 1989) 157. See Collins, *Daniel*, 24; Louis F. Hartman and Alexander A. Di Lella, *The Book of Daniel* (AB 23; Garden City, NY: Doubleday, 1978) 13; and André Lacocque, *The Book of Daniel* (trans. D. Pellauer; Atlanta: John Knox, 1979) 7.

4. Hartman and Di Lella, *Daniel*, 14.

5. Montgomery, *Daniel*, 15.

6. Collins, *Daniel*, 33.

pretation. The four beasts are four kings on the earth who are stripped of their dominion, and the kingdom is given to the saints of the Most High.

Three phrases that appear in Daniel 7 are worthy of note because they help elucidate the issue concerning the deity's age. The most important of the these phrases is the new divine epithet. We first encounter the "Ancient of Days" in Dan 7:9, when Daniel sees this figure in his night dream. The Aramaic construct chain is ʿattîq yômîn, in which the *nomen rectum* is the Aramaic reflex of the Hebrew yāmîm 'days', and the *nomen regens* is an adjectival form of the verb ʿtq 'to advance'.[7] This verb also appears in Ugaritic as the verb 'to pass' in the G stem and 'to become old' in the N stem and as the adjective 'perennial'.[8] Imperial Aramaic inscriptions attest an identical adjectival use.[9] The Akkadian verb *etēqu* denotes passing along, advancing, or even the passage of time.[10] The phrase is an Aramaic approximation of the epithet bāʾ(îm) bayyāmîm given to Abraham and Sarah in Gen 18:11, Abraham alone in Gen 24:1, and Joshua in Josh 13:1 and 23:1.[11] While 'Advanced of Days' is more precise, the usual English rendering, 'Ancient of Days', captures the sentiment.

In addition to the senescent epithet in Daniel 7, a second important phrase is kaʿămar něqēʾ (v. 9). This describes the hair of the Ancient of Days and is rendered in the RSV 'like pure wool'. Though the first word in the phrase clearly means 'like wool', with the prefixed comparative *kap*, the meaning of the second word is not as obvious. Traditionally, as seen in the RSV, the word has been rendered 'pure'.

Among the Greek translations of this text, Origen has *katharon* 'pure',[12] as does Theodotion,[13] while the Chester Beatty Papyrus attests *leukon katharon* 'pure white'.[14] The New Testament refraction of this scene in Rev 1:12–16 has *leukon* 'white' in v. 14. Origen and Theodotion

---

7. BDB 1108a; see also *HALOT* 1955.

8. *DUL* 191–92.

9. *DNWSI* 898. It is used of a document and possibly of foundations as well as wine and vinegar.

10. CAD E 384.

11. The *Targum Onqelos* of these texts uses forms of the verb ʿll 'to go or come in' when translating the Hebrew. See Alexander Sperber, *The Bible in Aramaic Based on Old Manuscripts and Printed Texts* (4 vols.; Leiden: Brill, 1959–73).

12. Sharon Pace Jeansonne, *The Old Greek Translation of Daniel 7–12* (Washington, DC: Catholic Biblical Association, 1988) 60.

13. Montgomery, *Daniel*, 300.

14. Frederic G. Kenyon, ed., *The Chester Beatty Biblical Papyri; Descriptions and Texts of Twelve Manuscripts on Papyrus of the Greek Bible* (Fasc. 7; London: Walker, 1937) 27.

render the phrase in light of an assumed Hebraization of the Aramaic. The word *katharon* itself is used in the pseudepigraphic work of Judith (10:5), where it is understood as white in the context of refined flour used to make "white bread."[15]

The notion of 'pure' is the meaning of epigraphic Hebrew and Jewish Aramaic *nqy* and probably suggests wool that is unblemished.[16] Some of the references among the epigraphic attestations of Jewish Aramaic refer to "pure," bread which may suggest a white bread.[17] Sokoloff departs from this tradition by arguing that *něqē'* here means 'lamb' and that the phrase simply means 'lamb's wool'.[18] He notes that many Aramaic dialects from Egyptian to Gaonic use *něqē'* to denote 'lamb', supporting earlier suggestions that posit an etymological link between this word and Akkadian *nīqu* 'offering [commonly of sheep]; libation'.[19]

Because the Awassi sheep (the most common and widespread breed of sheep in the ancient Near East) is usually white,[20] the translation 'lamb's wool' probably suggests a white color like the color of the hair in old age. Positing this meaning has the added advantage of a parallel with the raiment's color analogous with snow in the previous stich. Whether the word is a noun meaning 'lamb' rather than an adjective, whether 'pure' or 'white', the focus of the metaphor is captured by the Greek papyrus's rendering 'pure white', which denotes, as does the comparison to lamb's wool, the hair of the deity portrayed as an old man.

The third important phrase in Daniel 7 is the figure referred to as "one like a son of man." Before moving to the discussion regarding this person's identity, we should look at a small but not unimportant text-critical issue in Dan 7:13 involving the Greek textual evidence vis-à-vis the text of the MT. Papyrus 967, manuscript 88, and the Syro-Hexapla attest an interesting variant of the Greek tradition that departs from the MT and Theodotion.[21] Instead of reading *heōs palaiou hēmerōn* 'unto

---

15. Henry George Liddell, Robert Scott, and Stuart Jones, *A Greek-English Lexicon* (hereafter LSJ; 9th ed.; Oxford: Clarendon, 1996) 850b.
16. *DNWSI* 757–58.
17. Ibid.
18. Michael Sokoloff, "*'āmar něqê*, 'Lamb's Wool' (Dan 7:9)," *JBL* (1976) 278.
19. Ibid., 279.
20. Oded Borowski, *Every Living Thing: Daily Use of Animals in Ancient Israel* (Walnut Creek, CA: Altamira, 1998) 66–67. As the purple dyeing industry developed in Phoenicia, the demand for white wool increased, and thus the selective breeding patterns followed suit. See H. Epstein, "Domestication Features in Animals as Functions of Human Society," in *Readings in Cultural Geography* (ed. Philip L. Wagner and Marvin W. Mikesell; Chicago: University of Chicago Press, 1962) 292.
21. The Chester Beatty Papyrus has a lacuna from 7:11 to 7:14 and so cannot assist the discussion. The text of P 967 is published in Angelo Geissen, ed., *Der*

the[22] Ancient of Days' with Origen and Theodotion, they attest *hōs palaios hēmerōn* 'like the Ancient of Days', the difference being one letter. The upshot of these variants is that, contrary to the MT, the "son of man" and the "Ancient of Days" appear as a single individual.

Many have considered these variants to be errors.[23] Indeed, Papyrus 967 has other errors in this verse that call its testimony into question.[24] They may be mechanical errors, as Collins suggests,[25] perhaps from the influence of the initial *hōs* or deriving from aural misconstrual if the copyist was taking dictation. Others explain the difference as a theologically driven correction of the MT or of Theodotion's translation. Caquot maintains that the correction was made to enhance the character of the messianic figure.[26] Lust suggests that these texts preserve a different Vorlage that more accurately reflects a parallel with Daniel 2, whereby the stone that destroys the statue corresponds to the single heavenly figure in Daniel 7.[27] These assessments are, as Collins notes, too hasty and fail to account for the bigger picture.[28]

I suggest that the reading of Papyrus 967 is a scribal mistake. The other two variants that equate the two figures may be either mistakes or, what is more likely and quite different, a kind of midrash.[29] The New Testament book of Revelation attests a single figure with white hair referred to as "one like a son of man" in Rev 1:13–14.[30] Bruce suggests that these variants are all related and that they reflect a Christianizing of the text of Daniel.[31] While this is certainly possible, it may be that

---

Septuaginta-Text des Buches Daniel (Bonn: Habelt, 1968). See pp. 108–9 for the relevant text here.

22. The lack of the article here, where the MT has the Aramaic emphatic form, is not significant because the Old Greek tradition does not consistently render a construct chain that has the *nomen rectum* in the emphatic state with an article. Jeansonne, *Old Greek*, 98.

23. Montgomery, *Daniel*, 304. See also Collins, *Daniel*, 275 and 311.

24. Geissen, *Septuaginta-Text*, 109. It uses the dative in places where one expects the accusative so that the phrase is quite awkward.

25. Collins, *Daniel*, 311.

26. André Caquot, "Les quatre bêtes et le 'Fils d'homme' (Daniel 7)," *Sem* 17 (1967) 70. See also Johan Lust, "Daniel 7,13 and the Septuagint," *Ephemerides Theologicae Lovanienses* 54 (1978) 66.

27. Ibid., 70.

28. Collins, *Daniel*, 34.

29. Goldingay, *Daniel*, 145.

30. Whether this New Testament tradition is based on these readings or derived from a theological matrix involving an association of the Christ figure as Son of Man with God the father is not clear. Collins (*Daniel*, 311) suggests the former possibility.

31. F. F. Bruce, "The Oldest Greek Version of Daniel," *Oudtestamentische Studiën* 20 (1977) 26. All of these variants date to the common era. P 967 may be the oldest with a *terminus a quo* at 130 C.E. See the discussion of dating these texts in Jeansonne, *Old Greek*, 8–12.

the author of Revelation is simply reading the tradition of Daniel seen in Papyrus 967 and manuscript 88 rather than the tradition seen in Theodotion. If, however, the Revelation author is reading the Greek traditions that mirror the MT, it strikes me as odd to posit a Christianizing tendency that obscures a differentiation between God the father and the Messiah figure that is clear in the Aramaic Scriptures. Again, if the author of Revelation is reading the Greek tradition of Daniel reflected in Theodotion, it is more likely that he is fusing the separate descriptions of the heavenly beings in Daniel 7 and applying them to the Christ.[32] In any case, the MT and the main Septuagintal traditions (Theodotion and Origen) preserve the oldest Vorlage depicting two figures rather than one.

Now that we may safely assume that the Ancient of Days and "one like a son of man" are two distinct figures in the Aramaic text of Daniel 7, the identity of the latter, which has long been debated by commentators, can be addressed. The phrase "son of man," as virtually everyone now admits, simply means 'human being'.[33] It appears in the Sefire inscription with the meaning 'someone, anyone'.[34] Elsewhere in Aramaic it is used of mortals in opposition to deities.[35] There is a Ugaritic attestation as well.[36]

As Collins has noted, the son of man has generally been assumed in the history of interpretation to have one of three possible referents: an exalted human, the Jewish people as a whole, or a heavenly being.[37] Although the messianic interpretation, which identifies this son of man as the Anointed One, was the favorite among early interpreters down to the 19th century, most now regard this interpretation as unwarranted.[38] As Collins points out, there is no concern for the Davidic monarchy in the rest of the book of Daniel.[39] The view that suggested the figure was

---

32. Although Greg Beale does not mention these variants, this is his assessment of the use of Daniel in Revelation. See G. K. Beale, *The Use of Daniel in Jewish Apocalyptic Literature and in the Revelation of St. John* (Lanham, MD: University Press of America, 1984) 159.

33. Collins, *Daniel*, 304; and Goldingay, *Daniel*, 150.

34. KAI 224:16. Although its 2nd-century C.E. date is a few centuries later than Daniel (2nd century C.E.) a Greek-Aramaic bilingual inscription from Armazi also attests a similar usage. See KAI 276:9–10.

35. A 2nd–1st-century B.C.E. Phoenician inscription from Egypt has *bn 'dm* 'son of a human being' in opposition to *'lnm* 'gods' in a blessing. See KAI 48:4.

36. The text is KTU 1.169 from Ras Ibn Hani (RIH 78/20) where, in lines 14–15, *adm* seems to be in parallel with *bn adm*. See Johannes C. de Moor, "An Incantation against Evil Spirits," *UF* 12 (1980) 430.

37. Collins, *Daniel*, 308.
38. Ibid.
39. Ibid., 309.

a cipher for the collective Jewish people was based on the assumption that the "holy ones" in v. 10 and the son of man should be equated and that they would be given dominion as a people.[40] However, equating the son of man figure with a collective is not suggested by a straightforward literal reading of the text, which probably explains the relative paucity of this notion before the 19th century.[41] It has also been suggested that all three of these possibilities are in the mind of our author, so that a kind of synthesis is intended.[42]

It is more likely that the "one like a son of man" refers, like the Ancient of Days, to a single individual, who is presumed to exist outside the vision and is probably a heavenly being.[43] This coincides with the rise in prominence of angelic forces in the Judaism of the Hellenistic period, as attested in the texts from Qumran.[44] Whether this figure is the archangel Michael, who appears later in Daniel, as Collins argues, is not as clear. While I will have more to say regarding the nature of this son of man figure, suffice it to say for now that it appears to refer to an individual heavenly being.

The revolutionary nature of this text in the Hebrew Bible has been largely unappreciated. For the first time, Yahweh is explicitly portrayed as elderly: his hair is white, and he bears a title that effectively identifies him as one of advanced age. The long avoidance of old-age imagery for Yahweh has been reversed. It is now my task to explain why this reversal occurred.

Canaanite Antecedents of the Ancient of Days

Most scholars agree that the portrait of the Ancient of Days has its antecedents in Canaanite mythology, such as the portrayal of El at Ugarit, along with data preserved in the work of Eusebius. Despite this consensus, however, not all are so convinced. Arthur Ferch argues that there are too many differences between the Ugaritic texts and Daniel 7 to permit a connection.[45] Ferch assumes that the details of every deity involved in the supposed connection must be present to demonstrate continuity between both traditions. Surely, however, an author can borrow mythological motifs without appropriating every feature of a particular deity.

---

40. Ibid.
41. Ibid., 308.
42. Matthias Albani, "The 'One like a Son of Man' (Dan 7:13) and the Royal Ideology," in *Enoch and Qumran Origins* (ed. Gabriele Boccaccini; Grand Rapids: Eerdmans, 2005) 48.
43. Collins, *Daniel*, 305.
44. Ibid., 309.
45. Arthur J. Ferch, "Daniel 7 and Ugarit: A Reconsideration," *JBL* 99 (1980) 85.

Paul Mosca has suggested that the writer of Daniel 7 could draw on an ample supply of imagery within the Hebrew Bible itself and thus needed no other outside inspiration.⁴⁶ His more broadly conceived argument traces 16 motifs in the chapter to other parts of the Bible, thus demonstrating their domestic origin.⁴⁷ Number 8 on his list is the Ancient of Days, and here we see the chink in his rhetorical armor. In chap. 3, I noted that Mosca cites three texts (Isa 9:5, 40:28; Jer 10:10) that he believes demonstrate Yahweh's old-age features. Yet as I demonstrated, these texts speak of God's eternality and do not attribute to him any markers of old age. Mosca is forced to read his assumptions into the texts here because he can find no explicit old-age imagery used of Yahweh in the Hebrew Bible.

This being the case, one is able to question his broader argument about the innerbiblical development of all imagery employed in Daniel 7. First of all, in one of his major points, he posits (contra Collins) that a Jew of the 2nd century B.C.E. would not, on pious grounds, have sought literary assistance from foreign, heterodox writers, even though he would certainly have known of them.⁴⁸ This would especially be true, so the argument goes, if Daniel's target is Antiochus Epiphanes, a first-order pagan from the author's perspective. However, this premise fails to take into account the ways in which a writer may borrow and twist an opponent's words to serve a polemical purpose.⁴⁹ Examples of this sort of borrowing can be seen in the Hebrew Bible in the words of Hosea, who borrows Canaanite themes to counter idolatry.⁵⁰ Likewise Psalm 29 is probably a recasting of a hymn to Baal that proclaims Yahweh's supremacy vis-à-vis the Canaanite storm god.⁵¹ As already noted, Mosca assumes that the writer had no reason to seek out inspiration from his neighbors, because the Hebrew Bible provided all that he needed.

However, this is precisely where Mosca is wrong. The transformation seen between the "Ancient of Days" and the biblical texts that speak of Yahweh's eternality is too great to assume that no outside influence played a role therein. Because Yahweh's eternality did not occasion a portrayal of him as elderly in earlier biblical texts, it is difficult to assume that the transformation in Daniel 7 could be explained solely on

---

46. Mosca, "Ugarit and Daniel 7," 501.
47. Ibid., 500–501.
48. Ibid., 499.
49. John J. Collins, "Stirring up the Great Sea: The Religio-Historical Background of Daniel 7," in *The Book of Daniel in the Light of New Findings* (ed. A. S. van der Woude; Leuven: Leuven University Press, 1993) 123, 132.
50. Ibid., 132.
51. H. L. Ginsberg, "A Phoenician Hymn in the Psalter," *Atti del XIX Congresso Internazionale degli Orientalistici* (Rome: Senato, 1935) 472.

the basis of the biblical tradition itself. The idea of the "Ancient of Days" has no continuity with other depictions of Yahweh in the Hebrew Bible. It is clearly demonstrable that our writer is not bound by the pious restrictions retrojected upon him by Mosca.

If it is true that Daniel 7 departs from the traditional imagery used in depictions of Yahweh earlier in Israel's traditions, the question arises concerning the source for the transformation. Contrary to Ferch and Mosca, I am convinced that an external influence can best account for the change. I am suggesting that the source of Yahweh's old-age attributes in Daniel 7 is the depiction of El as attested in the texts from Ugarit. Before I make my case for this grounding of the imagery, it will be necessary to explain why other suggested external influences are less likely.

Helge Kvanvig has suggested that Daniel 7 has closer affinities with an Akkadian text entitled "Vision of the Underworld."[52] Kvanvig goes so far as to suggest Daniel 7's dependence on this Akkadian text, although he does not rule out the influence of other texts as well.[53] Positing this connection to a 7th-century Akkadian text has the advantage of a shorter chronological gap than with Late Bronze Age Ugarit, which has been the predominant liability of the Ugaritic connection.[54]

Yet as Collins points out, the differences between Daniel 7 and the "Vision of the Underworld" far outweigh the similarities. Both texts are presented as dreams, but Daniel 7 must be interpreted, whereas the "Vision" does not.[55] There are 15 creatures in the "Vision" but only 4 in Daniel 7. Kvanvig himself, in addressing the numerous differences between the two texts, says, "If we argue for a relationship between the two texts, the author of Daniel 7 must have interpreted the Akkadian vision according to a new setting and added new material."[56] Yet how much reinterpretation and putative new material can we tolerate before the hypothesis collapses under its own weight? It is much simpler to sug-

---

52. Helge S. Kvanvig, *Roots of Apocalyptic* (Wissenschaftliche Monographien zum Alten und Neuen Testament 61; Neukirchen-Vluyn: Neukirchener Verlag, 1988) 457.

53. Ibid. On the same page, Kvanvig makes the curious statement, "If we argue for a relationship between the Vision of the Nether World and Daniel 7 as a whole, it seems clear that other sources can have influence [*sic*] Daniel 7 in this sequence just as much or even more than the Akkadian vision." I could not agree more with the apodosis. The NW Semitic traditions expressed in the Ugaritic stories would serve as the best examples of these "other sources."

54. The date for this text is given in Alexander Heidel, *The Gilgamesh Epic and Old Testament Parallels* (Chicago: University of Chicago Press, 1946) 132. See also "A Vision of the Nether World," translated by E. A. Speiser (*ANET* 109).

55. Collins, "Stirring up the Great Sea," 129.

56. Kvanvig, *Roots of Apocalyptic*, 458.

gest that the many differences between Daniel and the "Vision of the Underworld" indicate that there is no connection between the two texts and that the source of Daniel's vision lies elsewhere.

An Iranian influence was first suggested by members of the *religionsgeschichtliche Schule*.[57] S. Mowinckel considered the "son of man" figure to be non-Jewish and thus argued that he was borrowed from Iranian and Chaldean sources.[58] Apocalyptic traditions were assumed to be of Iranian origin by many, especially before the discovery of the Ugaritic tablets in 1929.[59] The Manichean religion of ancient Persia was deemed to be the source for some of Judaism's features expressed in incipient form in the apocalyptic imagery of Daniel 7.[60]

The major obstacle to positing Persian influence on texts that derive from Palestine in the Second Temple period is the late dating of most of the extant texts from Persian religion, especially the Pahlavi texts.[61] Hultgård argues that the apocalyptic-eschatological ideas expressed in these late texts do indeed go back far enough in time to have been influential in Israel's late traditions.[62] Even so, he notes that there was "no direct and general borrowing of the Iranian apocalyptic eschatology as such by Judaism and Christianity" and the ideas merely "produced the necessary stimulus for the full development of ideas that were slowly underway in Judaism."[63] When we turn our attention to the ancient Kingdom of Ugarit, however, it is easy to see that the cultural connections with biblical Israel are numerous and demonstrable. While influence on biblical traditions could conceivably derive from cultures other than Ugarit, one must carefully consider the latter possibility first and foremost. Despite the proposed early connections with Iranian religion, pride of place must be reserved for a closer neighbor within Israel's sphere—Ugarit.

---

57. For a brief synopsis of the *Forschungsgeschichte* of this school, see Jürg Eggler, *Influence and Traditions Underlying the Vision of Daniel 7:2–14* (OBO 177; Fribourg: Universitätsverlag / Göttingen: Vandenhoeck & Ruprecht, 2000) 71–76.

58. S. Mowinckel, *He That Cometh* (trans. G. W. Anderson; New York: Abingdon, 1954) 432.

59. See, for example, Hugo Gressmann, *Die hellenistische Gestirnreligion* (Leipzig: Hinrichs, 1925) 19.

60. Idem, *Der Messias* (Göttingen: Vandenhoek & Ruprecht, 1929) 351–52.

61. Anders Hultgård, "Persian Apocalypticism," in *The Continuum History of Apocalypticism* (ed. Bernard J. McGinn, John J. Collins, and Stephen J. Stein; New York: Continuum, 2003) 31. The phrase "Pahlavi texts" is the common designation for the religious literature of the Zoroastrians compiled in the Sassanian and early Islamic periods (6th–7th centuries C.E.).

62. Ibid.

63. Ibid., 60.

El and Yahweh

The most obvious external analogue to the depiction of the two figures in Daniel 7, the one like a son of man and the Ancient of Days, is preserved in the Ugaritic tablets, in their depictions of the high god El and of Baal.[64] The author of the vision portrayed in Daniel wanted to represent Yahweh as conferring divine attributes upon a second figure.[65] In the Hebrew tradition, in which, as I have argued in chap. 3, Yahweh is in part a conflation of imagery used of El and Baal, the only option available to an orthodox Yahwehist is to fragment this conflation,[66] as it were, so as to distribute the divine attributes. In Daniel 7, the role of "cloud rider" is the fragment of Yahweh's personality that is conferred on this Son of Man, as well as the prerogative to have

---

64. Goldingay, *Daniel*, 151.

65. In subsequent traditions, more divine attributes are given to this figure. In *1 Enoch*, the Son of Man figure takes on the roles of eschatological king and judge, positions previously associated with God. See Erik Sjöberg, *Der Menschensohn im äthiopischen Henochbuch* (Lund: C.W.K. Gleerup, 1946) 88. Enoch speaks of the preexistence of the Son of Man (*1 En.* 48:3). See also H. Ludin Jansen, *Die Henochgestalt* (Oslo: Dybwad, 1939) 88–90. Jansen points out how the Son of Man is given the role of eschatological judge in *1 En.* 46:4. He is enthroned on a throne of glory in 47:3; see J. A. Emerton, "The Origin of the Son of Man Imagery," *JTS* 9 (1958) 236. The date of this section of *1 Enoch* (chaps. 37–71, "The Book of Parables" or "The Book of Similitudes") is usually placed between the 1st century B.C.E. and the 1st century C.E. See George W. E. Nickelsburg, "Enoch, First Book of," *ABD* 2:513. Loren Stuckenbruck has suggested that "The Book of the Giants" may predate Daniel 7, and he intimates that the *Enoch* text may have influenced the writer of Daniel 7. His argument is based on the lexical overlap of 8 items between Daniel 7 and the Aramaic fragment 4Q530 (which he says represents "The Book of the Giants" at Qumran) and theological and structural complexity. He suggests that the giant's vision is structurally and theologically less complicated than its counterpart in Daniel. See Loren Stuckenbruck, "The Throne-Theophany of the Book of Giants: Some New Light on the Background of Daniel 7," in *The Scrolls and the Scriptures: Qumran Fifty Years After* (ed. Stanley E. Porter and Craig A. Evans; JSPSup 26; Sheffield: Sheffield Academic Press, 1997) 216–19. I am not persuaded that the typology of structural and theological complexity that Stuckenbruck constructs can assist with chronology with that level of specificity. I am equally unpersuaded by the lexical overlap of words such as "throne," "1,000," "book," and "before" and verbs such as "sit down," "arise," and "serve," which serves as the basis of a posited common tradition. These elements are far too common to constitute a shared literary dependency.

66. Emerton, "The Origin of the Son of Man Imagery," 236. Emerton attributes the idea of fragmenting the divine characteristics to Nathaniel Schmidt. Emerton admits that this "seems" to be what Schmidt is saying. In his article, Schmidt notes that the Son of Man figure parallels Marduk as one who is triumphant over the sea. In this, perhaps Schmidt is intimating such a fragmentation of the divine attributes, but he nowhere uses this language. However, Emerton, in his reading of Schmidt, provides the exact wording to portray precisely what I believe is happening in Daniel 7. See Nathaniel Schmidt, "The 'Son of Man' in the Book of Daniel," *JBL* 19 (1900) 27.

eternal dominion. We noted above that riding the clouds was a Baal attribute also used exclusively of Yahweh in the Hebrew Bible—with the exception of Daniel 7.

I am not suggesting a direct borrowing from the Ugaritic traditions, so far removed in time from the Daniel author.[67] Clearly his own imagination and creativity played a role. However, a refracted tradition that is rooted in Canaanite mythology provides the best parallel for what takes place in Daniel's vision.[68] First of all, there is a relationship between the chief god El and the god Baal that involves dominion. Daniel 7 speaks of a deity and another to whom dominion is given. The Baal text from Ugarit speaks of Baal's eternal dominion and his kingship, yet El's status does not appear to be threatened by this. Baal is told to take "eternal dominion" in 1.2 IV 10. Anat tells El that "Baal is our king" in 1.3 V 32. Athirat says the same in 1.4 IV 43. It is clearly El, however, who must approve Baal's request for a house in 1.4 IV 50, a mere seven lines after Athirat's affirmation.

KTU 1.108 may also display this relationship between El and Baal in saying, *il . ytb . b ʿttrt il tpẓ . b hdrʿy*, which Cross translates 'El sits enthroned with Athtarte, El sits as judge with Haddu his Shepherd'.[69] Because the translation of this line is not agreed upon, the support it renders here is tentative.[70] Yet if *rʿy* is to be read as 'his shepherd', the notion of shepherd in this text conveys the role of agent that I am suggesting that the son of man fulfilled for the Ancient of Days. If the form *rʿy* is read 'his friend', there may be a parallel to the use of

---

67. In this sense, Ferch is right to question a direct borrowing. Yet borrowing a refracted motif from an ancient tradition does not necessitate complete overlap with an exemplar of this tradition that predates it by more than a millennium. It should come as no surprise that the use of the El-Baal imagery in Daniel 7 is different in some ways from the portrayal of these gods in the Ugaritic texts. See Ferch, "Daniel 7 and Ugarit," 81, 85.

68. There is sufficient overlap between the texts detailing Ugaritic lore and the later refractions thereof found in Eusebius's work, which is citing the work of Philo Biblius (70–160 C.E.) who in turn is citing someone named Sakkunyaton. While the accuracy of the transmission of these stories may be debated, Philo's Phoenician Sakkunyaton serves as another witness that this ancient lore was remembered centuries later. See Cross, *Canaanite Myth*, 13.

69. Cross, "The 'Olden Gods,'" 76.

70. Margalit suggests that the form *hdrʿy* is a place-name for Edrei in parallel with Ashtaroth, two locales in Bashan. See B. Margulis, "A Ugaritic Psalm (RS 24.252)," *JBL* 89 (1970) 293–94. Yet as Cross points out, *hdrʿy* would be a peculiar transcription of *ʾdrʿy* with a prothetic *ʾalep*. See Cross, "The 'Olden Gods,'" 76–77 n. 14. M. Pope points out that *hd* as a cognomen of Baal is always a B-word in poetic parallelism. Pope supports Margalit's suggestion that these are place-names; see M. Pope, "The Cult of the Dead at Ugarit," in *Ugarit in Retrospect* (ed. G. D. Young; Winona Lake, IN: Eisenbrauns, 1981) 172.

this word in the Hebrew Bible to refer to the close associate of the king (2 Sam 15:37, 16:16; 1 Kgs 4:5). Whether the Ugaritic text should be read 'shepherd' or 'friend', the close connection El has with Baal/Hadu is conveyed by this expression, tentative though the translation may be. Baal's status as El's agent is the best parallel available for the relationship portrayed in Daniel 7. Yahweh has come of age, taking on the elderly traits of the Ugaritic god El, demonstrating a renaissance of mythic imagery within the apocalyptic world of the Daniel author in the late Second Temple period.

To suggest, as Emerton does, that the Ancient of Days is actually El Elyon, who is the chief god over the subordinate Yahweh, the "one like a Son of Man," creates more problems than it solves.[71] First of all, the epithet *Elyon* is ambiguous in the Semitic traditions.[72] Baal is actually called 'Most High' (Ugaritic *ʿly*) in the story of Kirta (1.16 III 6-8) while El is nowhere referred to with this epithet in the extant Ugaritic texts.[73] Second, the likelihood that a postexilic apocalyptic writer would portray Yahweh as anything but the most powerful deity is quite small. Yahweh now takes on the role of aged God in order to confer a sort of agency on this son of man figure who, like Baal, does not supplant the older god but reigns with him. Emerton's position is derived from his insistence that Yahweh must be the son of man because he is said to ride the clouds, an epithet used only of Yahweh in the Hebrew Bible.[74] However, this divine role of "riding the clouds" is evocative of the divine quality conferred on the son of man by Yahweh. Interestingly enough, Emerton notes that, even though El confers kingship on Baal, this move

---

71. Emerton, "Origin of the Son of Man Imagery," 240. Emerton also overstates the Greek evidence that I addressed earlier in the discussion concerning MS 88, the Syro-Hexapla, and P 967. Emerton says that the LXX of Dan 7:13 equates the two entities (son of man and Ancient of Days). Yet the LXX is not monolithic, as the Theodotion text attests. See Emerton, ibid., 238, as well as the discussion of these texts in the earlier part of this chapter.

72. E. E. Elnes and P. D. Miller, "Elyon," in *DDD* 295.

73. Ibid. Of course there are other indications in the Hebrew Bible and the extrabiblical texts of the ancient Near East that do associate El with the title *Elyon*. See Gen 14:18-22, Ps 78:35, and Sefire I A line 11. The text from Kirta cited above reads:

l arṣ mṭr . bʿl	In the land the rain of Baal,
w l šd . mṭr . ʿly	and in the field the rain of the Most High.
nʿm . l arṣ mṭr . bʿl	Good for the land is the rain of Baal,
w l šd . mṭr . ʿly	and for the field the rain of the Most High.

74. Emerton, "Origin of the Son of Man Imagery," 232. It is interesting to note that, even if Emerton is correct that the portrayal here is Yahweh as the one like a son of man before the god Elyon, the concept of a deity's conveying dominion to his agent is still seen.

does not obviate the subordinate status of Baal, who must gain El's permission to have a house.[75] Yet Emerton fails to see that this is a more fitting analogue to the conferral of the divine attributes of "cloud rider" and eternal dominion on this son of man figure. Emerton notes further that "the Ancient of Days must, in Maccabaean times, have been understood to be [Yahweh]."[76] Given his assumption about the date of Daniel 7, his conclusions are quite curious.[77]

It remains to demonstrate the mechanism that brought the Canaanite imagery forward. Emerton posits the enthronement festival, which would have preserved the old traditions in the annual celebration.[78] A less culticly oriented explanation is more likely, however.[79] Our author is simply transmuting refracted ancient traditions seen already in the prophetic writings (see Isa 27:1, 51:9-10).[80] It is not inconceivable that these traditions were retained within certain circles in the postexilic community.[81] The trajectory that I am positing here is similar to the reemergence of cosmic imagery noted by Cross and others.[82] As older mythic notions were recycled into Israel's present during the postexilic period, refractions of older portrayals, long eschewed by the biblical tradents because of their association with heterodox religious expressions, were deemed admissible in their depiction of Yahweh.

It is not, however, as though these mythic components had disappeared in Israel for a time and then suddenly reemerged. It is likely that they were always present in every generation in Israel's past. However, among the circles in which the biblical texts were written and shaped, the Canaanite traditions that were perceived to support certain notions that threatened Yahweh's supremacy were kept at bay. By the Daniel writer's day, the monotheism of Deutero-Isaiah was sufficiently ensconced so as to permit a broader usage of Canaanite mythic elements. The perceived threat that the imagery constituted in the minds of the Israelite tradents of an earlier time was no longer applicable. In order to portray a conferral of some divine attributes on a being who rides the

---

75. Ibid., 239.
76. Ibid.
77. He suggests a 165 B.C.E. date for Daniel 7. See ibid., 225.
78. Ibid., 231.
79. Goldingay (*Daniel*, 151) suggests that the link with the temple cult (i.e., Emerton's thesis) is not likely.
80. Susan Niditch, *The Symbolic Vision in Biblical Tradition* (HSM 30; Chico, CA: Scholars Press, 1980) 202.
81. Goldingay, *Daniel*, 151.
82. Cross, *Canaanite Myth*, 343. See also Paul Hanson, *The Dawn of Apocalyptic* (Philadelphia: Fortress, 1975) 17.

clouds and appears before God, the Daniel writer employs an ancient model known from Canaanite traditions.

This practice of borrowing cosmic imagery to illustrate Yahweh's work in the world is already seen in the depiction of Yahweh as the vanquisher of Rahab in Isa 51:9, for example, and as the slayer of Leviathan in Isa 27:1.[83] Just as the Isaianic authors felt free to use these traditions, the Daniel writer used a different set of these stories to illustrate Yahweh conferring agency upon a subordinate being. This idea of Yahweh as transferring some of his divine attributes to another being likely suggested an analogy to the writer—one known from ancient Canaanite lore. This relationship between Yahweh and his agent evoked a scene also attested in the Ugaritic tablets where El, the father of years, reigns, and so does the youthful warrior Baal. The Daniel writer probably knew a refracted permutation of this scene that is preserved in Ugaritic. Its analogy to the vision he wanted to recount in Daniel 7 suggests that borrowing and applying a model from the ancient tradition occasioned no theological conundrum for him. When applying the model, he endowed Yahweh and the son of man with the relative ages of El and Baal in Canaanite traditions.

Yahweh the Father

Paralleling the reemergence of imagery from Canaanite traditions, a second trajectory of development that led to the portrayal of Yahweh with explicit old-age imagery was the portrayal of him as a father. The use of fatherhood imagery coincided with an inner-Israelite development that allowed for a portrayal of this sort. It is necessary to plot this transformation within the Hebrew Bible to demonstrate the point fully. In what follows, I examine the relevant texts and chart the path that the depiction of God as father took in the course of Israel's traditions.

There is a palpable reluctance in the text of the Hebrew Bible to present Yahweh as a father. Only 18 passages portray him this way or compare him explicitly to a father.[84] In what follows, I examine each of these 18 passages in order to chart the development of the idea of God as father. It is not my intent to provide exhaustive exegesis of these verses, but merely to elucidate the aspect of fatherhood that each one

---

83. See Jeremy M. Hutton, "Isaiah 51:9–11 and the Rhetorical Appropriation and Subversion of Hostile Theologies," *JBL* 126 (2007) 271–303. In this article, Hutton suggests that the reuse of Canaanite mythic themes was "intentional, methodical, and purposeful, performed by human agents with a specific literary and theological purpose in mind."

84. Deut 32:6; 2 Sam 7:14; Jer 3:4, 19; 31:9; Isa 63:16 [2×]; 64:7; Mal 1:6; 2:10; Ps 68:6; 89:27; 103:13; Prov 3:12; 1 Chr 17:13; 22:10; 28:6; 29:10.

portrays. I intend to show that the trajectory of portraying God as old is related to the trajectory of depicting him as a father, so fully understanding the former is dependent on a firm grasp of the latter.

In the discussion of these texts that follows, I have ordered my treatment of them generally along the lines of the thematic portrayal of Yahweh as a father. So I have grouped a few texts that might be late with texts that might be early. Thus, the way each text portrays the fatherhood idea is the primary indicator of its placement in the order.

I begin with Deut 32:6:

> Will you repay this to Yahweh,
> O foolish people, ones without wisdom?
> Is he not your father, the one who created you,
> he who made you and established you?

The verbal form *qānekā* 'one who created you' that appears alongside "father" in the third line bears closer examination. It is from the root *qnh* 'to acquire'.[85] In the Greek translation of this verb, the LXX traditions attest *ektēsato*, which is from the root *ktaomai* 'to acquire'.[86] However, we know from Ugaritic contexts of *qny* with the meaning 'to create'. Athirat is called *qnyt ilm* (1.4 I 23) which surely does not mean 'acquirer of the gods' but, rather, 'creatress [or procreatrix] of the gods'.[87] KTU 1.3 V 9 reads *qny[.w]adn .[bn i]lm* 'creator and lord of the divine sons', in a damaged line around which debate has turned. Mark Smith suggests [ ]n[ ]l[ ] in place of KTU's rendering of this line.[88] CTA reads *qn[-?] (a/w)-n[-lt]*.[89]

That El is the referent in this line is clear from the previous line. Smith's remarks notwithstanding, KTU appears to be the most likely reconstruction. At the very least, the form *qn[ ]* is being applied to El, who is spoken of here as "creator and lord of the divine sons." Furthermore, the 8th-century Phoenician inscription at Karatepe describes El as *qn 'rṣ* 'creator of earth',[90] and the title seen in Karatepe is probably the form behind the Hittite myth *Ilkunirša*.[91] The distinction in meaning

---

85. BDB 888b.
86. LSJ 1001.
87. Cross, *Canaanite Myth*, 15–16.
88. See S. B. Parker, ed., *Ugaritic Narrative Poetry* (hereafter *UNP*; SBLWAW 9; Atlanta: Scholars Press, 1997) 116 and his suggestions on p. 169.
89. CTA numbers this line as 17 (A. Herdner, ed., *Corpus des tablettes en cunéiformes alphabétiques découvertes à Ras Shamra–Ugarit de 1929 à 1939* [hereafter CTA; MRS 10; Paris: Impremerie Nationale, 1963]).
90. See KAI 26A III 18, with the commentary in KAI 2:37.
91. Cross, *Canaanite Myth*, 16. See also M. Pope, "Ups and Downs in El's Amours," *UF* 11 (1979) 707.

is important in that it describes the function of "father" in this verse as either one who creates or one who acquires.

While either meaning is possible, the context of Deut 32:6 tips the balance in favor of the idea of creator-father. In v. 6d, *qnh* is paired with the verb *ʿśh* 'to make', lending strong support for understanding *qnh* here as 'to create'.[92] If Deut 32:6 can be assumed to be an early text, it can be seen as an early witness to God's portrayal as a father and creator in the Hebrew Bible. Smith has suggested that "El was originally the patriarch of both the divine family and many human families in ancient Israel."[93] If true, Deut 32:6 may be an old indication of this status for Yahweh attested at a time when Yahweh and El were considered by many to be the same deity.

In 2 Sam 7:14, Yahweh declares to David regarding David's son:

> I will become a father to him
> and he will become a son to me.
> When he does wrong, I will rebuke him with the staff of men
> and with the stripes of the sons of humankind.

The antecedent of "him" in the first line is the son of David. While the original oracle may have had David's descendants in mind as a collective, the Deuteronomistic editor has made the referent more specifically Solomon.[94] As many have noted, the "fatherhood of God" idea expressed here is not an attempt to deify the king.[95] Nor is it an indication of the practice of sacred marriage in Israel.[96] McCarter suggests that this is adoption language, the purpose of which is "to qualify the king for the patrimony Yahweh wishes to bestow on him."[97] I agree with Böckler that this father-son terminology "begründet ... nicht ontologisch die Legitimaität des irdischen Herrschers sondern umschreibt die wechselseitige Beziehung zwischen Gott und König."[98] As a son is expected to obey

---

92. See also Gen 4:1, where the verb *qnh* is used by Eve when she gives birth to Cain: "I have *created* a man."

93. M. Smith, *The Memoirs of God* (Minneapolis: Fortress, 2004) 156.

94. P. Kyle McCarter, *II Samuel* (AB 9; Garden City, NY: Doubleday, 1984) 205.

95. Ibid., 207. See also Robert P. Gordon, *1 & 2 Samuel* (Exeter: Paternoster, 1986) 239.

96. McCarter, *II Samuel*, 207.

97. Ibid. J. J. M. Roberts provides an interesting critique of assuming that the idea of adoption attends every usage of God calling the king his son. J. J. M. Roberts, "Whose Child Is This? Reflections on the Speaking Voice in Isa 9:5," *HTR* 90 (1997) 126. See the brief discussion of this point below, in the examination of Ps 2:7 at the end of this section.

98. Annette Böckler, *Gott als Vater im Alten Testament* (Gütersloh: Chr. Kaiser / Gütersloher Verlag, 2000) 377.

his father who provides for him, so the king was to follow Yahweh, his fatherly benefactor.

The use of father-son imagery here must also be considered against the backdrop of filial terminology that denoted subordination in political correspondence within the ancient Near East.[99] In the Hebrew Bible, King Ahaz of Judah says he is the son of the Assyrian king Tiglath-pileser III in 2 Kgs 16:7. Among the Mari texts, the vassal ruler Abi-Samar refers to Yadun-Lim of Mari as his "father," and Abi-Samar calls himself "his son."[100] The Amarna texts also indicate this usage. EA 158 begins, "To Tutu, my lord, [my] father. Message of Aziru, your son, your servant."[101] While this diplomatic nuance must be considered, perhaps Keel is correct that limiting the meaning to only the judicial or political is too confining and overlooks the emotional idea of sonship.[102] As ubiquitous and influential as the political idiom was in the ancient Near East, the emotional side of fictive kinship permitted the image of sonship to convey more than these words would have in the present day under the rubric "metaphorical."[103] The important relation that 2 Sam 7:14 bears to Psalm 89 will be addressed after I examine the latter.

In Psalm 89, the psalmist is paraphrasing a "vision," in which Yahweh spoke to his "faithful one." Ps 89:27 reads:

> He will call out to me, "You are my father,
> my God and rock of my salvation."

The Davidic king is the antecedent of "he" in this verse, and as such this line has resonance with 2 Sam 7:14, where God is portrayed as the father of the king. However, placing a firm date on the composition of this psalm is virtually impossible. Unlike 2 Sam 7:14, where the Davidic descendant is called the son of Yahweh, the psalmist attributes this status to David.[104] Perhaps the psalmist is deliberately clarifying the sonship established in 2 Sam 7:14, connecting it to David.[105] Sarna

---

99. J. D. Schloen, *The House of the Father as Fact and Symbol* (Studies in the Archaeology and History of the Levant 2; Winona Lake, IN: Eisenbrauns, 2001) 256.

100. Ibid. See Georges Dossin, *Archives Royales de Mari I: Correspondence de Šamši-Addu et de ses fils* (Paris: Imprimerie Nationale, 1950) 25, no. 2, line 6 on the obverse and line 14 on the reverse.

101. W. Moran, *Amarna Letters* (Baltimore: Johns Hopkins University Press, 1992) 244.

102. Othmar Keel, *The Symbolism of the Biblical World* (trans. T. J. Hallet; Winona Lake, IN: Eisenbrauns, 1997) 248.

103. Jon D. Levenson, *The Death and Resurrection of the Beloved Son* (New Haven, CT: Yale University Press, 1993) 40.

104. Nahum Sarna, "Psalm 89: A Study of Inner Biblical Exegesis," in *Biblical and Other Studies* (ed. Alexander Altmann; Cambridge: Harvard University Press, 1963) 38.

105. Not everyone is in agreement here, however. Mowinckel assumes that the psalm reflects an earlier enthronement festival. See Mowinckel, *He That Cometh*,

and Fishbane have suggested that Psalm 89 is an exegesis of Nathan's oracle.[106] Although it does not seem likely to me, there is the possibility that the psalmist knows of Nathan's oracle through a tradition other than the text of 2 Samuel 7.[107] Whether Psalm 89 is an exegesis of Nathan's oracle as it appears in 2 Samuel 7 or not, it appears quite likely that Psalm 89 is later than 2 Sam 7:14, because it makes clear what is ambiguous in the oracle: David, like his future sons, is also to be seen as a son of God.[108] Psalm 89 fills out the picture of Yahweh's fatherhood over the Davidic House and establishes a critical move in the development of the God-as-father portrayal. I suggest that the oracle, by saying that David's sons will be considered Yahweh's sons, implicitly assumes David to be God's son too, yet leaves it unstated.

The idea, while influenced by the ancient Near Eastern notion of the king's being the son of the deity, is probably rooted in the idea of the suzerain-vassal relationship encoded in the familial terms "father-son."[109] As noted above, political usage of the familial terms is amply attested in the Amarna correspondence as well as that of Mari. The covenantal terminology in the later psalm states clearly, whether the clarification is the intent of the verse or not, the connections to the dynasty's founder.

In a sermon that calls for Judah's repentance through the metaphor of marriage relationships, Jeremiah records the words of Yahweh addressed to the people. The Judahites stand accused of polluting the land, and as a result the rains will be withheld. On the heels of this condemnation, Jer 3:4 reads:

> Did you[110] not just now call to me,
> "My father, friend of my youth are you"?

100–101. Related to Mowinckel's point is Ahlström's assumption that Psalm 89 reflects a northern Canaanite royal liturgy (or perhaps a Jerusalem Jebusite tradition) that David appropriated upon his conquest of Jerusalem. See G. W. Ahlström, *Psalm 89: Eine Liturgie aus dem Ritual des leidenden Königs* (Lund: Ohlssons, 1959) 182–83. Both theories are deeply rooted in assumptions about the liturgical nature of the Psalms. Ahlström's theory has the added liability of an uncritical acceptance of the Jebusite hypothesis.

106. See Michael Fishbane, *Biblical Interpretation in Ancient Israel* (Oxford: Clarendon, 1986) 466; and Sarna, "Psalm 89," 38.

107. Marvin E. Tate, *Psalms 51–100* (WBC 20; Dallas: Word, 1990) 417. A fuller account is found in McKenzie's article, where he attempts to recover an original of Nathan's oracle that served as an independent source for the oracle in 2 Samuel 7 and Psalm 89. Positing a hypothetical text, to my mind, unnecessarily complicates the picture. See John L. McKenzie, "The Dynastic Oracle: II Samuel 7," *Theological Studies* 8 (1947) 195.

108. Böckler, *Gott als Vater*, 377.

109. Schloen, *The House of the Father as Fact and Symbol*, 256–57.

110. Reading 2fs, following the *Qere*.

Here the idea of "father" seems to be closer to a term of endearment because "friend of my youth" is used in Prov 2:17 of the spouse that the wayward woman has abandoned.[111] In fact, it is tempting to posit some sort of nuance for "father" here that indicates intimacy between lovers.[112] The rhetorical juxtaposition between father and lover seen here in vv. 2–3 and then again in 3:19–20 is suggestive. However, the evidence that "father" connotes this nuance is lacking.

McKane suggests that 'friend' here (Hebrew *'allûp*) and in Prov 2:17 in fact means 'teacher'.[113] From this, he understands the term *father* to have a similar connotation, as one who directs and guides.[114] McKane remains open to the idea that teacher here could be "husband *qua* teacher" of a youthful wife.[115] This is essentially Duhm's position as well.[116] It is more likely, however, that our writer is simply mixing his metaphors between father and son, on the one hand, and husband and wife, on the other.[117] There is no need for the kind of text-critical surgery suggested by Holladay that deletes "my father" as a gloss.[118] These mixed metaphors are used again in 3:19–20, as I alluded to above. The portrayal here and its juxtaposition with a more intimate metaphor seek to emphasize the close relationship that Yahweh has sought with his people, be it imagined in a father-child metaphor or that of lovers.[119] This double possibility parallels Hosea's portrayal of Israel as a spouse (Hos 2:21–22) as well as a child (Hos 11:1) of Yahweh.

Jer 3:4 appears to be preexilic, perhaps from the prophet himself.[120] Its use of "father" for God, however, does not seem to be related to the trajectory that I am positing for the imagery's development. The use

---

111. Jack R. Lundbom, *Jeremiah 1–20* (AB 21a; New York: Doubleday, 1999) 303.

112. Note that "father" is what the two women call El in KTU 1.23 43 in a sexually explicit context.

113. William McKane, *Jeremiah* (2 vols.; ICC; Edinburgh: T. & T. Clark, 1996) 2:61.

114. Ibid.

115. Ibid., 62.

116. Bernhard Duhm, *Das Buch Jeremia* (KHC 11; Tübingen: Mohr, 1901) 35.

117. Lundbom, *Jeremiah 1–20*, 317.

118. William L. Holladay, *Jeremiah 1* (Hermeneia; Philadelphia: Fortress, 1986) 115.

119. Ricoeur suggests that, "by this strange mutual contamination of the two kinship figures, the shell of literality of the image is broken and the symbol is liberated. A father who is a spouse is no longer a progenitor (begetter), . . . love, solitude, and pity carry him beyond domination and severity." Paul Ricoeur, "Fatherhood: From Phantasm to Symbol," in *The Conflict of Interpretations* (ed. Don Ihde; Evanston, IL: Northwestern University Press, 1974) 489.

120. McKane, *Jeremiah*, 1:xc. Duhm argues that it is at least prior to the Deuteronomistic reform. See Duhm, *Das Buch Jeremia*, 33. Although Holladay suggests that this verse may be directly from Jeremiah, perhaps early in his ministry (he suggests

here, whether it is a term of endearment or more closely aligned with the wisdom notion of "father" as teacher of his "son," the pupil, may only be tangentially related to the development. Thus, it should perhaps be grouped with the other attestations of metaphorical or comparative uses of fatherhood for God. However, it may be expanding the fatherly side of the picture that is implicit in Hosea, where Israel is imagined as a child. It can certainly be argued that Yahweh is functioning as a father in Hosea 11, even though the word *father* is not used of him there.

Later in this chapter, a promise of reunification is given to Judah and Israel. In this context, Jer 3:19 reads:

> And I (God) said, "Surely I will set you among the sons,
> and I will give you a desirous land, an inheritance that is most glorious of the nations."
> I said, "You will call me 'my father,'
> and you will not turn away from [walking] behind me."

Connecting sonship with the distribution of an inheritance is reminiscent of Deut 32:8, which follows the fatherhood portrayal in Deut 32:6, discussed above. The aspect of fatherhood put forward here seems to be the idea of passing on an inheritance, giving good land, the latter idea being picked up again in Jer 31:12–14. The "you" here is feminine, continuing the marriage motif introduced earlier in the chapter. The thrust of the fatherhood component here is a metaphorical expression intended to portray the extension of inheritance rights to someone who did not normally receive them[121]—a wayward wife. The *Qere*'s second-feminine singular forms are correct here when the text depicts the woman addressing God as father. The significance of her calling him father in this context is that it will guarantee her an inheritance normally reserved for sons.[122] This is what the previous line means by setting her among the sons. Now she is pronounced an heir, as are the sons.[123]

---

prior to 609 B.C.E.) he later identifies "my father" as a gloss. See W. L. Holladay, *Jeremiah 2* (Hermeneia; Minneapolis: Fortress, 1989) 122.

121. Holladay, *Jeremiah 1*, 122.

122. There are also examples of this arrangement whereby a woman calls someone "father" to guarantee an inheritance in a will at Emar. See John Huehnergard, "Biblical Notes on Some New Akkadian Texts from Emar (Syria)," *CBQ* 47 (1985) 430.

123. The sons probably appear here as a cipher for the abstract notion of the person who normally inherits a father's inheritance. There is no reason to insist that they represent the nations, as argued by Carroll. See Robert P. Carroll, *Jeremiah* (OTL; Philadelphia: Westminster, 1986) 152. Yet the possible resonance with Deut 32:8, where nations receive inheritance from a deity, presents an interesting potential connection.

The use of 'friend' (Hebrew *'allûp*) in v. 4 has an interesting parallel with another word rendered 'friend' (Hebrew *rēʿa*) in v. 20. Note that in each verse, the word for 'friend' follows the reference to God as father in both verses, although the latter, *rēʿa*, is not as close in proximity. The two appear as parallel synonyms in Mic 7:5 for someone in whom one places trust. As in Jer 3:4, the metaphors here are mixed between Yahweh as father to his sons and Yahweh as husband to his wife.

Holladay considers Jer 3:19 to have been included in the first dictated scroll of Jeremiah, positing a late-7th-century date.[124] If this date is accepted, this use of father for God represents the earliest usage of this sort in Jeremiah and the only remaining preexilic attestation along the trajectory besides Deut 32:6, 2 Sam 7:14, Ps 89:27, and perhaps Job 31:15. Böckler assumes that this text is later, however, suggesting that its imagery betrays a connection to an exilic preacher.[125] She points to the fact that this text, which is more focused on the giving of the land, departs from the older tradition, which centers on the exodus and the wilderness wanderings.[126] For Böckler, the concept of God as one who forgives bespeaks an exilic date as well.[127] Because treaty terminology, which employed father-son titles to denote the suzerain and vassal, was well ensconced in the Assyrian period, Jeremiah's portrayal of God as father is not too surprising. 2 Kgs 16:7 demonstrates that this terminology was known in Judah in Tiglath-pileser III's day. The first-person singular pronoun in the phrase "my father" is an interesting expression when paired with the later "our father" expression seen in Isaiah 63–64.

We now turn to Jeremiah 31, where Yahweh promises to gather the people from the farthest parts of the earth and return them to the land of Israel. Jer 31:9 reads:

> With weeping they entered, and with compassion I carried them.
> I made them walk along wadis of water,
> in a straight path in which they would not stumble,
> because I have become a father to Israel
> and Ephraim is my firstborn.

---

124. Holladay, *Jeremiah 1*, 3. Duhm grants this as well. See Duhm, *Das Buch Jeremia*, 41.
125. Böckler, *Gott als Vater*, 383.
126. Ibid., 315.
127. Ibid., 387. Of course, positing such a late date for this text allows Böckler to support her thesis that the idea of God as father is transformed in the exile in the absence of a Davidic monarch. If Jer 3:19 is preexilic, her position is weakened, because this would be testimony for God's portrayal as father for all his people prior to the demise of the Judahite monarchy.

The section of this verse describing fatherhood has been considered to originate with the prophet himself.[128] Yet some say it originated late in the exile.[129] The appearance of "Ephraim" leads many to posit an early date, but this could easily be a late addition. The strong affinity with Deutero-Isaiah supports a later date for this verse.[130] For Böckler, this verse completes the transformation between God's being the father of the Davidic monarchs to being father of the people as a whole.[131] The focus here is clearly on the compassionate ideal of a father who brings comfort to a troubled child,[132] provides sustenance (indicated by the "wadis of water") and helps the child to live an upright life. The idea of life as walking on a path has already been intimated in 3:19 in the phrase "you will not turn away from behind me," where the image is probably of a father leading a child.

The next text, Isa 63:16, appears in a context of Judah's appealing to Yahweh for his attention and compassion. It reads:

> For you are our father.
> For Abraham did not know us
> and Israel did not recognize us.[133]
> You, Yahweh, are our father, our redeemer; from long ago is your name.

---

128. John Bright, *Jeremiah* (AB 21; Garden City, NY: Doubleday, 1965) 281. Bright assumed that vv. 7–14 were from Jeremiah in their entirety. Duhm believed that 9b was a Jeremiah fragment inserted in later material. See Duhm, *Das Buch Jeremia*, 245.

129. E. W. Nicholson, *Jeremiah 26–52* (CBC; Cambridge: Cambridge University Press, 1975) 63. Kilpp says the text is a *Mosaikbild* created out of mostly exilic sources. See Nelson Kilpp, *Niederreißen und aufbauen: Das Verhältnis von Heilsverheißung und Unheilsverkündigung bei Jeremia und im Jeremiahbuch* (Biblisch-theologische Studien 13; Neukirchen-Vluyn: Neukirchener Verlag, 1990) 144. McKane appears to accept this date as well. See McKane, *Jeremiah*, 2:793.

130. McKane, *Jeremiah*, 2:793. See also Duhm, *Das Buch Jeremia*, 246; and Böckler, *Gott als Vater*, 274.

131. Ibid, 275.

132. The pair of terms expressed in the phrase "with weeping they entered and with compassion I carried them" cannot be joyous, as Holladay suggests (following Qimḥi and Jerome). They are employed in Jer 3:21 as a response to "perverting their ways." See Holladay, *Jeremiah 2*, 185.

133. All the major ancient translations of the MT, supported by 1QIsa^a, read a perfect or suffix conjugation of the verb here. The MT's imperfect or prefix conjugation attestation was probably occasioned by the mistaken assumption that the *yod* in the previous verb, *yĕdāʿānû*, was marking the prefix conjugation as well as the first letter of the verbal root. The translation here reflects the emendation (emend to *hikkîrānû*) in favor of the ancient versions and 1QIsa^a.

In Isaiah 63–64, we encounter three occasions on which Yahweh is expressly called "our father"—yet another feature that sets Third Isaiah apart from the other two classical divisions first suggested by Duhm. This postexilic formulation is an important step in the transition between the early, infrequent depiction of God as father and its acceptance in the later periods. This theological uniqueness of Third Isaiah may be related to developments in the postexilic community that involved the renaissance of imagery associated with Canaanite religion.[134] In 63:16, both times the locution is "our father," which heightens the personal tone of the title. The thrust of God's portrayal as "our father" in this part of Isaiah is his living presence juxtaposed with the patriarchs.[135] As this present living father, Yahweh knows his people and their needs and desires.

The second text from Third Isaiah is Isa 64:7[8]. It follows a confession of sin and the people's neglect of Yahweh. It reads:

> And now, Yahweh, you are our father,
> we are the clay and you are our potter,
> and all of us are the work of your hand.

The idea of the father here as a "maker," specifically as a potter, carries a slightly different nuance (maker versus redeemer) from what is seen in 63:16.[136] It has an interesting resonance with Deut 32:6's notion of father-creator.

The book of Malachi begins with affirmations of God's love for Israel. It moves quickly, however, to addressing sins among his people. Mal 1:6a reads:

> A son honors a father and a servant [does so to] his lord.
> If I am a father, where is my honor?
> If I am a lord, where is the respect due me?

Despite the rhetorical dress that expresses these lines in the form of a conditional sentence, Malachi's words assume that the idea of God as father is accepted by his audience. This acceptance demonstrates an affirmation of the depiction of God as a father that is not surprising among these late texts of the Hebrew Bible, texts that arise from the postexilic period (late 6th century and later). While many of the texts we have seen thus far present Yahweh as doing things for Israel, this passage

---

134. Hanson, *Dawn of Apocalyptic*, 17.
135. See Claus Westermann, *Isaiah 40–66* (trans. David M. C. Stalker; OTL; Philadelphia: Westminster, 1969) 393.
136. Westermann (ibid., 397) argues that this line is a corrective designed to obviate any misconception concerning God's physical fatherhood.

plays on the notion of "father" as someone who deserves the respect of his children, as the Decalogue demands (Exod 20:12, Deut 5:16).

Later in this same book, Malachi sets forth an indictment of the priests for the way they have treated the people. Mal 2:10a reads:

> Is there not one father of us all?
> Has not one God created us?

This statement of solidarity becomes the basis for his condemnation of this priestly ill-treatment of fellow Israelites. The juxtaposition of father and creator here is reminiscent of Deut 32:6, Job 31:15, and Isa 64:7.[137] The portrayal of God as father in 1:6a and 2:10a has an interesting connection with the last verse of the book, which says that Elijah will come on the day of Yahweh and turn the hearts of fathers to their children and the hearts of children to their fathers.[138] Portraying Yahweh as a father earlier in the book adumbrates the kind of relationship he seeks from his people and the reconciliation he desires. Note again the first-person-plural pronominal suffix "us," which resonates with Isa 63:16 and 64:7, expressing in similar ways a collective understanding of Yahweh as being the father of "all of us."

We now turn to 1 Chr 17:13, a parallel account of Nathan's words to David in 2 Samuel 7. 1 Chr 17:13 reads:

> I will become a father to him and he will become a son to me, and I will not remove my love from him as I did from the one who was before you.

The first eight words of the original Hebrew in 1 Chr 17:13 are a verbatim rendering of the first words of 2 Sam 7:14, and they have long been assumed to be an adoption formula.[139] Yet as we will see in our discussion of Psalm 2 below, we need not exclude the metaphor of true,

---

137. Jer 2:27 provides a subtle equation of the status of father and creator, when Jeremiah derides the people for idolatry, saying, "Who says to a tree, 'you are my father' and to a stone, 'you gave me birth'?" Here it is clear that the people were ascribing fatherhood to their object of worship, and so even heterodox worship practice is illustrative of equating father and creator.

138. Although the significance of Malachi's usage of *ʾēl* for Yahweh here cannot be known with certainty, it is an interesting choice, given El's paternal portrayal in the Ugaritic texts. Malachi uses *ʾēl* for God in 1:9, where he associates the name with graciousness, another trait attested of El. This delineation cannot be pressed far, because he also uses the epithet *ʾĕlōhîm* for God as a dispenser of justice (2:17) one to be served (3:14, 18) and tested (3:15), and as the *nomen rectum* in the phrase 'offspring of God' (*zeraʿ ʾĕlōhîm*, 2:15).

139. Sarah Japhet, *I and II Chronicles* (OTL; Louisville, KY: Westminster John Knox, 1993) 334.

natural parentage here, as Roberts notes.[140] The remaining words are a paraphrase of 2 Sam 7:15. As in the DH, the focus of fatherhood is on the offspring of David rather than the king himself. An interesting omission in this text is the sentence, "When he does wrong, I will discipline him," found in 2 Sam 7:15. Whatever the explanation for the Chronicler's omission of this phrase,[141] the substantive point for my purposes is that the aspect of fatherhood as a figure of discipline is missing here. Fatherhood and "love" are linked, but the nuance of the DH is not present. Note that, like the DH, the Chronicler views God as the father of the Davidic lineage in perpetuity.

In 1 Chronicles 22, David is speaking to his son Solomon regarding the building of the temple. In 1 Chr 22:8, David relays the words of Yahweh to his son concerning the justification of and the instruction for Solomon's building project. Concerning Solomon, 1 Chr 22:10 reads:

> He will build a house for my name and he will become a son to me, and I will become a father to him. I will establish the throne of his reign over Israel forever.

As noted above, the phrase regarding "becoming a father and becoming a son" has long been assumed to be an adoption formula. Yet Roberts's caveat cited in the discussion of 1 Chr 17:13 is applicable here as well. We will examine the details of this argument shortly. The political terminology of father and son as covenantal terms discussed in the section on Jer 3:19 is likely applicable here.

A further discussion of the temple's construction appears in 1 Chronicles 28. David, again, speaks of Yahweh's words to him regarding his son Solomon. 1 Chr 28:6 reads:

> He said to me, "Solomon, your son, is the one who will build my house and my courts, for I have chosen him for myself to be a son, and I will become a father for him."

Once again the stress is on God as father of the Davidic king alone, and the observation above about the political terminology is relevant for this text as well.

In 1 Chronicles 29 David, addressing the assembly of Israel's officials, speaks yet again of Solomon's task of building the temple. 1 Chr 29:10 reads:

---

140. Roberts, "Whose Child Is This?" 126.
141. Japhet (*I and II Chronicles*, 334) says it is to avoid addressing Solomon's sins, as described in 1 Kings 11, and to conform to the outlook of the Deuteronomistic redaction of 1 Kings, which sees God's promises as conditional.

David blessed Yahweh before all the congregation and David said, "Blessed are you Yahweh, God of Israel, our father, from the eternal past unto eternity."

The use of "our father" here is ambiguous with regard to its antecedent—God or Israel—the Masoretic notation notwithstanding. While one could argue that a similar use in 1 Chr 29:18 and 29:20 (where the plural "fathers" makes it clear that the referents are the patriarchs) suggests that "father" in v. 10 refers to Israel *qua* Jacob the patriarch, the post-exilic idea of God as "our father" is attested in Isa 63:16 and 64:7. If it is the former, the text does not merit our attention. Yet if it is the latter, the Chronicler departs from the adoption motif paralleled in the DH and assumes the expression that had become current in his day. In this case, his placement of "*our* father" on the lips of David retrojects this postexilic locution onto the eponymous founder of the dynasty. Instead of the portrayal of God as the father of the Davidic monarchs, as seen in preexilic texts, here David addresses the deity as if he has always been viewed as he was in the postexilic period—as *our* father. Commentators are mixed in their assessments of the antecedent.[142] The later reference to "fathers" as patriarchs in vv. 18 and 20 leads me to believe that the Masoretes are correct in their punctuation: the antecedent of "father" should be Israel, the eponymous ancestor, rather than God.[143]

The remaining three texts, from Psalms and Proverbs, are not as central to the line of development that I am suggesting. Their chronological provenance is, furthermore, difficult to assess. In light of these two facts, I have decided to place them at the end of this group of texts.

In a praise of Yahweh for his power, Ps 68:6 reads:

Father of the fatherless and judge of the widows is God in his holy dwelling.

Fatherhood in this portrayal is closer to a family representative who guarantees the rights of his dependents.[144] On several occasions, Yahweh

---

142. While he translates the line 'Blessed are you Yahweh, our father, the God of Israel', Braun does not provide sufficient argumentation for his opinion, merely noting the occurrences in Isaiah 63 and 64. See Roddy Braun, *1 Chronicles* (WBC 14; Waco, TX: Word, 1986) 285. Japhet says that it describes Jacob, their forefather. See Japhet, *I and II Chronicles*, 509. Curiously, Böckler omits analysis of this text, although she lists it in one footnote in a group of texts under the heading "Gott als Vater." See Böckler, *Gott als Vater*, 30 n. 77.

143. Gottfried Vanoni, *"Du bist doch unser Vater" (Jes 63,16): Zur Gottesvorstellung des Ersten Testaments* (Stuttgarter Bibelstudien 159; Stuttgart: Katholisches Bibelwerk, 1995) 46.

144. Böckler, *Gott als Vater*, 386.

says that he is the protector of these particularly vulnerable groups (Jer 49:11; Hos 14:4; Mal 3:5; Ps 10:14, 17–18; 146:9; Prov 15:25).

Ps 103:13 reads:

> As a father has compassion for his children, so Yahweh has compassion for those who fear him.

This comparison of Yahweh with a father presents a more intimate portrayal of fatherhood than does Ps 68:6. Here the passage employs fatherhood as a simile rather than directly claiming that Yahweh is a father. While this figurative use of fatherhood surely contributed to the full acceptance of the more direct references to God as father that are seen later, it is difficult to locate this verse on this line of development.[145]

Prov 3:12 reads:

> For Yahweh disciplines the one he loves; and as a father does the son who is favored.

There is a text-critical problem here with the final phrase, turning on the form *ûkĕʾāb*. The LXX has *mastigoi* 'flogs', which represents *ûkĕʾāb* as a verbal form,[146] either by emending the initial *waw* to *yod* or simply inserting a *yod* or retaining the consonantal text and suggesting that the *kʾb* be understood as a participle or suffix conjugation.[147] It is also possible that a verbal form of *kʾb* fell out by haplography.[148] Although emending the text in favor of the LXX does result in a nice chiasm with the first stich, the lack of any similar use of the verb *kʾb* in the Hebrew Bible favors the MT.[149] The portrayal of God as a father in this text is a simile, in that God is one who, like a father, disciplines.

Now that the relevant texts have been examined in detail, I want to plot the trajectory of development that I see at work here. Annette Böckler's work has been a helpful source for the development of "God

---

145. A reversal of this theme is seen in Hos 1:6, where Yahweh tells the prophet to name his child "Not Loved," which becomes a metaphor for God's relationship with his people Israel. See Alfred Jepsen, "Gnade und Barmherzigkeit im Alten Testament," *Kerygma und Dogma* 7 (1961) 263.

146. William McKane, *Proverbs* (OTL; Philadelphia: Westminster, 1970) 294.

147. This reading is suggested by Rabbi Eliezer ben Jacob in the Midrash on Ps 94:2, where the pointing *wĕkĕʾēb* (D stem, suffix conjugation) is given. The verb *kʾb* is not otherwise attested in the D stem, however. See Michael Fox, *Proverbs 1–9* (AB 18A; New York: Doubleday, 2000) 379.

148. Ibid., 152.

149. Clifford says that appeal to Job 5:18 in support of emendation is not relevant because it refers to injuring rather than discipline. Yet discipline is precisely what is intended in Job 5:18, as the previous verbs clearly indicate. See R. J. Clifford, *Proverbs* (OTL; Louisville, KY: Westminster John Knox, 1999) 50. Even so, the MT of Prov 3:12 has the more likely reading.

as father" imagery, and the influence of her work will be seen in my own opinion of the process. Sorting out the relative dates of these references to Yahweh as a father in these texts is a difficult undertaking. The order in which I have discussed these biblical passages indicates my assumptions about their relative dating. Yet, as I noted above, plausible arguments could be set forth to suggest a different chronological arrangement. Establishing the earliest text among this collection is the most difficult. Although I have suggested that Deut 32:6 holds this position, many will remain unpersuaded that this is possible. I make no claim that all of Deuteronomy 32 is older than all of the texts I have discussed above.[150] The portrayal of Yahweh in v. 6 as a father and creator does seem to me to derive from an earlier time. Some, no doubt, could suggest that v. 6 belongs with the other texts that portray Yahweh similarly (Isa 64:7 and Mal 2:10). Even so, I am persuaded that the combined evidence of the syntax of the poetry, the archaic vocabulary, and the portrayal of Yahweh in v. 8, especially in light of the texts of the LXX and the Dead Sea Scrolls 4QDeut^q and 4QDeut^j, indicate an older provenance.[151]

Therefore, Deut 32:6, in my opinion, is the earliest text in this group, portraying Yahweh in much the same way as El is seen at Ugarit. He is father and creator. So here we have the earliest biblical indication of Yahweh imagined as a father. Although this sort of understanding could be tolerated early in Israel's history, as Yahweh began to take on the conflated imagery used of El and Baal, fatherhood (like old-age features) was overshadowed by images of a warrior or storm god in the Iron Age. Other "national" gods from the ancient Near East were also viewed as warriors who protected their people in battle. The 9th-century Mesha Stela depicts the Moabite god Chemosh in this manner.[152] The Assyrian god Ashur is similarly portrayed.[153]

---

150. For an overview of the discussion of Deuteronomy 32's date, see Paul Sanders, *The Provenance of Deuteronomy 32* (Leiden: Brill, 1996) 1–98, especially pp. 96–98. For a briefer overview, see Böckler, *Gott als Vater*, 293–96.

151. For the translation of v. 8 in the MT, "he [the Most High] established the boundaries of the peoples according to the number of the sons of Israel," the LXX attests 'angels of God', which likely mirrors the attestation of 4QDeut^q, 'sons of God [El]', or of 4QDeut^j, 'sons of God [Elohim]'. The MT likely constitutes a later emendation by scribes who were bothered by the potential polytheistic implications seen in the traditions preserved in the LXX and the two Qumran scrolls. See Emanuel Tov, *Textual Criticism of the Hebrew Bible* (Minneapolis: Fortress, 1992) 269.

152. The name *Chemosh* may even mean 'conqueror' or 'subduer'. See Hans-Peter Müller, "Chemosh," *DDD* 187.

153. Thus Shalmaneser III confidently proceeded against an Aramean-Palestinian coalition in the sixth year of his reign: "upon the (oracle-) command of Ashur, the great lord, my lord, I fought with them (and) inflicted a defeat upon them" (from

For one thing, Yahweh could not be portrayed within the human life cycle due to avoiding portraying him in old age, which might imply weakness. Furthermore, Yahweh's traits that paralleled Baal could not partake of fatherhood imagery, because this feature was not compatible with the youthful warrior epitomized by Baal. Besides, Baal is not called "father" at Ugarit.[154] Admittedly, the abstract idea of *fatherhood* does not immediately connote old age. Yet, it probably did mark an objectifiable point in human development that denoted a status approaching the status of *zāqēn*. Futhermore, given the presumed marriage patterns, and the average life expectancy of males in Syria-Palestine, fatherhood would probably not have predated by much the status achieved with the demarcation of *zāqēn*. Certainly, the details can be debated, as I have suggested in the first chapter. The customary picture of an old father/creator god that is also seen in the Ugaritic El and of Yahweh in Deut 32:6 and similarly in Job 31:15 yielded to the more expedient depiction of the warrior imagery in the Iron Age.

The next point along the trajectory is seen in 2 Sam 7:14, where Yahweh says the Davidide will be called his son. This transformation is influenced by the use of "son" to denote subordination seen in diplomatic correspondence in biblical texts as well as among the Mari letters and Amarna correspondence. This Israelite permutation of the *sonship* concept in the greater ancient Near Eastern milieu demonstrates the transformation of God as the father of the Davidic ruler, namely, Solomon. Refractions of this development are seen in Ps 89:27, where the sonship is specifically applied to David, making explicit what is merely implied in Nathan's oracle in 2 Samuel 7. This preexilic psalm shows David, the monarchy's eponymous founder, in the special relationship that Yahweh had with this ruling line as its divine father. Though the use of the father-son relationship is metaphorical, it transcends the limitations that we would perhaps place upon a portrayal referred to as "metaphorical." So the emotional side cannot be disconnected in a world where fictive kinship was more easily conceived.[155]

A crucial stage in this trajectory is one that I have not fully addressed specifically in the above texts: texts where Israel or the king is imagined

---

the Black Obelisk inscription, trans. A. Leo Oppenheim, *ANET* 279). Likewise, in his seventh year, Sargon II crushed rebel Arabs "upon a trust (-inspiring oracle given by) my lord Ashur" (annalistic inscription, trans A. Leo Oppenheim, *ANET* 286). Sennacherib also credited the success of his third campaign, directed against Ḫatti, to "the awe-inspiring splendor of the 'weapon' of Ashur, my lord" ("Oriental Institute Prism," trans. A. Leo Oppenheim, *ANET* 287–88).

154. Böckler, *Gott als Vater*, 382.
155. Keel, *The Symbolism of the Biblical World*, 248.

as a child of Yahweh, even though Yahweh is not specifically called "father." Ps 2:7 depicts God as speaking of his king, presumably the Davidide, whom he has set on his holy hill. He says to the king, "You are my son; today I have begotten you." Often commentators, pointing to the word "today," assume that this psalm employs an adoption formula.[156] J. J. M. Roberts has noted that the insistence that this is an adoption formula is based on specious arguments.[157] Roberts suggests that the language of literal birth be taken seriously and that this language need not have implied any similarity between Yahweh and Egyptian gods, who were said to give birth physically to kings.[158] Roberts's criticism is accurate, and his suggestion that aspects of physical fatherhood can be interpreted metaphorically with the same ease as aspects of adoptive fatherhood rings true.[159] Though Yahweh is not specifically addressed as a father in this verse, the physicality of fatherhood in Ps 2:7 adds a nuance to the depiction of God as father of the Davidic king established in Psalm 89.

Hos 11:1-3 and Exod 4:22 are two other critical citations where paternal portrayals are latent examples that eventuate in expressly imagining Yahweh as a father of the people as a whole. While the date of Exod 4:22 is debated, Hos 11:1-3 is certainly preexilic,[160] and as such represents an early attestation of Israel as a collective being portrayed as Yahweh's son. The fact that Yahweh is not specifically given the title *father* in these texts, especially if Exod 4:22 is as early as Hosea 11, is telling of the hesitant sensibility with which the writers/editors approached this imagery. It seems almost as though Hosea 11 reflects an intermediate stage in which the imagery of fatherhood could be used but not the title *father* itself.

The next text in the trajectory, Jer 3:4, is a bit perplexing because the meaning of father therein is not immediately evident. I suggested above that the word *father* is used as a term of endearment in parallel

---

156. See, for example, Artur Weiser, *Psalms* (trans. H. Hartwell; OTL; Philadelphia: Westminster, 1962) 113. H. J. Boecker says that, even though adoption was unknown in the legal system of biblical Israel, Ps 2:7 and 2 Sam 7:14 are adoption formulas. See Hans Jochen Boecker, "Anmerkungen zur Adoption im Alten Testament," *ZAW* 86 (1974) 88.

157. Roberts, "Whose Child Is This?" 126. Roberts cites Shalom Paul, who notes the meager evidence of adoption in the Hebrew Bible. See Shalom Paul, "Adoption Formulae: A Study of Cuneiform and Biblical Legal Clauses," *Maarav* 2 (1979–80) 173–85.

158. Roberts, "Whose Child Is This?" 126.
159. Ibid.
160. A. A. Macintosh, *Hosea* (ICC; Edinburgh: T. & T. Clark, 1997) lxxiii.

with 'friend' (*'allûp*) and the context suggests a title used of a spouse or lover. Jer 3:4 is a preexilic text, and it may parallel the dual imagery used in Hosea of Israel as spouse and child of Yahweh.

The more substantive move is seen in Jer 3:19, in which Yahweh says that Israel will call him "my father," and Israel is imagined as a wife who is legally made an heir. As the Judahite kingdom shrinks toward the extinction realized in 586 B.C.E., the fatherhood of God is expanded from the earlier notion of father of the Davidide ruler to father of the nation. The diffusion of Assyrian treaty terminology that employs fatherhood imagery to indicate the suzerain could have also played a role in the development in Jeremiah's day. Because the suzerain is the "father," and Yahweh was believed to be Israel's suzerain, it would naturally follow that Israel's God was a father. 2 Kgs 16:7 is a clear indication of the use of treaty terminology in Israel and Judah.

Jer 31:9, an exilic text, represents the completion of the picture of Israel as the child of Yahweh, its father. The imagery of compassionate caregiver intimated in Hosea 11 without the explicit title of *father* given to Yahweh is now made complete. The proclamation used in Nathan's oracle to denote the Davidide's status is used here to similar effect. Now, however, it is the nation as a whole that has become the child.

The postexilic permutation of the fatherhood-of-God imagery is epitomized in three locations in Isaiah 63–64, possibly four if we include 1 Chr 29:10. Yahweh is now depicted as "our father" in Isa 63:16 (2×) and 64:7. The postexilic expressions regenerate the viewpoint of Deuteronomy 32 and the greater Canaanite environment. Isa 64:7 also reconstructs the concept of *God as maker* with the imagery of the potter with the clay, again reminiscent of the idiom of Deut 32:6 with Yahweh as the creator.

The trajectory continues into Malachi, where Yahweh's fatherhood is so ensconced in the postexilic community it can now be used to great rhetorical effect as the basis of a conditional sentence. Yahweh says, "If I am a father, where is my honor?" As in Isa 64:7, Mal 2:10 speaks of God as "our creator," yet again demonstrating the reimagined depiction of Yahweh in Deut 32:6.

At this point, the resuscitation of the earlier portrayal has come full circle. Although not unimportant, less significant is the use of fatherhood as a comparison for Yahweh's attributes. I consider Ps 68:6, 103:13, and Prov 3:12 to be in this category and so omit them from the direct line of development that I am suggesting for the Hebrew Bible.[161] Again, not irrelevant but less demonstrative are the occurrences in the

---

161. This is Böckler's position as well. See Böckler, *Gott als Vater*, 385.

Chronicler's work. The remaining texts clearly show the pattern of development along my posited trajectory. Yahweh as father, so reminiscent of El's depiction at Ugarit and considered orthodox by Israel's earliest poets, reemerges into the tradents' circles, even though it has never fully disappeared from the popular imagination, as I will demonstrate in the remainder of this chapter.

Yahweh as Father: The Onomastic Evidence

Now that I have plotted a trajectory of development using the texts of the Hebrew Bible that depict God as father, I want to examine that trajectory in the light of the onomastic evidence. When seeking to determine the various ways in which Israel's God was portrayed, we will find that analyzing the names of people within the biblical texts as well as names from epigraphic sources can be quite helpful. Often names provide a more candid look into the common assumptions among everyday people in ancient Israel, as opposed to the assumptions held by the individuals writing the texts gathered in the Hebrew Bible. Personal names containing the theophoric element "Baal" are indicative of a candid view that proved too heterodox for some of the biblical tradents, who substituted the word *bōšet* 'shame' for this element to mark their displeasure. The name *Mephibosheth* is a good example here (2 Sam 4:4,[162] 21:8). Yet some Baal-names persisted in the text and provide a glimpse into the sensibilities of people in ancient Israel prior to the 9th-century condemnation of Baal adherents embodied in the tales of the prophets Elijah and Elisha.

An examination of personal names is also helpful for understanding the development of God as father, since the names may provide a window into the uncensored quotidian world of ancient Israel. Yet caution is in order when using names to determine points of view among ancient Israelites. While biblical sentence-names have meanings, in actual usage, personal names throughout the ancient Near East may not have retained their literal significance as they were handed down from generation to generation, or across generations, as in cases of papponymy. With this caveat in mind, in what follows I examine four names in the Hebrew Bible as well as names from extrabiblical sources that combine the word *father* with a theophoric element. As Böckler points out, it is not clear from the names precisely what is meant by the use of "father."[163] As we have seen above, "father" can connote sovereign or suzerain, defender of rights, or leader, as well as biological father. I will address these polyvalent possibilities after I examine each name.

---

162. The Lucianic tradition of the LXX gives his name as *Memphibaal*.
163. Böckler, *Gott als Vater*, 165.

We begin with Eliab, a name given to six people in the Hebrew Bible. One of these individuals is a leader in the tribe of Zebulun (Num 1:9; 2:7; 7:24, 29; and 10:16). Another is the father of Dathan and Abiram (Num 16:1, 12; 26:8; Deut 11:6) and still another is the son of Jesse (1 Sam 16:6; 17:13, 28 [2×]; 1 Chr 2:13; 2 Chr 11:18). The remaining three only appear in the Chronicler's work: a descendant of Kohath, an ancestor of Samuel (1 Chr 6:12); a Levite (1 Chr 15:18, 20; 16:5); and a Gadite, one of David's officers (1 Chr 12:10). There are also attestations of this name outside the Bible, as we will see below.[164]

Central for my purposes is to determine what the name Eliab meant. That is, does the name Eliab express the phrase "my God is a father," or is the *î* in the name something other than a first-person-singular pronominal suffix? One may suggest that the *î* is merely an anaptyctic vowel employed to resolve a consonantal cluster among two monosyllabic nouns. This would permit the translation 'El is a father', a name (that is, *ilib*) that appears among the deity lists in the Ugaritic corpus (see KTU 1.47 2; 1.109 12; 1.118 1; and 1.148 23). Yet there are several examples of names attested in the epigraphic sources where the theophoric element *ʾl* is used with another monosyllabic noun, such as *ʿz* 'strength' (Avigad *HB* #17+18, ##72–74, 90) or *ṣr* 'rock' (Beersheba 2:1) without any orthographic indication of an anaptyctic vowel.[165] Of course, this does not mean that an anaptyctic vowel was not there. This sort of scribal practice is seen in Ugaritic where the first-person-singular pronominal suffix is not indicated in the orthography but is clearly present in the context.[166] So while we cannot rule out the possibility that the *î* is only an anaptyctic vowel, it seems more likely that it is a pronominal suffix.[167] It seems best, therefore, to read this name 'my god is a father'.[168] The more traditional understanding of this name would be 'the [divine] father is my god'.

---

164. This is true despite Böckler's insistence to the contrary. See ibid., 79.

165. Nahman Avigad, *Hebrew Bullae from the Time of Jeremiah* (Jerusalem: Israel Exploration Society, 1986); S. Gogel, *Grammar of Epigraphic Hebrew* (Resources for Biblical Study 23; Atlanta: Scholars Press, 1998) 403.

166. Josef Tropper, *Ugaritische Grammatik* (AOAT 273; Münster: Ugarit-Verlag, 2000) 215. See his example (KTU 1.3 IV 54) which is actually quite close to the discussion here. Tropper notes that this phenomenon is seen in poetry and prose.

167. Scott Layton suggests this, noting the high frequency of pronominal suffixes in personal names, especially in the initial element of the compound. See Scott Layton, *Archaic Features of Canaanite Personal Names in the Hebrew Bible* (HSM 47; Atlanta: Scholars Press, 1990) 148.

168. Böckler, *Gott als Vater*, 80. Actually Böckler translates the name 'my god is [my] father', which may, in fact, be what is indicated. Yet the second 'my' is obviously not present.

A name similar to Eliab is Abiel, given to two people in the Hebrew Bible. The first Abiel we encounter is Saul's grandfather, the father of Kish (1 Sam 9:1).[169] This same Abiel was the father of Ner (1 Sam 14:51), who was the uncle of Saul.[170] The second person so named, Abiel the Arbathite, appears in a list of David's warriors (1 Chr 11:32).[171] This name is not attested outside the Bible.[172] The meaning of this name could be 'my father is God' or 'my father is [the god] El'. Gesenius further suggested 'my father is strong', understanding *ʾēl* as an adjective from the root *ʾwl*.[173] Although Gesenius's translation is possible, the preponderance of evidence throughout the Near East where a theophoric element is used with "father" suggests that *ʾēl* in Abiel should be taken as a noun, 'god', or the divine name 'El'. If the former, the name may indicate some kind of ancestor worship,[174] in which case the theophoric element would have a general meaning of 'deity'. If it is the latter possibility, the name would mean '[the god] El is my father'. Noth sees a name like Abiel as simply analogous to names such as Marduk-ilu, Sin-ilu, and Šamaš-ilu, which merely indicate that, to the name-bearer, these figures are deities.[175]

Another name of importance here is Abijah, given to nine individuals in the Bible. The first person so named is the grandson of Benjamin according to the Chronicler (1 Chr 7:6, 8). The second is the younger son of Samuel (1 Sam 8:2, 1 Chr 6:13). The third is a priest appointed by David to oversee the eighth division serving in the temple (1 Chr 24:10). Jeroboam I and Rehoboam have sons whom they name Abijah (1 Kgs 14:1 and 14:31, respectively). Rehoboam's Abijah reigned after his father died, and the DH refers to this Abijah as Abijam (1 Kgs 14:31; 15:1, 7, 8).[176] The Chronicler calls him Abijah (1 Chr 3:10; 2 Chr 11:20, 22; 12:16; 13:1, 2, 3, 4, 15, 17, 19, 22, 23) and Abijahu (2 Chr 13:20, 22).

---

169. The Chronicler refers to this Abiel as Jeiel (1 Chr 9:35).

170. There is a bit of confusion regarding the exact relationship between Saul and Abner and Ner. The above conclusion is suggested by P. K. McCarter, *I Samuel* (AB 8; Garden City, NY: Doubleday, 1980) 256.

171. This same person is called Abi Albon in 2 Sam 23:31. The BHS note on 1 Chr 11:32 suggests reading Abiel as Abi Baal, citing 2 Sam 23:31. The BHS editor might have intended to cite J. Wellhausen, *Der Text der Bücher Samuelis* (Göttingen: Vandenhoeck & Ruprecht, 1871) 215, on this verse, where the suggestion is made that the original name was *ʾbybʿl*, of which Abi Albon is a garbled form.

172. Böckler, *Gott als Vater*, 85.

173. Ibid. See W. Gesenius, *Thesaurus philologicus criticus linguae hebraeae et chaldaeae Veteris Testamenti* (vol. 1; Leipzig: 1835) 42, 48.

174. Böckler, *Gott als Vater*, 85.

175. Cited in ibid., 86.

176. The Vaticanus LXX has *Abiou* in all four passages, while N and several minuscules (b, g, h, n, o, u, and c_2) along with the Ethiopic attest *Abia*.

Böckler assumes that the DH's Abijam is the best reading, but more likely is Gray's suggestion that the *mem* derives from a misread *waw* in the old orthography which could explain the MT and the Vaticanus's rendering of 1 Kgs 14:31; 15:1, 7, 8.[177] Abijah is also the name of two women. One is the wife of Hezron (1 Chr 2:24), and the other is the mother of Hezekiah (2 Chr 29:1, 2 Kgs 18:2). Some have rightly questioned the reading of the former woman's name.[178] The latter is not without its problems either. Only the Chronicler calls Hezekiah's mother Abijah, whereas the DH calls her Abi. Two priests bear this name in the postexilic period. The first is attested under Nehemiah's governance (Neh 10:8) and the second is attested as a member of the group returning from Babylon with Zerubbabel and Jeshua (Neh 12:1, 4, 17).

Extrabiblical evidence for the name Abijah and variants thereof are well attested. A possible early attestation of this name is found on the Gezer Calendar, from the 10th century B.C.E.[179] The form 'by[ ] appears in the margin along with what also appears to be a name, *pnyh*[ ]. A 6th-century B.C.E. inscription from Arad (Arad 27 6) attests the name '*byhw*.[180] The name has two possible understandings. One is 'my father is Yahweh', while the other is 'he is my father', where the *hw* may stand for the third-masculine pronoun. This name, if it bears the former meaning, is consistent with the 6th-century B.C.E. date for Jer 3:19, where Yahweh is addressed as 'my father'. This name is also found on two Aramaic papyri from the 5th century at Elephantine.[181] An 8th-century B.C.E. Samaria ostracon (52, line 2), a late-8th-century Hebrew seal,[182] and Bordreuil Cat. 40 attest the name '*byw*.[183] The biblical name Abijah is to be understood as 'Yahweh is my father'. The Masoretes doubled the *yod* in all the biblical attestations of the name in order to show the presence of the pronominal suffix as well as the initial letter of the

---

177. Böckler, *Gott als Vater*, 82; John Gray, *I and II Kings* (OTL; Philadelphia: Westminster, 1963) 315.

178. Williamson considers the name a gloss. See H. G. M. Williamson, "Sources and Redaction in the Chronicler's Genealogy of Judah," *JBL* 98 (1979) 355. Curtis and Madsen emend the text to read *Abihu* 'his father'. See Edward L. Curtis and Albert A. Madsen, *The Book of Chronicles* (ICC; Edinburgh: T. & T. Clark, 1910) 92.

179. See KAI 182 II.

180. See Gogel, *Grammar of Epigraphic Hebrew*, 394.

181. See A. E. Cowley, *Aramaic Papyri of the Fifth Century* (Oxford: Clarendon, 1923) 2, 20 and 24, 17.

182. This seal is no. 72 in Herr's Hebrew seal collection. See Larry G. Herr, *The Scripts of Ancient Northwest Semitic Seals* (HSM 18: Missoula, MT: Scholars Press, 1978) 115.

183. Pierre Bordreuil, *Catalogue des Sceaux ouest-sémitiques inscrits de la Bibliothèque Nationale du Musée du Louvre et du Musée biblique de Bible et Terre Sainte* (Paris: Bibliothèque Nationale, 1986) #40.

divine name. The inscriptional form, *'byw*, is likely to indicate 'Yahweh is my father' in keeping with the Masoretic notion.[184] The fact that this name is attested in the 8th century is early evidence that some people were considering Yahweh as a father in this time period.

Joab is yet another name that needs to be considered here. It is given to three men in the Hebrew Bible, the most famous of whom is the son of Zeruiah, David's field commander, who is mentioned 141 times in the DH (he first appears in 2 Sam 2:13). Another man bearing this name, a Judahite, is cited in 1 Chr 4:14, and the other is a man who appears in Zerubbabel's day (Ezra 2:6, 8:9; and Neh 7:11). Outside the Hebrew Bible, the phrase *lyw'b* 'to [or belonging to] Joab' appears on a seal.[185] The theophoric element *yô-* is the hypocoristic form that Yahweh takes in the preformative position in personal names. So the name is to be understood as 'Yahweh is a father'.[186]

If my thesis that the God of Israel was not imagined as a father figure in Israel's early history is true, aside from Deut 32:6, I must explain these names in light of the development I am positing. It must be admitted that placing a firm date on the biblical texts in which these names appear is fraught with difficulty. If we take the names at face value as onomastic attestations within the time frame in which they appear in the biblical chronology, then we have attestations of people with names marking the deity as "father" within the time period during which, I have suggested, this notion was overshadowed.

We have two, perhaps three persons named Abijah before the monarchy (Benjamin's grandson in 1 Chr 7:6, 8; Samuel's son in 1 Sam 8:2; 1 Chr 6:13[28]; and, if the MT of 1 Chr 2:24 is to be read, which I doubt, the wife of Hezron). This is in keeping with my thesis. That the name is used again of two sons of kings in the beginning of the divided monarchy in the 10th century may appear to be counterevidence. However, for a crown prince to bear this name is in line with the theology expressed in Nathan's oracle in 2 Samuel 7. That both of these sons are given this name may even indicate the awareness of this theology in both houses. Jeroboam's use of the name for his son may express an attempt to transfer the blessing of Yahweh as father of the king to himself and his heirs. The Chronicler also attests an individual so named in

---

184. Layton, *Archaic Features*, 148.

185. See Francesco Vattioni, "I sigilli ebraici," *Bib* 50 (1969) 361, #9. While Diringer says the writing is in Punic letters, he suggests no date for the seal. See David Diringer, *Le Iscrizione antico-ebraiche palestinesi* (Florence: Le Monnier, 1934) 171. Böckler overlooked this citation in her work. See Böckler, *Gott als Vater*, 75.

186. Layton suggests that whether one referred to a deity in a personal name as 'my father' or merely 'father' did not significantly affect the overall meaning of the name. Layton, *Archaic Features*, 147.

David's day, as well as Hezekiah's mother. The person in David's day is to be expected, because the process of overshadowing the idea of God as father would only have been in its early stages in the period after the monarchy was well established.

The names given to the two women in Chronicles are, admittedly, exceptions to the pattern. Yet as exceptions they do more than prove the rule. These names actually provide examples of people who were not influenced by the tendency of the writers who eschew the portrayal of Yahweh as a father of the people. The priestly names in the postexilic period, like the premonarchic names, do not invalidate my thesis. The epigraphic attestations of variants of Abijah are, like the biblical testimony, scattered within the time period under examination. If the Gezer Calendar exemplar is to be read as ʾbyh, its 10th-century provenance precedes the time when this usage would have been overshadowed by the tradents. Likewise, the Aramaic papyri from the 5th century do not affect my thesis, because this locution fits with the renaissance of fatherhood imagery for God. The Samaria ostracon and the Hebrew seal both derive from 8th-century contexts, at a time when, I have suggested, this kind of expression was eschewed by those writing the traditions. Like the names given to the women in Chronicles, they serve as exceptions and prove that this pattern of avoiding the concept of God as father was not complete among all Israelites. Yet these exceptions might suggest that the tradents are intentionally avoiding such a portrayal, and the absence of references to Yahweh as a father is not merely fortuitous. The Arad attestation ʾbyhw, if it is to be understood as 'Yahweh is my father' rather than 'he is my father', has a 6th-century provenance and should be at home with the pattern that I have suggested in Jeremiah, when the Judahite kingdom was about to end. The biblical attestations of Eliab, Abiel, and Joab do not challenge the proposed pattern and thus do not merit further discussion.

The names that are borne by people who lived between the advent of the Davidic monarchy and the exile and who are not royalty do pose a challenge to the pattern. Böckler's suggestion, that some of these references to "father" may indicate mere sovereignty or compassionate equity that Yahweh epitomizes, may account for this contrary evidence on some level.[187] It is probably too facile a solution to account for all of them, however. While the position I am taking appears to me to be a more honest assessment of the data, it also has the advantage of supporting the larger picture of my historical reconstruction. While these names may appear to be counterevidence, I suggest that they are simply

---

187. Böckler, *Gott als Vater*, 52.

proof that the influence of the writers who dispensed with this portrayal of Yahweh was not complete. I even suggest further that these names that appear to question the proposed pattern might actually demonstrate that the tradents were intentionally avoiding a portrayal of this sort. The names in question simply indicate that the official portrayal of God as a warrior did not overshadow his depiction as a father to the people. These names exist as testimony to the older assumptions about Yahweh that are attested in Deut 32:6. That is, they may be remembrances of the older way of seeing Yahweh as a father-creator. In this way, these names are analogous to the Baal names I mentioned above. They represent expressions that were not attuned to the expediency of depicting Yahweh as a warrior, an impulse possessed by the men who held the reins of the theological depictions of Yahweh in Israel during the monarchy. These officials who passed on the depictions of Israel's God needed their deity to be a warrior, while the individuals who were seeking a name for their child had no such need. Their desire for a portrayal of God was more likely as a personal deity to whom they could direct their prayers.

Popular familial notions of the deity may have influenced these exceptions to the pattern. That is, kinship societal structure may have also played a role in the popular view of God as a father. Cross has argued that Israel is portrayed as the "kindred of the LORD" and that this portrayal is rooted in West Semitic kinship structures.[188] The patrimonial household has been elucidated in biblical Israel as well as in Ugarit by Schloen.[189] When one notes that the ʿam of Israel is structured as a patrimonial household writ large, it seems only natural to assume that the head of the family would reflect the head of most of the individual families within the larger framework. This being the case, one could conceivably assume that the head of the family is a patriarchal figure. Because there is good evidence to support the notion that each 'house of the father' (*bêt ʾāb*) in Israel consisted of joint families (that is, multi-generational nuclear families)[190] who were led by the paterfamilias, it is obvious that family heads were usually father figures. When one notes the portrayal of Israel's God in the Hebrew Bible, therefore, one would conceivably expect their God to reflect the kind of imagery one sees in the paterfamilias. That is, one would likely expect the God of a people who is proclaimed to be the leader of a family to take on the

---

188. Frank Moore Cross, "Kinship and Covenant in Ancient Israel," *From Epic to Canon* (Baltimore: Johns Hopkins University Press, 1998) 12.

189. Schloen, *The House of the Father as Fact and Symbol*, 77.

190. P. King and L. Stager, *Life in Biblical Israel* (Louisville, KY: Westminster John Knox, 2001) 36.

characteristics of a father. So it comes as no surprise that the people would probably have viewed their God as a father and indicated this view in the names they bestowed on their children. Even so, as I noted above, Israel's tradents rarely found these paternal depictions for Yahweh helpful. The names that appear as exceptions to the suggested pattern, therefore, may actually help to elucidate the intentions of the writers of the preserved traditions.

Hellenistic Antecedents for the Ancient of Days?

In addition to the two trajectories that I have suggested for explaining this transformation of the portrayal of God in Israel's tradition, the 2nd-century B.C.E. date for Daniel 7 leads to a consideration of Hellenistic influence. If the Greeks had a higher regard for old age, perhaps this could partially explain the new openness to portraying God with senescent attributes. Although the Greek treatment of old age in society and in literature is quite complex, a negative assessment of old age was quite common. More favorable treatment of the elderly is seen, for example, at Sparta, where in classical antiquity it was said, "Only Sparta is a most fitting abode of old age," and "Only in Sparta does it pay to grow old."[191] Some have argued that Sparta honored old age because there were few elderly around, a fact that is well documented.[192] The fact that the laws in Sparta were not written allowed the gerontocracy to be viewed as the repository of law and tradition in the city-state.[193] While Sparta does stand out as an exception, it is becoming increasingly clear that even here the privileges of old age were limited to the aristocracy.[194]

Literarily, old age is portrayed as a liability in the main in the Greek world. This is true despite the longevity of many Greek writers.[195] The mythological Geras, the personification of old age, is the offspring of Night and issued from the same womb as Doom, Fate, Death, and other antisocial monstrosities, according to Hesiod (*Theogony*, 211–25).[196] While Nestor, the senior adviser to the Greek overlord Agamemnon in Homer's *Iliad*, was the prime Greek archetype of the senescent male,

---

191. E. David, *Old Age in Sparta* (Amsterdam: Hakkert, 1991) 1.
192. Ibid., 46.
193. Ibid., 52.
194. Ibid., 103. This aristocratic status was doubly important because a Spartan citizen had the right to give his land away to anyone and therefore could exert much pressure on his children if they did not obey him. See ibid., 55.
195. Sophocles wrote his last play at 90 while Euripides died at 80, Plato at 81, and Isocrates at 98. See Thomas M. Falkner and Judith de Luce, eds., *Old Age in Greek and Latin Literature* (Albany, NY: State University of New York Press, 1989) 6.
196. Robert Garland, *The Greek Way of Life* (Ithaca, NY: Cornell University Press, 1990) 253.

old men are not a regular feature of Greek mythology.[197] Nestor is portrayed as wise, but he is also garrulous. Kirk points out that Odysseus's father, Laertes, who is depicted as dirty and unkempt, is never even considered as a replacement for Odysseus, even though he had ruled before he passed the throne to his son years before.[198]

In the same vein, Hesiod's golden age has no old age, and Classical Greek love poetry has little regard for the aged.[199] In the plays of Aristophanes, old men often appear, and they are a favorite target of mockery.[200] Gender plays a role here as well, with elderly Greek women bearing a heavy burden in old age. Aristophanes' last two plays are replete with jokes on the elderly, especially on the sexual desire of old women.[201] As suggested by Hubbard, the fact that many Greek choruses are composed of elderly actors points to the painful ambiguity of old age—having wisdom but being unable to affect the course of human affairs.[202]

What is true on the literary level is paralleled in Greek artistic portrayal. Vases depict Heracles subduing a dwarf or, less commonly, a giant named Geras 'old age', whose genitals are grotesque and swollen.[203] From approximately 470 B.C.E. onward, Athenian vase painting manifests a vogue for depicting elderly satyrs with permanently erect penises, which they direct with a vengeance towards maidenly maenads.[204] While this depiction intimates potency among these elderly figures, the larger portrayal suggests that they are viewed with repulsion. Prior to the Hellenistic period, Greek sculptors habitually eschewed the portrayal of the elderly and the physical deterioration and degeneration that they embodied.[205]

It is clear that Hellenization was pressed upon Palestine around the time that Daniel 7 was being written. 2 Maccabees 6 speaks of an envoy sent to Jerusalem by Antiochus IV Ephiphanes to rededicate the Jerusalem temple to Zeus Olympius.[206] Other sites within Palestine also attest

---

197. Geoffrey S. Kirk, "Old Age and Maturity in Ancient Greece," *Eranos Jahrbuch* 40 (1971) 128.

198. Ibid. Odysseus's dog Argos is also a picture of old-age neglect.

199. Ibid., 135, 139.

200. Thomas K. Hubbard, "Old Men in the Youthful Plays of Aristophanes," in *Old Age in Greek and Latin Literature* (ed. T. M. Falkner and J. de Luce; Albany, NY: SUNY Press, 1989) 90.

201. Stephen Bertman, "The Ashes and the Flame: Passion and Aging in Classical Poetry," in ibid., 160.

202. Ibid.

203. Garland, *The Greek Way of Life*, 254, fig. 39.

204. Ibid., 270.

205. Bertman, "The Ashes and the Flame," 160.

206. F. Graf, "Zeus," *DDD* 938.

the presence of a Zeus cult probably dating back to the Maccabean period.[207] Although there may be facets of Zeus's depiction that overlap with Yahweh's, the elderly depiction of the Ancient of Days does not appear to be among them. Numismatic evidence suggests that Zeus's depiction in Palestine was similar to the depiction seen in Phidias's statue of Zeus Olympius from the 5th century B.C.E.[208] No clear markers of old age appear in any of these depictions.

The substantive point of the evidence, both literary and artistic, from the Greek world shows that, at the very least, respect for old age was not common. If the transformation seen in Daniel 7 is to have been influenced by the Greek world, it would not have been from a Classical model. It is also unlikely that the Hellenization of Palestine in the 3rd and 2nd centuries can account for the change in Yahweh's depiction. In other words, if Greek traditions played any role in influencing the author of Daniel, we can be certain that they were not old traditions rooted in depictions of deities from the Classical period.

Conclusion

Yahweh's coming of age is a complex journey through Israel's traditions extending back to its earliest poets, through its most ardent defenders of Yahwistic orthodoxy, and down to the author of Daniel who, like some of the prophets before him, resurrects cosmic notions and uses them to reveal God as the Ancient of Days. Yahweh could not be represented as an elderly figure early in the traditions because he was imagined as a youthful warrior, much like Baal. Although he was, like El, considered a father early on, ideas of this sort were overshadowed quite early by the biblical tradents to avoid associating him with the human life cycle, which could lead to assumptions about his age. These Israelite tradents deemed it necessary to employ warrior imagery, as is true of the depiction of the gods of their neighbors. As a result of this political expedience, the warrior imagery overshadowed other portrayals among the writers and redactors of the tradition. Yet onomastic evidence demonstrates this impulse to be less than complete at the popular level, suggesting that the depictions were embraced by some but not by the men who wrote and shaped the traditions.

As cosmic imagery was welcomed back into Israel's literary circles, refracted portrayals of God came too. The idea of Yahweh as a father,

---

207. Achim Lichtenberger, "Artemis and Zeus Olympios in Roman Gerasa," in *The Variety of Local Religious Life in the Near East in the Hellenistic and Roman Periods* (ed. Ted Kaiser; Leiden: Brill, 2008) 134–35.

208. Ibid., 134; see plate L. The description of the Zeus statue destroyed in the 5th cent. C.E. appears in Pausanias's *Guide to Greece* 5.11.1–8.

once embraced by the poet of Deuteronomy 32, had undergone a similar transformation in which, over time, it was also welcomed back. By the time of the author of Daniel 7, the defenders of orthodox portrayal of their God had changed their stance, so that Yahweh's association with old age and fatherhood no longer posed a contradiction to his portrayal as a warrior earlier in their history. By the middle of the 2nd century B.C.E., Yahweh's fatherhood was well ensconced, and cosmic imagery was at home with the tradents of orthodoxy. These two trajectories, the concept of God as a father and the return of cosmic motifs, intersect in Daniel 7, whose author could use cosmic imagery to set the stage for Yahweh's portrayal as an aged deity, much like the Ugaritic El, conferring an agency of sorts on a divine being who receives some of his divine attributes, much like the Ugaritic Baal. The Canaanite traditions are transmuted to convey Israel's God and his divine agent, who is given a divine epithet and eternal dominion. Internal developments coincide with external motifs to produce a novel depiction of Yahweh, the Ancient of Days.

Yahweh has, in this sense, come of age. As a result, the inevitable process of aging that all beings face is even applied to the God of Israel. This study has examined the view of old age in the Hebrew Bible, surveying terms for senescence and the topoi of old age. In this overview, I noted that the view of old age is multifaceted, sometimes portraying old age in a positive light and sometimes depicting it as a time of decline and weakness. The depiction of advanced age in the Ugaritic evidence, though not as common as in the Hebrew Bible, also demonstrated a varied treatment of old age. As in the Hebrew Bible, it was a time of wisdom for some, while for others it was seen as a time of weakness.

With these two understandings of old age in mind, I turned to the question why Yahweh was not portrayed explicitly with old-age imagery in Israel's early traditions. I noted that the imagery used of Yahweh was, in many ways, a compilation of imagery used of Baal and El. However, because not all of their depictions were compatible when combined, some had to be discarded. The senescence seen in El was one of these features that was deemed unsuitable for a god who was predominantly a divine warrior. I also suggested that the advanced age seen in El may have been eschewed by the biblical authors because of its association with other gods and perhaps with old-age weakness.

The practice of avoiding old-age imagery by the biblical tradents is abandoned in Daniel 7, where Yahweh is called "the Ancient of Days." After examining Daniel 7's connection to the epic imagery expressed in Ugaritic, I suggested that the portrayal of God as old is a transmuted refraction of the depiction of El. The Daniel writer employed an analogue from ancient Canaanite lore to depict Yahweh as an elderly God, before whom appears a divine being who rides the clouds and is given eternal dominion. That such ancient traditions were still known as late as the 2nd century B.C.E. is indicated in the citations of the Phoenician Sakkunyaton as preserved in Eusebius. The analogy of the relationship between the youthful god Baal and the aged god El served as a fitting expression for the message of Daniel 7. Yahweh confers some of his divine attributes on this being called "one like a son of man." This usage of mythic material is an example of the recycling of older mythological elements that is seen in the work of the earlier prophets.

A second trajectory along which Yahweh's coming of age may be plotted is related to his depiction as a father. Biblical evidence suggests that Yahweh was imagined as a father by the writers of the Hebrew Bible, for the most part, only in the later period. I suggested that Deut 32:6 is an early witness to God's representation as a father before the biblical tradents began avoiding portrayals of this sort. The early traditions eschewed this depiction probably to avoid associating God with the human life cycle. Although this avoidance was the official stance, some onomastic data provide evidence of a common perception that did not correlate with the texts of the tradents. The trajectory of portraying God as a father opened the door, as it were, to understanding him as an aged deity. This trajectory intersected with the trajectory of resurrected cosmic imagery in Daniel 7, and together they paved the way for the depiction of Yahweh as "the Ancient of Days."

Indexes

Index of Authors

Abou-Assaf, A. 11
Aharoni, Y. 96
Ahlström, G. W. 125
Ajayi, J. 6, 7
Albani, M. 113
Albright, W. F. 71
Alster, B. 49
Aquila 19, 54
Aristotle 25, 34
Assmann, J. 94
Avigad, N. 97, 140

Beale, G. K. 112
Bertman, S. 147
Biggs, R. 70
Böckler, A. 123, 125, 128–29, 133–36, 138–44
Boda, M. J. 72
Boecker, H. J. 137
Bordreuil, P. 11, 96, 142
Borowski, O. 110
Braun, R. 133
Braunwald, E. 35
Brichto, H. 22, 57, 73
Briggs, C. A. 19
Bright, J. 129
Brown, F. 19
Bruce, F. F. 111

Calment, J. L. 15
Caquot, A. 70, 111
Carroll, R. P. 127
Charles, R. H. 108
Chiriboga, D. 19–20
Cintas, P. 79
Clifford, R. J. 97, 134

Cogan, Mordechai [Morton] 36, 38, 42, 100
Collins, J. J. 108, 111–15
Conrad, J. 8, 9, 11
Cornelius, I. 80–81, 100
Cowley, A. E. 10, 142
Craigie, P. C. 95
Crenshaw, J. 42, 46, 55, 92
Cross, F. M. 27–28, 62–63, 67, 69–71, 79, 93–97, 99–100, 103, 105, 118, 120, 122, 145
Curtis, A. H. W. 86
Curtis, E. L. 142

Dandamayev, M. A. 15
David, E. 26, 146
DeVries, S. J. 36–37
Dietrich, M. 75
Dijkstra, M. 72, 105
Di Lella, A. A. 108
Diringer, D. 143
Dobbs-Allsopp, F. W. 99
Donner, H. 93
Dossin, G. 124
Driver, S. R. 19
Duhm, B. 126, 128–30
Dulin, R. Z. 6

Eggler, J. 116
Eissfeldt, O. 62–63
Elnes, E. E. 119
Emerton, J. A. 117, 119–20
Eng, M. 7
Epstein, H. 110
Euripides 146
Eusebius 113, 118, 150

Evans, D. G. 36

Fabry, H.-J. 9, 11
Falkner, T. M. 146
Ferch, A. J. 113, 115, 118
Finnegan, R. 61
Fischer, D. H. 5
Fishbane, M. 125
Fitzmyer, J. A. 8-10
Fleming, D. E. 81, 103
Foner, N. 8
Fowler, J. D. 96, 101-2
Fox, M. 47, 49, 134
Franklin, B. 5

Gachet, J. 79
Gammie, J. G. 108
Garland, R. 146-47
Gaster, T. H. 25
Geier, M. 53
Geissen, A. 110-11
Ginsberg, H. L. 114
Ginsburg, C. 47
Gogel, S. 140
Gogel, S. 97, 105, 142
Goldingay, J. E. 108, 111-12, 117, 120
Good, R. M. 69
Gordis, R. 47, 50, 52-54
Gordon, C. 10, 62-63, 97
Gordon, R. P. 123
Graf, F. 147
Gray, J. 85, 142
Green, A. R. W. 82
Gressmann, H. 80-81, 116
Groening, M. 5
Gulick, J. 14
Gullette, M. 5
Gutmann, D. 8, 14, 20, 23, 33, 36, 64-65

Hachlili, R. 16
Hackett, J. A. 64-65
Hadley, J. M. 105
Hamilton, M. 34
Hanson, P. 120, 130

Harrington, D. J. 10
Harris, J. G. 6, 26
Harris, R. 14
Hartman, L. F. 108
Hayajneh, H. 98
Healey, J. F. 72, 98
Heidel, A. 115
Heltzer, M. 77
Herdner, A. 70, 122
Herr, L. G. 142
Hesiod 54, 69, 146-47
Hestrin, R. 84-85
Hoffmann, H.-D. 28
Hoftijzer, J. 8
Holladay, W. L. 39, 126-29
Holmes, E. R. 8, 15
Holmes, L. D. 8, 15
Hubbard, T. K. 147
Huehnergard, J. 46, 101-2, 127
Hultgård, A. 116
Hutton, J. M. 121

Ibn Ezra 53
Isocrates 146

Jacob, E. ben (Rabbi) 134
Jacobsen, T. 17
Jansen, H. L. 117
Japhet, S. 131-33
Jastrow, M. 51
Jeansonne, S. P. 109, 111
Jepsen, A. 134
Jeremias, J. 105
Jirku, A. 62-63
Jones, H. S. 31, 110
Jongeling, K. 8

Kaminsky, J. 21
Kanael, B. 80
Kantorowicz, E. H. 34
Kautzsch, E. 53
Kedar-Kopfstein, B. 19
Keel, O. 81-85, 99, 103-4, 124, 136
Kenyon, F. G. 109
Kilpp, N. 129

Kimball, S.   8
King, P.   84-85, 103, 145
Kirk, G. S.   147
Köckert, M.   102
Korpel, M. C. A.   98, 101, 104
Kraus, H.-J.   42
Krüger, T.   49-50
Kugel, J.   46
Kvanvig, H. S.   115

Laroche, E.   95
Layton, S.   140, 143
Leeb, C.   13
Lemaire, A.   96, 99
Levenson, J. D.   27-28, 124
Lewis, T.   68
Lichtenberger, A.   148
Liddell, H. G.   31, 110
Lohfink, N.   47
Loretz, O.   75
Lowenthal, M. F.   19-20
Luce, J. de   146
Lundbom, J. R.   126
Lust, J.   111
Luther, M.   53

MacDonald, J.   13, 20, 28
Macintosh, A. A.   137
Madsen, A. A.   142
Malamat, A.   11, 36
Margulis, B.   118
McCarter, P. K.   32-33, 123, 141
McKane, W.   126, 129, 134
McKenzie, J. L.   14, 125
Meissner, B.   9
Millard, A.   11, 19
Miller, P.   100-101, 119
Montgomery, J. A.   108-9, 111
Moor, J. C. de   67, 72, 76, 80, 85, 99, 103-4, 112
Moran, W.   9, 63, 124
Mosca, P.   92, 114-15
Mowinckel, S.   116, 124
Müller, H.-P.   135
Murphy, R.   55

Nicholson, E. W.   129
Nickelsburg, G. W. E.   117
Niditch, S.   120
Nielsen, K.   57
Noth, M.   27-28, 102, 141
Nougayrol, J.   77, 95

Ogden, G. S.   48-49
Oldenburg, U.   62, 69
Olmo Lete, G. del   10, 66-67, 69
Olyan, S. M.   69, 91, 105
Oppenheim, A. L.   136
Origen   109, 111-12

Pardee, D.   62, 67
Parker, S. B.   61, 63, 68, 74, 82-85, 122
Paul, S.   10, 40, 137
Pausanias   148
Peckham, B.   28
Philo Biblius   118
Plato   26, 146
Pope, M.   43-44, 55, 62, 68-71, 76, 80, 95, 118, 122
Preuss, H. D.   93
Pritchard, J. B.   26, 85

Rad, G. von   21, 24
Rashi   53
Reiner, E.   9
Rendtorff, R.   96
Renfroe, F.   75, 97
Reviv, H.   13, 36, 40
Ribichini, S.   95
Ricoeur, P.   126
Roberts, J. J. M.   123, 132, 137
Röllig, W.   93
Roth, M. T.   14
Rowley, H. H.   108

Sakkunyaton   100, 118, 150
Sanders, P.   135
Sanmartín, J.   10, 66, 69
Sarna, N.   124-125
Sasson, J.   57
Sawyer, J. F. A.   48-49

Schaeffer, C. F.-A.   73, 78, 84, 100
Scharbert, J.   17, 29
Schloen, J. D.   61-62, 124-25, 145
Schmidt, N.   117
Schottroff, W.   32, 34, 45
Scott, R.   31, 110
Seesemann, O.   14, 40
Segert, S.   69-71
Selms, A. van   70
Seltzer, M.   61
Seow, C.-L.   47-54
Simmons, L.   7, 8, 22, 23, 56, 64
Sjöberg, E.   117
Skinner, J.   17
Smith, M.   63, 67, 69-71, 82, 84, 92-94, 97-99, 105, 122-23
Smith, P.   16
Soden, W. von   9
Sokoloff, M.   110
Sophocles   146
Speiser, E. A.   17, 21, 24
Sperber, A.   109
Spronk, K.   76
Stager, L.   12-13, 20, 25, 79, 84-85, 103, 145
Stähli, H.-P.   13
Stol, M.   45-46
Stuckenbruck, L.   117
Sukenik, E. L.   80
Sznycer, M.   70

Tate, M. E.   125
Theodotion   109-12, 119

Thurner, M.   19-20
Toorn, K. van der   72
Torczyner, H.   102
Tov, E.   135
Tropper, J.   68-69, 98, 140

Uehlinger, C.   81-85, 99, 103-4

Vaihinger, H.   53
Vanoni, G.   133
Vattioni, F.   143
Vita, J.-P.   77

Walls, N. H.   76, 82, 85-86
Watson, W. G. E.   67
Weiser, A.   42, 137
Wellhausen, J.   17, 32, 141
Westermann, C.   17, 21, 25, 130
Williams, R. J.   53
Williamson, H. G. M.   142
Willis, T.   13
Witzenrath, H.   48
Wolff, H. W.   15, 39
Wyatt, N.   62, 78

Xella, P.   95
Xenophon   25

Yon, M.   78-80

Zevit, Z.   102
Zias, J.   16
Zöckler, O.   53

Index of Scripture

Genesis
1-11   17-18
2:7   54
3:19   54
3:23   54
4:1   123
6:3   15
6:4   93
7:11   51
8:2   51
11:10   18
14:18-22   119
14:19   96
15:15   9, 22
16   65
17   19
17:17   18
18   19
18:11   18, 21, 29, 109
18:25   95
18:27   54
19:4   12, 20
19:30-38   20
19:31   20, 29
19:31-35   106
19:37-38   21
21:2   23
21:7   21, 23
21:10   20
21:33   93
23:7   26
24:1   21, 29, 109
24:2   21
25:8   9, 22-23, 43
27   22
27:1   22, 31
27:1-2   29
27:2   22
27:5-29   106

Genesis (cont.)
28:1   23
30:41   34
31:35   26
35:17-19   23
35:28   23
35:29   23, 43
37:3   23
37:31-32   23
42:38   9
43:27   24
44:20   23-24
44:29   9
44:31   9
47:9   24
48:1   24
48:10   24
48:19-20   24
49   25
49:24   101-2
50:22   29

Exodus
4:22   137
6:16   25
6:18   25
6:20   25
7:7   25
10:2   25
10:6   25
10:9   12, 25
15   100
20:12   131
32:4   102
33:10   26
34:6   98

Leviticus
19:3   25
19:32   10, 26

Leviticus (cont.)
27:3-7   26-27

Numbers
1:2-3   27
1:9   140
2:7   140
3:1   51
4:3   27
7:24   140
7:29   140
8:24   27
10:16   140
11:16   12
14:11   52
14:23   53
16:1   140
16:12   140
16:30   53
23:22   102
24:8   102
26:2   27
26:8   140
33:38-39   27

Deuteronomy
4:40   28
5:16   28, 131
5:23   12
6:2   28
8:4   19
9:16   102
9:21   102
11:6   140
11:9   28
11:21   28
21:2   12
25:15   28
28:50   12, 28
29:4   19

Deuteronomy (cont.)
29:9   12
30:18   28
30:20   11, 28
31:2   28
31:9   12
31:20   53
31:28   9, 12
32   135, 138, 149
32:6   96, 121–23,
   127–28, 130–31,
   135–36, 138, 143,
   145, 150
32:7   12
32:8   127
32:19   53
32:25   10, 28
33:2   105
33:2–5   100
33:5   98
33:26   99
33:26–29   100
33:27   93
34:7   28

Joshua
9:13   19
10:12–13   100
13:1   29, 109
23:1   29, 109
23:2   12, 29
23:14   29
24:1   12
24:29   29

Judges
2:8   30
5   25, 100
5:4   105
5:5   105
5:28   48
6:31   99
8:32   9
11:27   95
19   30, 61
19:16   30

Judges (cont.)
19:17   30
19:20   30
19:22   30

Ruth
1:11   57
1:12   56
2:8   57
2:19   56
2:22   56
3:2   56
3:10   57
3:14   52
4:4   12
4:9   12
4:11   12
4:15   56

1 Samuel
2:17   53
2:22   30–31
2:23–25   31
2:31–32   31
3:2   31
4:13   31
4:15   31
4:18   30–31
8:1   30, 33
8:2   141, 143
8:4–5   33
8:5   32
9:1   141
12:2   11, 30, 33
14:3   31
14:51   141
16:6   140
17:12   30, 33
17:13   140
17:28   140
20:24   96
20:41   26
24:13   96
24:16   96
25:41   26
28:14   33

2 Samuel
2:13   143
3:4   96
3:27   35
4:4   139
6:16   48
7   125, 131, 136,
   143
7:6   97
7:14   121, 123–25,
   128, 131, 136–37
7:15   132
8:16   96
12:14   53
15:37   119
16:5–8   35
16:16   119
17:15   12
17:27   31
19:33   31, 32
19:34   32
19:35   44
19:36   31, 32
19:38   32
20:10   35
21:8   139
22:7–18   100
23:31   141

1 Kings
1   33, 76
1–2   7, 61
1:1   34
1:4   34
1:5   34
1:6   34
1:11   34
1:15   33
2:6   10, 35
2:9   10, 35
2:27   31
3:5   35
3:6–10   45
3:11   11
3:11–14   45
3:14   35–36

1 Kings (cont.)
  4:3 96
  4:5 119
  4:17 96
  11 132
  11:4 35, 59
  12:6 36
  12:8 36
  12:28 102
  12:32 102
  13 37, 103
  13:11 37
  13:25 37
  14:1 141
  14:4 11, 37
  14:7–16 37
  14:31 141–42
  15:1 141–42
  15:7 141–42
  15:8 141–42
  15:23 37
  18–19 100
  18:27 99
  19:12 100
  21:8 12
  21:11 12
  22:41–42 96
  22:42 96

2 Kings
  4:14 38
  7:2 51
  7:19 51
  9:30 48
  10:1 12
  10:5 12
  16:7 124, 128, 138
  18:2 142
  18:27 38
  23:18 37

1 Chronicles
  2:13 140
  2:24 142–43
  3:3 96
  3:10 141

1 Chronicles (cont.)
  4:14 143
  6:12 140
  6:13 141, 143
  7:6 141, 143
  7:8 141
  9:8 96
  9:35 141
  11:32 141
  12:2 69
  12:6 96
  12:10 140
  15:18 140
  15:20 140
  15:25 12
  16:5 140
  17:13 121, 131–32
  18:15 96
  22 132
  22:5 59
  22:8 132
  22:10 121, 132
  23:1 59
  24:10 141
  27:16 96
  28 132
  28–29 35
  28:6 121, 132
  29 132
  29:1 59
  29:10 121, 132, 138
  29:18 133
  29:20 133
  29:28 9, 59

2 Chronicles
  1:11 11, 59
  11:18 140
  11:20 141
  11:22 141
  12:16 141
  13:1 141
  13:2 141
  13:3 141
  13:4 141
  13:7 59

2 Chronicles (cont.)
  13:15 141
  13:17 141
  13:19 141
  13:20 141
  13:22 141
  13:23 141
  21:2 96
  24:15 15, 30, 59
  29:1 142
  36:17 11

Ezra
  2:4 96
  2:6 143
  2:57 96
  3:8 58
  3:12 12, 58
  5 9
  5:5 10
  5:9 10
  6:7 10
  6:8 10
  6:14 10
  8:8 96
  8:9 143
  10:4 12
  10:8 12

Nehemiah
  7:11 143
  7:59 96
  9:18 102
  10:8 142
  11:4 96
  12:1 142
  12:4 142
  12:17 142

Esther
  3:13 12, 59
  5:9 51

Job
  3:16 49
  4:19 48

Job (cont.)
  5:18   134
  8:8   33, 55
  8:8–10   43
  12:12   11, 33, 44, 55
  12:12–13   44
  12:20   12
  13:28   19
  15:10   11, 43
  23:7   96
  27:18   48
  29   44
  29:8   11, 26
  29:18   11
  30:1   44
  31:15   96, 128, 131, 136
  32   43
  32:4   43
  32:6   11, 44
  32:6–7   43
  32:7   11
  32:9   40, 43–44
  33:28   49
  33:30   49
  35:33   44
  36:26   92
  38:21   11
  41:24   10
  42:16–17   43
  42:17   55

Psalms
  2   131
  2:7   123, 137
  7:12   95
  10:3   53
  10:13   53
  10:14   134
  10:17–18   134
  18:1   51
  21   42
  21:5   11, 41
  23:6   11, 41
  24:10   98
  29   114

Psalms (cont.)
  29:3–9   100
  32:3   19
  33   42
  36:10   49
  37:25   12
  47:9   98
  51:7   34
  55:24   41
  56:14   49
  61:7   41
  68   100
  68:5   99
  68:6   121, 133–34, 138
  68:8   96
  68:9   105
  69:24   51
  71   39, 42
  71:18   10, 41
  74:10   53
  75:8   95
  78:35   119
  78:38   98
  86:15   98
  89   124–25, 137
  89:27   121, 124, 128, 136
  89:46   41
  90:2   92
  90:3   54
  90:10   15, 41
  91:16   11
  92:15   10, 41
  93:5   11
  94:2   134
  102:24   41
  102:27   19
  102:28   92
  103:13   121, 134, 138
  103:14   54
  103:15   41
  104:3   99
  105:22   12
  106:19   102

Psalms (cont.)
  107:11   53
  111:4   98
  132:2   101–2
  132:5   101–2
  136:1–26   98
  137:1   58
  145:8   98
  146:9   134

Proverbs
  1:30   53
  2:17   126
  3:2   11, 45
  3:12   121, 134, 138
  3:16   11, 45
  4:10   11
  5:12   53
  10:27   45
  15:5   53
  15:25   134
  16:31   10, 45
  17:6   45
  19:26   45
  20:20   45
  20:29   10, 12, 45, 57
  23:22   45
  24:21   62

Qoheleth
  4:2   19
  4:3   19
  4:13   46
  6:3   12, 46
  6:6   46
  7:8   46
  10:16   46
  11   49
  11:7   49
  11:7–12:7   47, 49, 55
  11:8   50
  11:9   50
  11:10   50
  12:1   50
  12:1–7   47, 49, 55

Qoheleth (cont.)
12:2   50
12:3   50-52, 55
12:4   52
12:5   52

Song of Songs
4:2   55
5:14-15   55
6:6   55
6:11   52
7:13   52

Isaiah
1:4   53
1:24   101-2
3:5   12
3:14   12
5:24   53
7:20   38
9:5   92, 114
20:4   12
24:18   51
25:6   105
27:1   120-21
33:22   98
36:12   38
38:12   48
40:28   92, 96, 114
43:10   99
43:12   99
43:15   96
46:4   10, 38, 92
47:6   38
49:7   26
49:26   101-2
50:9   19
51:6   19
51:9   121
51:9-10   120
52:5   53
57:15   92
60:8   51
60:14   53
60:16   101-2
63   133

Isaiah (cont.)
63-64   128, 130, 138
63:16   121, 129-31, 133, 138
64   133
64:7   121, 130-31, 133, 135, 138
65:20   38

Jeremiah
2:27   131
3:2-3   126
3:4   121, 125-26, 128, 137-38
3:19   121, 127-29, 132, 138, 142
3:19-20   126
3:21   129
6:11   12, 39
10:10   92, 114
14:21   53
23:17   53
29:1   12
31   128
31:9   121, 128, 138
31:12-14   127
31:13   12, 39, 57
33:24   53
38:1   96
49:11   134
51:22   12, 39
51:23   39

Lamentations
1:1   58
1:19   12
2:6   53
2:10   58
2:21   12, 58
4:16   12
5:3   58
5:12   12
5:14   12, 40, 57-58
5:17   51
5:20   11

Ezekiel
7:26   12
9:6   12, 39, 57
27:9   12

Daniel
2   108, 111
3:33   98
5   108
5:19   51
6:27   51
7   18, 58, 91-92, 100, 107-21, 146-50
7:1-18   108
7:9   58, 109-10
7:13   58, 110, 113, 119
7:22   58

Hosea
1:6   134
2:19   99
2:21-22   91, 126
7   40
7:9   10, 40
8:5-6   102
11   127, 137-38
11:1   126
11:1-3   137
13:2   102
13:3   51
14:4   134

Joel
1:2   40
1:14   40
2:13   98
2:16   12, 40
3:1   12, 40

Jonah
4:2   98

Micah
7:5   128

Habakkuk
   2:7   51
   3:3   105
   3:3–15   100
   3:6   92

Zechariah
   8:4   11
   8:4–5   12

Malachi
   1:6   121, 130–31
   1:9   131
   1:14   98
   2:10   121, 131, 135, 138
   2:15   131

Malachi (cont.)
   2:17   131
   3:5   134
   3:10   51
   3:14   131
   3:15   131
   3:18   131

New Testament

Revelation
   1:12–16   109
   1:13–14   111

Apocrypha

2 Maccabees
   6   147

Judith
   10:5   110

Pseudepigrapha

1 Enoch
   37–71   117
   46:4   117
   48:3   117

Index of Other Ancient Literature

Ugaritic Literature

KTU
- 1.1 II 18   97
- 1.1 III 6   97
- 1.1 III 22   97
- 1.1 III 24   62
- 1.1 III 26   64
- 1.1 IV 13   64, 97
- 1.1 IV 18   64, 97
- 1.2 I 10   62
- 1.2 I 23-24   76
- 1.2 I 33   64
- 1.2 I 35-36   76
- 1.2 I 50-52   76
- 1.2 III 5   97
- 1.2 IV 8   99
- 1.2 IV 10   98, 118
- 1.2 IV 15-35   100
- 1.2 IV 29   99
- 1.3 II 40   99
- 1.3 III 38   99
- 1.3 III 44   85
- 1.3 IV 4   99
- 1.3 IV 54   140
- 1.3 V 1-2   65-66
- 1.3 V 2   64-65
- 1.3 V 3   65
- 1.3 V 7-8   97
- 1.3 V 9   122
- 1.3 V 24-25   10, 64-65
- 1.3 V 27   76
- 1.3 V 28   65
- 1.3 V 30   63
- 1.3 V 32   95, 98, 118
- 1.3 V 36   98
- 1.4 I 23   122
- 1.4 II 10   97

KTU *(cont.)*
- 1.4 III 11   99
- 1.4 III 18   99
- 1.4 III 31   97
- 1.4 IV 23   75
- 1.4 IV 23-24   66, 97
- 1.4 IV 24   62, 98
- 1.4 IV 38   98
- 1.4 IV 38-39   66
- 1.4 IV 41   63
- 1.4 IV 43   98, 118
- 1.4 IV 44   95
- 1.4 IV 48   98
- 1.4 IV 50   118
- 1.4 IV 50-51   66
- 1.4 IV 58   97
- 1.4 V 1-2   63
- 1.4 V 4   10
- 1.4 V 8   100
- 1.4 V 60   99
- 1.4 VII 31   100
- 1.4 VIII 49   98
- 1.5 II 7   99
- 1.5 V 4-5   85
- 1.5 V 18   85
- 1.5 VI   97
- 1.5 VI 11   97
- 1.6 I 34-35   97
- 1.6 I 36   62, 98
- 1.6 I 49   97
- 1.6 I 63   105
- 1.6 II 6   86
- 1.6 III 4   97
- 1.6 III 10   97
- 1.6 III 14   97
- 1.6 IV 11   97
- 1.6 V 18   75
- 1.6 VI 20-31   100
- 1.6 VI 39   97
- 1.6 VI 54   98

KTU *(cont.)*
- 1.10 I 7   99
- 1.10 III 1   86
- 1.10 III 36   99
- 1.15 I 5   86
- 1.15 II 14   97
- 1.15 III 18   97
- 1.16 III 6-8   119
- 1.16 IV 9   97
- 1.16 V 10   97
- 1.16 V 23   97
- 1.16 VI 16   74
- 1.16 VI 59   98
- 1.17 I 26-33   71
- 1.17 I 45-49   72
- 1.17 II 1-8   72
- 1.17 II 16-23   72
- 1.17 VI   64
- 1.17 VI 48-49   97
- 1.17 VI 49   62, 98
- 1.17 VI 56   98
- 1.18   64
- 1.18 I 11-12   64-65
- 1.18 I 15   97
- 1.19 I 31   75
- 1.19 I 43-44   99
- 1.19 I 46   100
- 1.22 I 8   101
- 1.23   67, 70-71, 78, 86
- 1.23 33   75
- 1.23 33-34   66, 69
- 1.23 34   75
- 1.23 35   75
- 1.23 35-36   67
- 1.23 37   68-70
- 1.23 38-39   70
- 1.23 39   68
- 1.23 40   68-70
- 1.23 41   70

KTU *(cont.)*
  1.23 43   68, 126
  1.23 43-44   70
  1.23 44   69-70
  1.23 47   68-70
  1.23 48   70
  1.23 49-52   70
  1.23 51-52   68
  1.23 56   68
  1.47 2   140
  1.65   63
  1.82 8   75
  1.92 40   99
  1.108   118
  1.108 2-4   95
  1.108 5   95
  1.109 11-14   73
  1.109 12   140
  1.114   106
  1.114 16·   73, 80
  1.114 18-19   73
  1.114 21   73
  1.116 VI 30-38   74
  1.116 VI 43-53   74
  1.118 1   140
  1.128 15   95
  1.129 4   64
  1.148 23   140
  1.169   112
  2.23 20   11
  2.71 14   75
  2.72 18   75
  4.63 I 9   101
  4.98 17   10
  4.115 9   98
  4.133 2   98
  4.141 II 9   10
  4.165 13   98
  4.183 II 26   10
  4.261 10   98
  4.382 28   98
  4.607 16   98
  4.609 23   10
  4.616 2   98
  4.631 18   101
  4.659 8   98

KTU *(cont.)*
  4.775 10   101
  4.787 10   10
  5.18 9   98
RIH
  78/20 14-15   112
RS
  8.295   78-79, 81
  11.839 21   101
  16.126B+ ii 41   101
  16.145 5   101
  16.145 10   101
  17.288 27   98
  18.20 15   98
  19.70 8   98
  20.239   77
  24.440   79
  27.053 9   101
  88.070   79

Other West Semitic Inscriptions

Aharoni, *Arad Inscriptions*
  27 4   96
Aḥiqar
  line 6   10
  line 17   10
  line 26   10
  line 35   10
Arad inscription
  27 6   142
Avigad, *HB*
  #17+18   140
  ##72-74   140
  #90   140
Beersheba inscription
  2:1   140
Bordreuil, *Catalogue*
  40   142
Cowley, *Aramaic Papyri*
  2, 20   142
  24, 17   142
Diringer, *Iscrizione*
  171   143

Gezer Calendar   142
Herr, *Scripts*
  no. 72   142
Jerusalem Jar
  Inscription 1   97
KAI
  2:37   96, 122
  26A III 18   96, 122
  48:4   112
  182 II   142
  224:16   112
  276:9-10   112
Khirbet Beit Lei
  inscription B   99
Kuntillet Ajrud
  15:7   11, 105
Mine M no. 358 (Cross, *CMHE*, 19)   93
Samaria ostracon
  52 line 2   142
Sefire
  I A 11   119
  II B 8   8
Tell Fekheriyeh
  inscription   19
  lines 7-8   11

Akkadian and Mesopotamian Inscriptions

Amarna Letters
  137:29   9
  158   124
  250:43   63
Epic of Gilgamesh
  I 101   54
Creation of Man by the Mother Goddess
  Assyrian version
    lines 14-20   54
  Babylonian version
    lines 15, 12   54
Hammurabi, Code of
  §§171-72   45

Akkadian and Mesopotamian Inscriptions (cont.)

Instructions of
   Suruppak 46
Publications of the
   Babylonian Section
   8/1 16 46
Sargon II, annalistic
   inscription 136
Sennacherib, Oriental
   Institute Prism 136
Shalmaneser III,
   Black Obelisk
   inscription 136
Texts in the Iraq Museum
   4 27 45
Vision of the
   Underworld 115, 116

Classical Sources

Hesiod
   Theogony 54, 69
   211–25 146
Homer
   Iliad 69
Pausanias,
   Guide to Greece
   5.11.1–8 148
Plato, Republic 26

Dead Sea Scrolls

1QIsa^a
   Isa 63:16 129
4Q530 117
4QDeut^j
   Deut 32:6, 8 135
4QDeut^q
   Deut 32:6, 8 135
"Book of the
   Giants" 117

Egyptian Sources

Insiger Papyrus 32
Instruction of Ani 26, 45
Instruction of
   Ptahhotep 46
Merneptah Stela 99
Job Stela 80

Rabbinic Sources

Midrash
   Ps 94:2 134
Talmud, Babylonian
   B. B. Bat. 91a 57
Targum of Ruth 57

green press INITIATIVE

Eisenbrauns is committed to preserving ancient forests and natural resources. We elected to print this title on 30% post consumer recycled paper, processed chlorine free. As a result, for this printing, we have saved:

2 Trees (40' tall and 6-8" diameter)
1 Million BTUs of Total Energy
181 Pounds of Greenhouse Gases
819 Gallons of Wastewater
52 Pounds of Solid Waste

Eisenbrauns made this paper choice because our printer, Thomson-Shore, Inc., is a member of Green Press Initiative, a nonprofit program dedicated to supporting authors, publishers, and suppliers in their efforts to reduce their use of fiber obtained from endangered forests.

For more information, visit www.greenpressinitiative.org

Environmental impact estimates were made using the Environmental Defense Paper Calculator. For more information visit: www.papercalculator.org.